Understanding Organizational Change

Jean Helms Mills, Kelly Dye and Albert J. Mills

Routledge
Taylor & Francis Group

LONDON AND NEW YORK

First published 2009
by Routledge
2 Park Square, Milton Park, Abingdon, Oxon, OX14 4RN

Simultaneously published in the USA and Canada
by Routledge
270 Madison Avenue, New York, NY 10016

*Routledge is an imprint of the Taylor & Francis Group, an informa
business*

© 2009 Jean Helms Mills, Kelly Dye and Albert J. Mills

Typeset in Times by RefineCatch Limited, Bungay, Suffolk, UK
Printed and bound in Great Britain by
TJ International Ltd, Padstow, Cornwall

Library of Congress Cataloging-in-Publication Data
Helms-Mills, Jean.
    Understanding organizational change/Jean Helms Hills, Kelly Dye
and Albert J. Mills
        p. cm.
    Includes bibliographical references and index.
    1. Organizational change.   I. Dye, Kelly.   II. Mills, Albert J.,
194.   II. Title.
    HD58.8.H458 2008
    658.4′06—dc22   2008008883

ISBN 10: 0–415–35576–1 (hbk)
ISBN 10: 0–415–35577–X (pbk)
ISBN 10: 0–203–00220–2 (ebk)

ISBN 13: 978–0–415–35576–6 (hbk)
ISBN 13: 978–0–415–35577–3 (pbk)
ISBN 13: 978–0–203–00220–9 (ebk)

Understanding Organizational Change

This ex

tional c

book p

about t

impact

change

The bo

- Th
- Ty
  Six
- Th
  fas
- Th
- Ui

The au

Atlant

and ex

import

organi

Jean Helms Mills is a Professor of Management at Saint Mary's University, Canada. Her research interests are organizational culture and change, gender, the cold war and critical sensemaking. She is the author of *Making Sense of Organizational Change* (Routledge).

Kelly Dye, PhD, is a faculty member at Acadia University, where she teaches organizational behaviour and change management.

Albert J. Mills, PhD, is Professor of Management and director of the PhD program at St Mary's University in Canada.

Contents

Figures

Acknowledgements

From Kelly Dye:

I wish to thank my husband and daughter for their unwavering support and encouragement. Without them, projects like this would never be possible. I would also like to thank my co-authors for their hard work and advice. I couldn't ask for better partners. Finally, I would like to thank a special student, Jessica Vaughan, for her help with the manuscript.

From Jean Helms Mills and Albert Mills:

Without an editor a book wouldn't be possible and we would like to thank Francesca Heslop for her encouragement in helping us bring this book to fruition. Also thanks to our many students, whose insights we have tried to incorporate into the book. In particular, Sheila Sutherland, for your help in reviewing the final manuscript.

1 Making sense of organizational change

Objectives of this chapter:

By the end of this chapter, you should:

1 Understand what is meant by programmatic change
2 Be able to define organizational change
3 Be familiar with the development of the field of change management
4 Understand the importance of change management
5 Be familiar with developments in both the theory and practice of change management
6 Understand and be able to apply the sensemaking framework

Business as usual. A day in the life of the business world

Tuesday, June 7, 2005 was, as things go, a fairly normal day in the world of business and political affairs. In the news Alexander Solzhenitsyn, the former Soviet dissident, had emerged from years of obscurity to warn that Russia was ripe for a new pro-democracy revolution; Tony Blair, Britain's Prime Minister, clashed with President Jacques Chirac of France over changes to the constitution of the European Union; the United States government considered banning the use of marijuana for medical purposes; and Canada's Ontario Provincial Government announced plans to end mandatory retirement at age sixty-five.

Meanwhile, innumerable companies were going about their business and those that were large enough, important enough and/or interesting enough made it into the business pages of the major newspapers. That day *The Times* of London reported on the affairs of forty-three leading companies; *The New York Times* covered fifty-five companies; and Canada's *Globe and Mail* focused on one hundred and forty companies. Interestingly, of the two hundred and five individual companies featured (see Figure 1.1) only twenty-seven drew the attention of more than one of the three newspapers. Of these twenty-seven, only a quarter were newsworthy because of their success. Of the successful companies, five had expanded their operations by taking over other companies, including media company *E. W. Scripps* (purchased the online comparison-shopping site *Shopzilla*), US real estate investment trust *ProLogis* (bought *Catellus Development*), US savings and loan company *Washington Mutual* (purchased the credit card company *Providian Financial*), the London-based drinks company *Diageo PLC* (took over *Allied Domecq*), and the oil-drilling outfit *Weatherford International* (bought two divisions of *Precision Drilling Corporation*). Two other companies announced expansion plans – *Flybe*, the UK regional airline, ordered a large number of new aircraft, and US home improvement giant *Lowe's* revealed plans to open branches in Canada in 2007. For four other companies the news was mixed. *Daimler-Chrysler* announced above average growth overall but a drop in its Mercedes sales; *Pfizer* reported that the US government had both approved extension of sales of Viagra for pulmonary hypertension and fined the company for price-fixing; *Citigroup* announced the take-over of *ABN/Amro*, and the loss of important data; and, similarly, *Time-Warner* had taken over another company – *Adelphia*, and was experiencing data security failure.

The majority of the twenty-seven companies were undergoing challenges of a different kind. Several faced bankruptcy or takeover, including *Adelphia Communications Corp., Allied Domecq, Catellus Development, Precision Drilling Corp., Providian Financial Corp.* and *Shopzilla*. Data security failure, i.e. lost or stolen data, dogged four companies (*Citigroup, Time-Warner, Bank of America, Wachovia*). Five companies faced corruption charges that included accusations of doctored accounts (*American International Group*), a criminal probe into false reporting on sales and stockpiling (*Bristol-Myers Squibb*), investigation by the US Justice Department (*Quest Diagnostics*), and price-fixing fines (*Pfizer; Serono Inc.*). *Boeing* was newsworthy for laying off employees and selling one of its plants to *Onex*. *Morgan Stanley* was going through a series of resignations by executives and was dropped from a group handling the sale of *France Télécom*. *United Airlines* was reportedly using pension law loopholes to hide its economic problems; and *Microsoft* was ordered to pay $8.9 million to a Guatemalan inventor in a patent case, and there was reportedly near agreement with the European Commission to comply with anti-trust legislation.

This tip of the business iceberg reflected much that was going on in the remaining 178 companies featured in the business news that day. Competitiveness and expansion characterized more than sixty per cent. Some companies were newsworthy because of their market position (e.g. *WB* 'one of the big six broadcasters' in the US), financial standing (e.g. *TransCanada Power* a 'blue-chip trust') or share value (e.g. *Canadian Tire Corp.*, 'a good investment'). Others made the news for takeovers (e.g. *Aga Foodservice* purchased rival *Waterford Stanley*) and mergers (e.g. UK drug distributor *Alliance Unichem* joined with Portugal's *National Association of Pharmacies*), expansion (e.g. *Asda*'s expansion into Northern Ireland) and exploration (e.g. *Dragon Oil*), new strategies (e.g. *CVS Corp*), new leaders (e.g. the appointment by *Kodak Canada* of a new CEO and President), and new products (e.g. Swiss company *Novartis'* development of an anti-malaria drug). On the dark side of the coin, seventeen companies were reported to be involved in some form of corrupt business practice, fifteen reported loss of business, slumping sales, or excess capacity, while a further ten declared bankruptcy or were taken over; five companies reported data security problems, three were involved in top leadership problems, two each experienced financial problems, trade disputes, or injunctions against them; two companies were involved in an advertising controversy, one faced a discrimination claim, and one declared lay-offs. In other words, one third of the featured 178 companies, were undergoing some form of change that brought them negative attention. And for those in charge, June 7 was either a good or a bad day, depending on which company they led.

That day *The Times*, the *Globe and Mail* and *The New York Times* reported the affairs of seventy-one business leaders – sixty-seven men and four women (see Figure 1.2). Of these, only two men and one woman were of interest to more than one newspaper. Debby Hopkins, the Chief of Operations and Technology for *Citigroup* came off well. True, *Citigroup* was involved in a data loss problem but that was somewhat overshadowed by the announcement that the company was taking over *ABN/Amro*. Maurice Greenburg (former head of *AIG*) and John Houldsworth (former head of *General Reinsurance Corp*'s Dublin operations) did not fare so well: Greenburg reportedly had been forced to retire due to 'regulatory scrutiny', while Houldsworth pleaded guilty to criminal conspiracy. Greenburg and Houldsworth were not the only ones to receive negative press. Richard M. Scrushy (co-founder and former CEO of *HealthSouth*) was on trial, indicted on eighty-five counts of accounting irregularities, and Frank Quattrone (Chief Technology Banker at *Credit Suisse First Boston*) was on trial for fraud and obstruction of justice. Scrushy was later found innocent on all counts but Quattrone was sentenced to eighteen months for obstruction of justice. However, the great majority of business leaders who were front-and-centre received positive press for announcing advances in their companies' fortunes. By all accounts, business was doing well.

The operations of companies and other organizations are impacted by a variety of factors, including leadership change, merger, growth and expansion, downsizing, the introduction of new products, technological change, industrial disputes, competition, changing political climate and legislation, changing consumer tastes, legal intervention and many other factors. Some of these factors – such as changed strategies, downsizing, and new leadership – are responses to a changing environment. Some – such as new or increased competition and changing consumer tastes – are the triggers of organizational change. Some – such as new technologies, changed strategies and new leaders – are both responses to perceived change and powerful triggers of organizational change. And, on Tuesday, June 7, 2005, all of these factors were of sufficient impact to be newsworthy for a number of leading companies. Interestingly, what was not mentioned was *programmatic change, i.e. pre-packaged change programmes, such as Total Quality Management and Business Process Re-engineering, which focus on changing core organizational processes through the application of a series of elaborate rules and guidelines.* On June 7, 2005 none of the companies were mentioned as having adopted or applied programmes of Culture Change (CC), Total Quality Management (TQM), Business Process Re-engineering (BPR), the Balance Scorecard (BSC) or Six Sigma (SS).

Change is an everyday occurrence but it is not just any change that catches attention and forces organizational leaders and other stakeholders to take action. It is usually not the everyday occurrence that makes an impact on the thinking of those in charge of organizations. When we think about organizational change we are referring to that level of difference that makes a significant or substantial impact on the way people think about their organization. It is a change that affects some aspect of peoples' jobs and the way they carry out those jobs. Thus, *organizational change can be defined as an alteration of a core aspect of an organization's operation.* Core aspects include the structure, technology, culture, leadership, goal or personnel of an organization. An alteration or change to any or all of these elements can range from the restructuring of a single department through to a restructuring of the entire company; the introduction of new machinery to a complete change in the way production is organized; a change in the thinking

◆ = Culture change ■ = TQM ◆ = Balanced Scorecard ● = Reengineering ◎ = Six Sigma
Abbott Laboratories Inc ■◆
ABC (One of 'big six broadcasters')
ABN/Amro ■◆
Adelphia Communications ●CPM
Aeroplan (Income trusts tip)
Aga Foodservice (Purchases rival *Waterford Stanley*)
Airbus ■
Alliance Atlantis (Media competitor)
Alliance Unichem (UK drug distributor joins with Portugal Nat'l Assoc. of Pharmacies)
Allied Domecq (Potential bidder steps aside to let *Pernod Ricard* purchase rival company: To sell *Montana* to *Diageo*)
American International Group ■
Ameritrade (In merger talks with *TD Bank*)
Apple ■◆
ARXX Building Products (Reference to former leader now at *Lowe's*)
Asda (Expands into Northern Ireland, buys former *Safeway* stores from *Morrison's*)
Asset Strategics (Big purchase of another company)
Astral Media (Largely owned by BCE; media competitor)
ATI Technologies Inc (Falling revenues; shares drop 10%; strategy problem; competition; seasonal decline; stock market slump)
Bank of America ■◎
Bank of England (Raised interest rates due to economic slowdown)
Battery Ventures (Bidding for *Nymex* share)
Bayer Corp ■
BCE ◆
Beaver Lumber Co. (Reference to former leader now at *Lowe's*)
Belhaven (Independent brewer expanding properties)
Bell Globemedia (BGM) (Threat of sale by BCE)
Berkshire Hathaway Inc (General RE unit; accused of corruption)
Best Buy Inc. (Reference to earlier takeover of *Future Shop*)
Bick's Pickles (Controversial advertisement – see *Ogilvy & Mather*)
Big Rock Brewery Income Trust (Puts brewery up for sale; excess capacity)
Blackstone Group (Bidding for *Nymex* share)
Blizzard Energy Inc (Purchased by *Shiningbank*)
BMO Nesbitt Burns (Investment dealer)
Boeing ◆■◆
Bombardier ◆●◎
Bonavista Energy (Potential financial problems)
Boots (Britain showing signs of slowdown)
Bristol-Myers Squibb (To settle criminal probe over inflated sales)
British Retail Consortium (Falling High Street sales)
Canadian Pacific Ltd. (Good investment tip – see Rankin)
Canadian Pacific Railway Ltd (Expansion plans)
Canadian Tire Corp. Ltd ◆
CanWest Global Communications (Purchase of Black's media empire in 2000; wins injunction against *MTG*)
Capital Economics (Reports British economy slowdown)
Catellus Development Corp (Bought by *ProLogis*)
CBS (One of 'big six broadcasters')
Centrica (British utility group buys Dutch energy supplier *Oxxio*)
Cessna Aircraft (In same town as *Mid-Western*)
CGI Group Inc. (Outsources to *Uni-Sélect Inc*)
ChoicePoint (Data security failure)
Chrysler ◆■●◆
CHUM (Purchase of *Craig Media* in early 2000s)
CIBC World Markets ◆■◆
CitiFinancial (Client data goes missing in *UPS* package)
Citigroup ●◎
Cobequid Life Sciences Inc. (Good investment tip – see Rankin)
Comcast (Purchased bankrupt *Adelphia* – see also *Time Warner*)
Connors Bros. Income Fund (Dip in share price)
Corus (Media competitor)
Craig Media (Taken over by *CHUM*)
Crestview Partners (To buy assets from *Adelphia* and *ML Media Partners LP*)
CVS Corp (New strategy)
Daimler-Chrysler ●
Daimler-Chrysler AG (above average growth)
Dairy Queen Canada Inc.(Announces marketing strategy)
Diageo (Buys *Pernod* asset and agrees to stay out of *Domecq* fight)
Dragon Oil (Approached for shares stake)

Figure 1.1

E*Trade Financial Corp. (Takeover attempt of *Ameritrade*)
E.W. Scripps (Buys *Shopzilla*)
Easy Cruise (Adding second ship)
eBay (Buys *Shopping.com*)
Embraer SA (Sales to *Flybe*)
Empresa Brasileira de Aeronáutica (Gets order for 14 passenger jets from *Flybe*)
Enron Corp. (Jailed employee)
Entrée Gold Inc (Opportunities in Mongolia)
Erdene Gold Inc. (Opportunities in Mongolia; strategic alliance with *Erdenet Mining Corp.*)
Erdenet Mining Corp (Strategic alliance with *Erdene Gold*)
Eurotunnel (Seeking help from European Transport Commission to stave off bankruptcy)
Experian (Data lost by *CitiFinancial*)
Flybe (British regional airline orders 14 passenger jets from *Embraer*)
Ford Motor Co. ◆■●◆◎
Fox (One of 'big six' broadcasters)
FPI Ltd (To spin off as publicly trade company – *Ocean Cuisine International*)
France Telecom (France willing to sell as much as 8% of France Telecom)
Future Shop (Takeover by *Best Buy*)
GE Aviation Materials (Corporate bias case)
General Electric ◆■●◆◎
General Motors ◆■●
General Re Corporation (Senior executive pleads guilty to helping *American International Group* 'doctor' its books)
Gold Fields (Merger with *Norilk Nickel* blocked by S. African Government)
Good Technology Inc (*RIM* competitor)
Google Inc. (Runaway success)
Grant Thornton (Announces new Senior Manager)
Group Five (Wins Dubai airport expansion contract)
GW Pharmaceuticals (Lost appeal to launch cannabis therapy)
Hanover Investments (Seized control of the chemical company *Elementis*)
HealthSouth (Trial of former chief executive Richard M. Scrushy)
Hoare Govett (Defectors to *Citigroup*)
Hollinger Inc (Leadership trying to get rid of Board member)
Home Depot ◆■
Home Hardware (Earlier purchase of *Beaver Lumber*)
Honda (Competitor to *GM*)
HSBC Bank Canada (Owned by *HSBC Holdings Plc* ●)
HSBC Financial Corp (Buys *Invis Inc*; owned by *HSBC Holdings Plc*; and sister of *HSBC Bank Canada*)
IBM◆■●
Intel Corp. (Competitor for *ATI*)
Invis Inc (Bought by *HSBC Fin. Corp*)
Ivanhoe Mines Ltd (developing gold-copper deposits – see Entrée Gold)
J.P Morgan◆■
Jean Coutu Group (PJC) Inc. (Good investment)
King Pharmaceuticals Inc. (Price-fixing fine)
Kodak Canada Inc. (New President and CEO)
LexisNexis (Data security failure)
Lowe's (Plans to open first Canadian store in 2007; gender strategy)
Mamma.com Inc (Cease trade ban lifted)
Mapeley (Property group selling new shares)
Marks & Spencer (Showing signs of slowdown)
Mediapost (Comments on big broadcasters reducing commercial rates)
Microsoft ◆■
MidOcean Partners (Buy assets from *Adelphia* and *ML Media*)
Mid-Western Aircraft Systems (Subsidiary of *Onex*)
Milo's Knitwear International (U.S. trade dispute with China regarding textiles)
Minerva (Property group agree to sell to rival)
Mirkaie Trikshret Group (MTG) (Loses injunction by *CanWest*)
ML Media Partners LP (Sell assets to *MidOcean* and *Creastview*)
Moffat Communications Inc (Illicit gains – see Rankin)
Molson Co. ●
Montana (To be sold to *Diageo PLC*)
Morgan Stanley ■
Motorola ◆■
MTU Aero Engineers (Shares rose more than 2 percent)
NBC ◆
Nokia Corp (*RIM* competitor)
Nortel (Stockmarket slump)
Novartis (Develops anti malaria drug)
Nvidia Corp. (Competitor to *ATI*)

Figure 1.1   Continued

Nynex ◆
OAU Yukos (Corruption charges)
Ocean Cuisine International (To be publicly traded)
Ogilvy & Mather (Controversial advertisement – see *Bick's*)
Onex Corp (Buys *Boeing* plant; lay offs)
Pearson PLC (Seen as potential partner by *BGM*)
Pernod Ricard SA (Sell Bushmills to Diageo)
PetroKazakhstan (Order to return misappropriated oil)
Pfizer ◆●
Pizza Pizza (Income trusts)
Precision Drilling Corp. (Selling to *Weatherford*)
Premier Foods (Buys *Marlow Foods*)
Prologis (Buys *Catellus Development Corp.*)
Providian Financial (Bought by *Washington Mutual*)
Pure Digital (Strategy at CVS)
Quebecor (Media competitor)
Quest Diagnostics (Being investigated by Justice Department)
Ravelston Corp. (Corruption charges; in receivership)
Raytheon Aircraft (In same town as *Mid-Western*)
RBC Securities Dominion Bank (Insider trading)
RCS Media Group (Prepare for corporate take over)
Reitmans (Canada) Ltd (Good investment)
Renewable Energy Holdings (Smaller stock to watch)
Rentokil (Appoints new CFO)
RIM (Facing competition from *Microsoft*; stock-market slump)
Rogers Communications (Media competitor)
Rona Inc. (Canadian rival to *Lowe's*)
Roots store (Mentioned in passing – see Rankin)
Royal Bank of Canada ●
Royal Dutch/Shell (Replaces technology advances with security threats as strategy)
Samsung Electronics Co. Ltd (Referenced as supplier to *Pure Digital*)
Saputo (Sales affected by higher prices)
SAS ◆
Schering-Plough Corp. (Price-fixing fine)
Schlumberger Ltd (Major competitor for *PDC* and *Weatherford*)
Serono Inc. (Price-fixing fine)
Serono SA (Parent of *Serono* Inc)
Seven Networks Inc. (*RIM* competitor)
Shiningbank Energy Income Fund (Buys *Blizzard Energy Inc.*)
Shoppers Drug Mart Corp. (Good investment)
Shopping.com (Purchased by *eBay*)
Shopzilla (Bought by *E.W. Scripps*)
Sony Ericsson Mobile Communications AB ◆■●◎
Starwood ●◎
T. Eaton Co. ◆■
Textile Council of Hong Kong (U.S. trade dispute with China regarding textiles)
The Ivy (London restaurant opening in NYC)
Time Warner ◆
Toronto-Dominion Bank (Take over bid for *Ameritrade*)
Torstar (Media competitor)
TransCanada Power (Blue-chip trust)
Uni-Sélect Inc (Outsourcer for *CGI*)
United Airlines ◆■
United Parcel Service Inc ◆■●
UPN (One of 'big six' broadcasters)
Vancity Enterprises (Big contract)
Vancouver City Savings Credit Union (Parent of *Vancity*)
Visco Corp. (*RIM* competitor)
Visionary Vehicles (Want to import cars from China; two top executives leave after falling out with head of company)
Visteon Corp (Restructuring; staff back to Ford)
Volswagen AG (Cost-cutting)
Wachovia (Data security failure)
Wachovia Corp. (Stolen data)
Walt Disney Company ◆■●
Washington Mutual (Buys *Providian Financial*)
WB (One of 'big six' broadcasters)
Weatherford Int'l (Buys 2 segments of *Precision Drilling*)
Windmill Development Group (Big contract)
Woolworth's Group (Sales down because of decrease in DVD sales)

Figure 1.1 Companies in the news (Tuesday, June 7, 2005).

Source: Compiled from the business sections of *The New York Times*, *The Times* and the *Globe and Mail* for 7 June, 2005

Note: Bracketed statements are edited comments from the respective newspapers for 7 June, 2005

Ackerley, Peter (President – *Erene*) Ballmer, Steve (Chief Executive – *Microsoft*)
Balsillie, James (Chair and Co-CEO – *RIM*)
Belleghem, Joe Van (Head – *Windmill*)
Bramson, Edward (Founder – *Hanover Investments*)
Bricklin, Malcolm (Head – *Visionary Vehicles*)
Bridgeford, Greg (Executive VP of Business Development – *Lowe's*)
Buffett, Warren (Head – *Berkshire Hathaway*)
Caring, Richard (Owner – *Ivy Restaurant*, New York)
Clark, Ed (CEO – *TD Bank*)
Crowe, Greg (Pres – Entreé)
Crowley, Patrick (CFO – *ATI*)
Davis, Chuck (CEO – *Shopzilla*)
Disney, Roy E. (Large investor – *Walt Disney Company*)
Ducey, Michael P. (Former President and Chair – *Kodak Canada*)
Dutton, Robert (CEO – *Rona*)
Eddington, R (Outgoing CEO – *British Airways*)
Eisner, Michael D. (Outgoing CEO – *Walt Disney Company*)
French, Jim (MD – *Flybe*)
Givens, Beth (Director – *Privacy Rights Clearing House*)
Godin, Serge (Chair and CEO – *CGI*)
Gold, Stanley P. (Financial advisor to Roy E. Disney)
Gounon, Jacques (Chair – *Eurotunnel*)
Greenberg, Maurice R. (Former Chairman of *A.I.G.*)
Hawkins. Kevin (Director General – *British Retail Consortium*)
Heyer, Stephen (CEO – *Starwood*)
Hopkins, Debby (Chief Operations and Technology – *Citigroup*)
Hopkins, Keith (Chairman –*Elementis*)
Houldsworth, John (Former Executive – *General Re Corporation*)
Jobs, Steven P. (Founder, Head – *Apple*)
Jones, Digby (Director-General *CBI*)
Kaplan, Jonathon (CEO – *Pure Digital*)
Kessinger, Kevin (Executive VP – *Citigroup's* global consumer group)
Khodorkovsky, Mikhail (Head – *OAO Yukos*)
Khouri, Jacques (President and CEO – *Vancity*)
Killinger, Kerry K. (CEO – *Washington Mutual*)
Kravis, Henry (Co-founder – *Kravis Roberts*)
Leve, Brian R. (Appointed to board – *Grant Thornton*)
Lin, Willy (Managing Director – *Milo's Knitwear International*)
Lowe, Kenneth (CEO – *E.W. Scripps*)
Lutz, Robert (Vice Chair – *GM*)
Mandese, Joe (Editor – *Mediapost*)
McFarlane, Andrew (CFO – *Rentokil*)
Mey, Susan E.C. (President and Chair – *Kodak Canada*)
Mohapatra, Surya N. (Chairman and Chief Executive – *Quest Diagnostics*)
Monty, Jean (Former boss – *BCE*)
Morningstar, Bill (Executive VP for Media Sales – *WB*)
Newsome, James (President – *Nymex*)
Niblock, Robert A. (CEO – *Lowe's*)
Otellini, Paul (CEO – *Intel*)
Pischetrieder, Bernd (CEO – *Volkswagen*)
Pohl, Eric (Co-Head – *Dresdener Kleinwort Wasserstein*)
Pouzilhac, Alain (CEO – *Havas*, French advertising group)
Quattrone, F. (Former Executive of *Credit Suisse/First Boston*)
Robinson, Doug (President – *Lowe's Canada*)
Sabia, Michael ("Boss" – *BCE*)
Saputo, Lino (CEO – *Saputo*)
Schofield, Robert (CEO – *Premier Foods*)
Scrushy, Richard M. (Chief Executive – *HealthSouth*)
Slakinski, Ray (Independent Apple developer)
Swartout, Hank (Founder, CEO – *PDC*)
Taylor, Bernard (Former Executive – *Glaxo*; Founder – *Cambridge Laboratories*)
Tellier, Paul (Former CEO – *Bombardier*)
Thomas, Marcel T. (Chief Executive – *GE Aviation Materials*)
Topper, David (Executive – *Morgan Stanley*)
van der Veer, Jeroen (Chief Executive – *Royal Dutch Shell*)
Verschuren, Annette (President – *Home Depot Canada*)
Wagoner, Rick (CEO – *GM*)
Walker, Ulrich (Head of Smart Division – *Daimler-Chrysler*)
Walsh, Paul (CE – *Diageo*)
White, Peter (Board member– *Hollinger*)

Figure 1.2 Business leaders in the news.

Source: Compiled from the business sections of *The New York Times*, *The Times* and the *Globe and Mail* for 7 June, 2005

of a group or department to a fundamental revamping of the corporate symbolism; the replacement of a CEO or the introduction of an entirely new management team; the introduction of a new product or service through to a rethink of the fundamental way it does business; and organizational change can range from the closing of selected departments through to the expansion of all departments. It is not so much the scale of the change that is important but the extent to which its impact is felt within the organization.

The development of change management

It has long been recognized that change is an important factor in the success and survival of organizations and this has led to the development of ways to manage organizational change. As we shall see in following chapters, the earliest attempts to develop a systematic approach to change management began in the era following the Second World War, with the work of Kurt Lewin and his work on leadership style,[1] sensitivity training, action research and force field analysis. Lewin's focus on change management developed from his interest in addressing such things as patterns of aggressive behaviour, and racial and religious intolerance. Researchers in the management field have subsequently built on Lewin's work to address issues of workplace motivation, productivity and resistance to change. Within the literature on change management, Lewin's focus on leadership style, sensitivity training, action research and force field analysis remains. However, the underlying motivation for the research has changed from a broader interest in community wellbeing to a specific concern with the successful operation of the business organization.[2]

Initially, change management research centred on discrete areas of behavioural change, focusing on leadership (e.g. leadership style), training (e.g. sensitivity training), and/or attitude change (e.g. participatory management). Eventually, various aspects of the emerging research on action research, laboratory training, participative management and survey feedback coalesced into a systematic approach aimed at the long-term change of organizational structure, beliefs and values. This new, systematic approach became known as Organizational Development, or OD, and was a forerunner of the programmatic change programmes that started to appear in the 1980s.

By the turn of the 1980s, an interest in organizational change was an established part of the thinking of business practitioners and educators but it was about to take several important turns. Whereas previously change was seen as an ongoing, incremental problem, requiring changed attitudes and behaviours, it was beginning to be perceived as an *imperative*, i.e. something that managers needed to do; something they ignored at their peril. With the onset of 'globalization' business educators and practitioners began to focus on the power of external change factors to influence the life and death of the organization. The management of change became an essential part of the business education of the manager and with it came a number of *programmatic* change strategies and models, starting with a focus on corporate strategizing and the management of corporate culture (CC), through a series of change techniques that include Quality of Working Life (QWL), Total Quality Management (TQM), Business Process Re-engineering (BPR), the Balance Scorecard (BSC), and Six Sigma. As organizational change came increasingly to mean programmatic change, change management became big business in itself, garnering billions of dollars for consultancy firms and the authors of 'how-to' books.[3]

The importance of change management

The management of change is important for a number of reasons. As we have seen from our list of newsworthy companies, a number of factors trigger a perceived need for change. Managers need to deal with issues of changing technologies and customer tastes, government regulation, industrial relations issues, competition, cash flow issues and accounting practices, data security, leadership change and a host of other issues that may either threaten or enhance the survival and growth of the organization. This means that managers and other organizational stakeholders need to be aware of the variety of factors that can affect the way they do business. They also need to be aware that how they make sense of those factors is an important determinant of how their organization experiences change.[4] For example, in the mid-1980s senior management at *Coca-Cola* were acutely aware that changing tastes, amidst fierce competition from other soft drinks manufacturers, could lead to a drop in demand for their cola product. How they made sense of that awareness was another problem. They decided to be proactive and drop their established Coke in favour of 'New Coke'. In the process they faced widespread anger from customers demanding the reinstatement of the old Coke, or the 'Classic Coke' as it was renamed. Thus, awareness of potential problems is part of the problem of managing change. Making sense of the problem is the other crucial part.

Sensemaking is also a critical element in programmatic change. Decisions about whether and when to introduce programmatic change often depend on how senior managers make sense of the issues they face and their perception of the value of any given change programme. For example, when Louis Comeau took over as the CEO of *Nova Scotia Power* in the early 1980s his perception was of a company lacking in cohesion and unity of purpose. This was reinforced when he commissioned a workplace survey, which confirmed a general lack of morale. There were a number of ways that Comeau could have dealt with this perceived problem. The action he chose was to introduce a programme of culture change. This decision was greatly influenced by the fact that culture change was popular among business leaders at the time, including industry leader *Florida Light & Power* and the highly successful local communications company *MT&T*. In other words, Comeau's sense of the situation and its resolve was influenced by the popular practices of the time.

The management of change, particularly with the advent of programmatic change, has become a powerful business in its own right. For consultants it can mean billions of dollars in programme development, implementation and training fees. For senior managers it can mean solutions to survival, growth and profitability. For customers it can mean improved and efficient service, and for employees it can mean opportunities for job improvements. As we shall see, all of these things make the management of change an attractive field of endeavour. But there are also downsides that we can learn from. For example, where organizational change is deemed to have failed this can lead to the firing of senior managers and falls in shareholder equity;[5] whether a success or a failure, many important change initiatives can result in employee lay-offs, demotion and job dissatisfaction as new ways of working are introduced; and customers can become dissatisfied as they experience an unwanted change, or a decline, in service.[6] The process of organizational change today is as much shrouded in threat and fear as it is in opportunity and promise. In theory and practice, change management is part of a powerful discourse of management in today's world.

In practice

As we shall see throughout this book, a large number of companies adopt not just one but a variety of organizational change programmes over time.[7] This is true of a large number of the companies, including those featured in Figure 1.1. *BCE, Canadian Tire, NBC* and *Nynex*, for example, have adopted a culture change programme at some point in recent years. *Airbus, American International Group*, and *Morgan Stanley* have all adopted TQM programmes. *Molson, Royal Bank of Canada* and *Sony* have reengineered their companies. *ABN/Amro, Apple Computers* and *Citigroup* have adopted the Balanced Scorecard approach, while *Bank of America, GE, Ford* and *Starwood Hotels* adopted Six Sigma. Many companies – including *Boeing, Chrysler, CIBC* and *Citigroup* – have adopted most or all of the various programmatic change strategies, earning the title 'serial changers'.[8]

In the process, these companies have become exemplars of change and have contributed to a growing industry of change management that has developed from a piecemeal approach to a billion dollar industry.[9] This has been assisted through innumerable press releases, website messages, 'how-to' books, the growth of the consulting business and the extensive highlighting of company successes throughout business texts, course materials and a range of scholarly articles. The *CIBC* website, for example, links 'consistent, sustainable performance over the long term' to the 'disciplined measurement of . . . performance' through a Balanced Scorecard approach[10] and *ING*'s Head of Management Accounting, Popko de Vlugt, contends that the introduction of the Balanced Scorecard has led to a greater 'focus on the commercial effectiveness of management'.[11] Six Sigma has been heralded by *Air Canada Jazz*'s Vice President of Corporate Strategy, Jolene Mahody, as 'an ingrained part of the culture' of the company,[12] while *General Electric* CEO,

Jack Welch, claimed that Six Sigma saved his company five billion dollars.[13] Wayne Crawley, the former Director of Internal Auditing for *Nova Scotia Power Inc.*, claims that the elimination of jobs through re-engineering made his company more cost-effective and customer-focused.[14]

The message is effective. At the start of the twenty-first century, fifty per cent of Fortune 1,000 companies had adopted the Balanced Scorecard as one of several change strategies;[15] and many of the top corporations were listed as 'six sigma companies'.[16]

In theory

Since the mid-1970s, there has been a rapid growth in the number of scholarly books and journal articles on organizational change, including ways to manage change, ways to overcome resistance to change and specific programmatic methods of change. A look in any management journal, business section of the newspaper, management text or magazine (e.g. *Fortune* or *Forbes*) confirms that organizational change has become a key management discourse. Between January 1994 and February 1995, over 1,200 articles were published on re-engineering alone[17] and from January 1994 to February 1996 over 1,000 articles were published on Total Quality Management.[18] Between 1960 and 2006, the number of change management books housed in the US Library of Congress alone went from zero to 3,404 (see Figure 1.3). Over the same time period, there was a massive growth in the number of books written on specific change programmes, including Organizational Development (OD), Quality of Work Life (QWL), Organizational Culture (OC), Corporate Culture (CC), Business Process Re-engineering (BPR), Total Quality Management (TQM), the Balanced Scorecard (BSC) and Six Sigma (SS) – see Figure 1.4. A similar trend was evident from a website search in 2002 which indicated that just

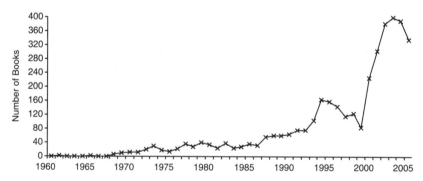

Figure 1.3 Organizational change books housed in the US Library of Congress, 1960–2005.

Source: Adapted from Helms Mills (2003: 78) and compiled from books referencing either 'organizational change' or 'organisational change' in the online references of the US Library of Congress

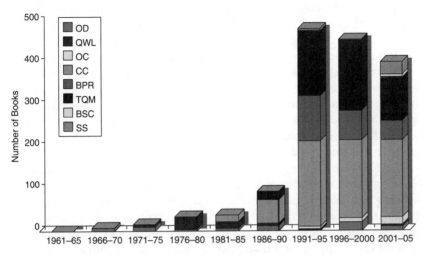

Figure 1.4 Growth of books on organizational change.

Source: Adapted from Helms Mills (2003: 79) and compiled from online references of books housed in the US Library of Congress that reference Organizational Development (OD), Quality of Work Life (QWL), Organizational (OC) or Corporate (CC) Culture, Business Process Re-engineering (BPR), Total Quality Management (TQM), the Balanced Scorecard (BSC) and Six Sigma (SS)

under 2,000 articles had been published on organizational change in the previous five years.[19] While the focus may vary, the underlying message is the same. If your company has not been involved in some sort of change initiative, it may not be living up to its potential. Indeed, those who have been successful at promoting change have been elevated to guru-like status, as change fads and fashions come and go.[20]

Although today's discourse of change contains many of the elements of the earlier, pre-1980, approach to change, the difference between then and now is that organizational change has come to be thought of as a holistic, rather than piecemeal, approach to organizational effectiveness. The focus of change used to be on strategies for managing. Organizations engaged in OD techniques to improve the behavioural or structural levels of the company. It was a way to ensure that a company capitalized on its effectiveness. Nowadays, the emphasis on organizational effectiveness and customer satisfaction is often rooted in a drive to be seen as cutting-edge. Through application of the latest techniques, the senior manager can derive satisfaction from knowing that he or she will be seen as forward-thinking in their attempts to ensure company survival and growth in a global economy.

So how did this happen? Over time, globalization has forced organizations to re-evaluate their strategic direction. This has caused a shift away from a concern for the individual to the broader concerns of how to deal with competition and the instability of the business environment. During the late 1980s and early 1990s, privatization was seen as the logical solution. But it brought with it a new set of issues and problems, which helped to redefine the definition of change as a 'planned or unplanned response to pressures and forces'[21] and created a sense of urgency. With the publication of Tom Peters and Robert Waterman's (1982) seminal book *In Search of Excellence* the idea of creating 'excellent companies' through programmatic change captured the interest of the business community and solidified the need for managers to seek out pre-packaged solutions that would ready them for the unexpected and help them to manage it. The Peters and Waterman book was so popular that it became the first management book to take first place on the *New York Times* bestseller list and it was translated into sixteen different languages. It was no accident that companies, *Nova Scotia Power* included, were convinced by consultants of the benefits of implementing culture change in the mid-1980s.

Peters and Waterman's culture change was soon followed by other programmatic approaches on change and the popularity and acceptance of each approach was premised on the notion that the previous one was inadequate or harmful to the organization.[22] Over time, there developed a recurring theme of needing to find a change approach that emphasizes customer service and the use of 'expert' knowledge.

It is evident that the phenomenon of change has been driven, to a large extent, by economic factors. However, the popularity of organizational change management also owes much not only to management practices but also to its introduction to new generations of managers through business education. This has been increasingly the case as business schools have increased their attempts to blend with the business environment and focus on practical business applications. In fact, it has been suggested that management education and business school trends are guided by managers' needs.[23] Across a range of management textbooks, including introductory management texts, human resources management, organizational behaviour and organization theory, TQM, BPR and organizational culture are featured heavily.[24]

This blending of the academic and business community has allowed for the legitimization of management gurus, such as Peters and Waterman (OC), Hammer and Champy (BPR), and Peter Senge ('the learning organization'), to play a central role in bridging management theory with management practice.[25] But it is not only the business 'gurus' who are helping to normalize the process of programmatic change. At other levels, managers are informed of the benefits of such programmes by business publications (e.g. *Fortune, Forbes*), which in turn create a need for consultants, who are able to offer their expertise in implementing the programmes and are able to sell the idea of a ready-made solution to those facing a plethora of choice.

Objectives of this book

The exponential growth in both frequency and magnitude over the past twenty to thirty years, and the vast resources now committed to change programmes in companies around the globe, has created a need for today's students of business, as well as for managers and aspiring managers, to familiarize themselves with the phenomenon of organizational change.

A survey of North American-based companies involved in change programmes over the past twenty years indicates that thousands, including many top corporations, such as *Shell Oil, Mercedes Benz* and *McKinsey*, have engaged in some form of change programme.[26] According to a number of sources, programmatic change is important and vital and can have many benefits for the company and its various stakeholders. Numerous other accounts, on the other hand, claim that programmatic change is ineffective, costly and time-consuming. All agree that organizational change is a widespread and important topic of study.

Who is our audience?

First and foremost, this book is aimed at students of organizational change – the managers and employees of tomorrow. The book will provide the ability to assess the need for organizational change, master the techniques of programmatic change, manage organizational change and/or assist you in understanding and surviving the process of organizational change.

Anyone who is interested in organizational change in the twenty-first century needs to have a solid grounding in the early theories of organizational change, an understanding of the factors that contributed to its evolution from a series of techniques that provided a piecemeal approach to bettering the workplace to the full-scale management discourse that it is today. Therefore, this book is about more than learning how to 'manage' change. Instead, we will look at particular strategies of change and the historical background of change, to understand the development of this discourse. We will be focusing on theories aimed at 'organizational change' by exploring the symbiotic relationship between theory and practice.

Therefore, our purpose in writing this book is not to recommend or condemn specific change programmes, nor is it to pass judgement on whether change is good or 'bad', well managed or not, successful or unsuccessful. Instead, our goal, based on our own experiences in teaching courses on organizational change, is to provide you with a solid grounding in understanding the *process* of organizational change. This includes understanding why organizations engage in change, what factors influence the choice of specific change programmes, what factors contribute to and influence employees' understanding of these programmes and what we can learn from this.

In this book, we want to provide you with the knowledge and tools necessary to be able to make sense of and question the underlying assumptions of the elements that make up the organizational change discourse, so that you have a thorough understanding of the subject matter.

How to make sense of organizational change

It has been argued that change needs to be understood from a holistic perspective, one that can provide both a theoretical grounding and a practical application. In order to do this, we have adopted a 'sensemaking' approach in order to help us understand change.[27] This approach has been gaining popularity since the mid-1990s as a way to understand a variety of organizational processes. It is particularly helpful in this case because it not only provides a way of uncovering why individuals think and act but it also alerts managers to potential problems they could encounter in the change process. Whereas the traditional approach to the study of the management of change is mainly focused on issues of adoption, implementation and outcomes, sensemaking gives us the scope to explore the reasoning behind these issues.[28] For example, what are the factors that encourage managers to perceive a need for change and how do these perceptions influence the change process? What happens when a company adopts a particular change programme and what can we learn from this? With a sensemaking perspective, we attempt to answer these questions, as well as present a balanced account of the debates and issues surrounding change.

The sensemaking framework

What is a sensemaking perspective? There are in fact several approaches to sensemaking but our approach is based on the work of Karl Weick.[29] Weick contends that decision-making relies on seven, interrelated socio-psychological properties – retrospection, cues, ongoing sense, social sense, plausibility, identity construction and enactment.[30] To the list we have added an eighth property of projection.[31]

Drawing on the study of organizational change at *Nova Scotia Power*, the various properties can be explained in the following way:[32]

Retrospection: As Weick's research suggests, we tend to make sense of an act *after* it has occurred. We make *retrospective* sense of an event. Usually, we do this in an unconscious way but every now and then retrospective sensemaking surfaces where we say things like 'what was I thinking?' It is clear that people usually have an idea of what they are about to do and may well have planned it in advance. However, it is once they have acted that the sense of their action becomes meaningful. For example, Louis Comeau as CEO of *Nova Scotia Power* may have thought about introducing culture change to achieve a unity of purpose throughout the company. But we don't know that for sure. It was only once Comeau hired culture-change consultants to take action that we get a sense of that action. Why? Because, following an act, people reflect on what they have done as they attempt to explain and sometimes justify their actions. But they do not do this in an abstract way.

Cues: When we make sense of a situation we draw on selected cues to understand and explain action. For example, Comeau drew on cues that suggested that company morale was low, which signalled to him that a culture change was needed. However, our *selection* of cues is influenced by a number of factors, including an ongoing sense of a situation.

Ongoing sensemaking: When we make sense of anything we are influenced by what we 'know'. Ideas do not operate in a vacuum but arise in the context of pre-existing notions. Faced by low morale, Comeau did not invent the idea of culture change but rather drew on the power of an ongoing set of ideas throughout the industry and beyond that suggested that culture change was a solution to the types of problem *Nova Scotia Power* was experiencing. Likewise, ideas are not simple reflections of powerful ongoing ideas. Whether a particular act is pursued or not often depends on the set of social relations that the person is involved in.

Social sensemaking: When Comeau pursued the idea of culture change his company was a publicly owned 'Crown Corporation'. Thus, politically, he had to deal with government as well as customers and employees. These social groups helped to influence the cues that Comeau used to introduce culture change, as he emphasized a new culture that would value the province, the environment, the customer and the employee. However, by the early 1990s, *Nova Scotia Power* had been privatized and Comeau's social sensemaking experience was influenced by the new powerful shareholders and by an ongoing sense of the value of privatization. The previous cue of morale was replaced by a search for greater efficiencies as Comeau moved away from culture change and introduced Business Process Re-engineering.

Plausibility: At the heart of any successful action lies plausibility, a sense that something is believable or reasonable if not actually true. What makes something plausible is the ability of the actor (e.g. Louis Comeau) to sufficiently weave together a story or an account that in its utilization of cues adequately addresses the ongoing and social sense of a situation. When Comeau introduced culture change he was able to point not only to the results of an attitudes survey on morale but also to government and customer dissatisfaction. He was also able to cue the fact that the company consisted of geographically disparate entities that resulted from a series of mergers and takeovers. In other words, *Nova Scotia Power* needed help and part of the problem was the disparate nature of the different units. The introduction of re-engineering was more problematic. It was relatively easy to cue privatization, a new shareholding group and the need to be competitive to make a drive for efficiency plausible. It was less easy to deal with the fact that this new focus on efficiency (which resulted in a number of lay-offs) was in contradiction to the company's stated aim of valuing of employees. Here it was claimed that the re-engineering programme was not replacing the culture change but was in fact the second phase.

Identity construction: Any process of decision-making involves not only social pressures in the context of an ongoing sense but also an individual sensemaker who has to weigh the options. This will be affected in large part by the individual's experiences, values and beliefs, which form an integral part of his or her identity. Louis Comeau, for example, had been a federal politician before he took over as head of *Nova Scotia Power*. He was used to having to establish a rapport with people to gain their trust. As the Chief Executive Officer of *Nova Scotia Power* he inevitably drew on his previous experiences, which had shaped not only his identity but also his way of making sense of reality. Yet experiences are not fixed and concrete. They rely on selected cues, which are, in turn, influenced by ongoing and social sense-making. Senior managers have to learn how to become senior managers. They have to gain a sense of the job through a balance of experience, identity needs and dominant expectations of how a senior manager acts. By the time Louis Comeau took over as CEO of *Nova Scotia Power*, there was a powerful ongoing sense of the effective business leader as someone who could manage change in a global economy. The good manager was someone who anticipated change by consistently adopting the latest change techniques. The more quickly the manager adopted the latest programmatic change, the more cutting-edge he (and sometimes she) was seen to be. In that regard, Comeau was among the best; introducing attitude surveys in the early 1980s, culture change in the mid-1980s, and Business Process Re-engineering in the early 1990s.

Enactment: Making sense of a situation is only a part of the process. Enacting that sense is the critical part. Enactment refers to a situation where a sense of some thing or event is widely accepted. That is, that a particular sense (e.g. employment equity) is understood by a wide number of people. Clearly there can be various enactments of different senses of a situation. When *Nova Scotia Power* tried to introduce culture change to its militant Cape Breton unionized employees the workers staged a walk out. The union had successfully enacted a sense of the change as just another management ploy to get more out of the workers. In the meantime, employees in other regions of the company had seemingly bought into senior management's enactment of culture change as an attempt to value employees.

Projection: Enactment is influenced by a number of factors, not least of which is plausibility, but also the ability of more powerful actors to project their sense of a situation onto others, in the process shaping their understanding of the situation. The ability to project a sense onto a situation can be due to any combination of interpersonal skills, political power, social standing and/or economic power. Thus, an ongoing sense of a situation refers to a dominant view of reality. Enactment occurs through the shaping of ideas through a series of interpersonal relationships and the use of various media, including memos, company newsletters, annual reports, videos, newspapers, magazines, the web and other spaces where ideas are disseminated. At *Nova Scotia Power*, Louis Comeau was able to project a notion of the successful culture change on managers and employees by dint of his highly personable identity but especially due to the fact that he was the CEO and, as such, in overall charge of the flow of information and training throughout the company. Of course, it is not simply the power to project a sense of a situation that ultimately enacts it. Projection also depends on the exposure of others to a coherent alternative view, and the ability of other actors to project that alternative. In the *Nova Scotia Power* case the unionization of the Cape Breton workers provided the groundwork for an alternative social sense.

The sensemaking framework and organizational change

The sensemaking framework allows us to think more critically about organizational change. It encourages us to focus on organizational change as a *sense* of situation rather than a concrete fact: something that is both an interpretation and an outcome of interpretation. It directs us to go beyond the idea of manager as professional or expert to focus on his or her skill as a sensemaker. It leads us to question the notion of organizational change as a linear, wholly rational or necessary process, while requiring us to analyse the skills needed to successfully implement (or resist) organizational change. Table 1.1 lays out the sensemaking framework and its challenges for organizational change.

Table 1.1 Eight features of a sensemaking framework

Sensemaking Framework Feature	Definition	Implications for Change Managers
Sensemaking and identity construction	The different ways in which people make sense of the same organizational change events and how it is related to their understanding of the way their identities are constructed within organizations.	The 'top-down initiatives requiring dramatic changes of self (i.e. from humanist to efficiency locused) are highly problematic and need either to be avoided or handled with great skill'.
Social sensemaking	The need that people have to make sense of their situations not just as individuals but as social individuals is connected to a variety of influences on them such as supervisors, management, trade unions and so forth.	An understanding of social sensemaking highlights the need for managers to identify the social factors that influence sensemaking in their organizational contexts.

(Continued overleaf)

Table 1.1 Continued

Sensemaking Framework Feature	Definition	Implications for Change Managers
Extracted cues of sensemaking	The need for managers of change to be aware of the way people draw on a variety of 'cues' or ideas and actions, perhaps taken from the external environment, in order to make sense of various decisions.	Change managers need to identify appropriate cues and match them to intended change programmes. The way in which these cues are interpreted, however, may inadvertently create problems for staff in accepting the legitimacy of the change programme and its intended purposes.
Ongoing sensemaking	Sense-making changes over time as new cues are experienced and events addressed.	Change managers need to understand 'that ongoing sensemaking stabilizes a situation and how change acts as a shock, generating emotional response and new acts of sensemaking'.
Retrospection	Reference to Karl Weick's argument that people make sense of their actions retrospectively.	Change managers need to understand that different groups will apply their own retrospective sensemaking in order to understand emerging organizational events.
Plausibility	The way that change management programmes need to be sold so that the 'story' about the change is plausible rather than necessarily accurate.	Change managers need to understand the way the context and power relations impact on their ability to provide plausible stories that gain widespread acceptance of the need for change.
Enactment	Whereas the above aspects of sensemaking act as influences on sensemaking, 'enactment is about imposing that sense on action'.	Enactment alerts change managers to the need to connect sensemaking to actions.
Projective sensemaking	The ability of a powerful actor to project sensemaking onto a situation, shaping the interpretation of others.	The implication of this is that using legitimate power to impose sensemaking on parts of the organization may be an important aspect of understanding the implementation of change.

Source: Adapted from Palmer, Dunford and Akin (2006, pp.191–2)

End of chapter questions and exercises

1   Do an Internet and library search of those managers listed in Figure 1.2. Make notes on any contributions they are reported to have made to organizational change; any statements they have made on organizational change; and which company they now work for if they have changed companies since June 2005. Write some brief notes on what this tells you about leadership and organizational change.

2   Do an Internet and library search of those companies listed in Figure 1.1. Make notes on which organizational change strategies they have adopted over time, and what they say about those changes; note any differences and similarities in company statements about different change strategies. Write some brief notes about what this tells you about the importance of organizational change strategies and some of the differences between them.

3   From the companies referenced in Figure 1.1 make a list of the various factors that can be said to influence organizational change. What does this tell you about the management of change?

4   Using the business section of a national newspaper, make a list of the companies that the paper reports on and of the reasons why they made the news. Compare this list with your answer to question 3. Make a note of any new triggers of organizational change and if any of the companies are the same as the ones reported in Figure 1.1. What does this tell you about how different companies react to change? What does this tell you about how companies react to change over time?

5   Using the same national newspaper, make a list of the top managers that the paper reports on and of the reasons why they made the news. What percentage of the managers are women and what does this tell you about gender and leadership? What does this tell you about leadership and the management of change?

6   Now look at the front, 'news', section of the same national newspaper and make a list of the main issues discussed. Which, if any, of those items are likely to have an important influence on business operations in the future and how is that likely to affect organizational change and how it is managed?

7   Define change management.

8   Why do you think that change management is important to (a) business educators, (b) senior managers, (c) employees and (d) consultants?

9   How do you think that the notion of change management has changed over time, and why?

10   Who are the main stakeholders in the development of change management strategies, and why?

11   Identify a current change in an organization from the list in Figure 1.1. Think about what sensemaking changes might need to be enacted and how you would go about doing it. Assess this in terms of the sensemaking framework we have outlined at the end of this chapter.[33]

2 The discourse of change: from theory to practice

Objectives of this chapter:

By the end of this chapter, you should:

1   Be familiar with the scientific management approach
2   Be familiar with the human relations approach
3   Be familiar with socio-technical systems theory
4   Be familiar with contingency theory
5   Understand what is meant by the discourse of change
6   Understand the types of change and levels of change
7   Be familiar with different job design strategies

Air Canada and change

Between 1940 and 1970, *Air Canada*, the flag carrier of Canada, operated reservations offices in a number of different cities. The job was a popular one because of the higher than average pay and benefits, yet once hired, many of the agents found the work itself monotonous, repetitive and restrictive. The initial three-week training course taught agents how to make air, hotel and car reservations. This included preliminary training on how to calculate domestic and international fares. Agents who showed an aptitude for doing these fare calculations could be selected for more in-depth training and might be transferred to one of the specialized departments. But for the majority, they were assigned general telephone sales duties. Productivity was measured on the number of calls answered during an eight-hour shift. These calls were periodically monitored by quality assurance agents to ensure that customers were being given information in a courteous and efficient manner.

In the early 1970s, a new computer system was installed and *Air Canada* implemented a variety of job redesign strategies designed to enhance customer service and help to increase sales. These techniques included 'customer care programmes' and management training courses. During the mid-1980s, the airline restructured their 'special accounts' departments to give agents more autonomy and ownership of the accounts of frequent flyers and travel agency bookings. Instead of one agent doing the air booking, one doing the hotel booking, another doing the car rentals and another handling the ticketing, one agent would be responsible for all the steps of a passenger's travel arrangements, including the follow-up after the journey was completed.

Privatization in 1989, followed by deregulation, increased competition and technological advances forced the airline to once again re-evaluate its strategic direction. In 1991, this led to the closure of most of the reservations offices and the centralization of the remaining three offices. At the same time, a number of employees were offered either early retirement or severance packages. In late 1999, *Air Canada* merged with *Canadian Airlines*, in what some described as a hostile takeover on the part of *Air Canada*. More lay-offs occurred, along with pay cuts. Efforts were made to merge the two distinct cultures and to sort out seniority issues amongst the various unions. Change initiatives, such as Six Sigma and the Balanced Scorecard were some of the ways that *Air Canada* tried to address their problems. But events such as September 11 and the SARS outbreak in Toronto led to a decrease in travel and the airline filed for bankruptcy in 2003.

By 2005, a newly restructured *Air Canada* emerged from bankruptcy protection. The new airline was more focused on profitability and customer satisfaction, as indicated in the opening remarks of Robert Milton, CEO, during their 2005 annual meeting: 'You shared our vision of a new air services company. You shared our vision to capitalize on *Air Canada*'s restructuring, seize new business opportunities, unlock shareholder value and generate profitability in the aviation services sector'.[1] This means more change initiatives for *Air Canada* in the coming years as it, like many other companies, continues to engage in ongoing change at a number of levels throughout the organization, according to current change fashions.

In order to make sense of how the notion of organizational change, in particular programmatic change techniques, has become a panacea for organizational effectiveness and survival, we first need to have an understanding of the theoretical underpinnings of what currently constitutes change management literature. We then need to understand the forces that have driven change management, the types and the levels of change and the 'champions of change', in order to be able to understand how organizational change has moved from a piecemeal approach, utilizing a variety of management theories, to the global phenomenon it has become today.

Since the organizational change literature is non-linear, and it is our intention to present the story in a comprehensive manner, we will begin this chapter by showing how the influence of early management theories led to the development of specific change techniques and work redesign strategies. Specifically, in this chapter, job design strategies evolving from scientific management and the human relations approach will be discussed to show how dissatisfaction with universalist approaches of these early change techniques led to the development of more employee-centred theories, such as socio-technical system theories and job enrichment. We will then discuss different types of change and the levels of change that can be effected within the organization. This will be followed by a discussion on how internal and external forces for change, including the role of business schools, management gurus and consultants, have contributed to the creation of pre-packaged solutions and elevated the popularity of the organizational change discourse. We will conclude by examining some of the problems associated with traditional models of change and what can be done to overcome them.

Early management theories and the changing nature of work

It could be argued that *all* management theories are at the root of today's discourse of change. Ever since the industrial revolution, with the advent of power-driven machinery, which changed the nature of work and society, the need for organizing and for ways to increase productivity have become ongoing issues for management. The move away from an agrarian society to the relocation and centralization of work in factories created not only a new 'working class' but also the need for more formalized organizational structures and led to what we now know as the division of labour. The organizational hierarchies that resulted from the horizontal divisions of labour were seen as necessary to control worker behaviour and output and have evolved into what is known today as the employer/employee relationship.

Classical theory: scientific management

During the early part of the 20th century, Frederick Taylor, an American industrial engineer, was seeking ways to increase productivity by scientifically studying and measuring the most expeditious way to complete work tasks. Taylor, who is best known for developing *scientific management*, believed that achieving maximum efficiency for both the organization and the workers was the way to achieve maximum prosperity for both. To do this, Taylor felt that the ideal organization needed to have more control systems in place, that managers needed to hire employees based on their abilities (not friendship or favouritism), and that 'systematic soldiering' – employee attitudes about work norms[2] – needed to be regulated. He concluded that the best way to do this was by including a management hierarchy that bound managers together by a system of rules so that authority became objective rather than personal. He also believed that managers should manage and workers should work. Therefore, the job of managers was to be involved in the design of work processes, the selection and training of employees and the creation of incentive plans to motivate workers to work harder and to eliminate systematic soldiering.[3] Taylor firmly believed that because workers were motivated solely by money, they would work hard to achieve economic prosperity by taking advantage of any bonus schemes that could be put into place.

When he was hired as a management consultant for the *Bethlehem Iron* plant of Pittsburgh in 1898, Taylor was able to implement his ideas. Through the reorganization of the pig iron lifters,[4] he created an environment that demonstrated the power of his beliefs and confirmed his notion of 'economic man' by demonstrating that workers were driven by money, as they worked harder to achieve the bonuses. The work processes of the pig iron lifters were then broken down into their most fundamental elements, including a finely detailed set of instructions for how to lift the shovel and how many movements to make while transferring the pig iron to the rail cars. These tasks were then assigned to those workers who were the most highly skilled for each one, and incentives were put in place to reward performance that exceeded what was required to carry them out. By doing this detailed analysis and ensuring that his workforce was highly trained and specialized, Taylor was able to achieve maximum efficiency. So successful was the restructuring of the pig iron area of the plant that productivity increased by as much as 60%, workers' pay had increased from $1.15 to $1.88 a day and the workforce was cut by nearly 70%.[5]

The Gilbreths

At the same time that Taylor was implementing scientific management principles, Frank and Lillian Gilbreth,[6] associates of Taylor's, were also engaged in studies that explored the technical aspects of work simplification. The focus of the Gilbreths' *time and motion studies* was on the categorization of various observable elements in work processes, so that unnecessary motions could be identified and worker fatigue could be eliminated. Whereas a hallmark of Taylor's scientific management was the use of the stopwatch to define worker efficiency, the Gilbreths believed that getting the elements of the work process right would naturally speed up the workers. If anyone has read the book *Cheaper by the Dozen*[7] they will realize that it was written by two of the Gilbreth children and shows how their parents incorporated many of their work-saving techniques into their family life. Today, one hundred years later, there is still interest in the work of the Gilbreths. *The Gilbreth*

Network[8] is an online site devoted to bringing together people who want to read more about their work and share their ideas.

Making sense of scientific management

Following his successes at *Bethlehem Iron*, Taylor wrote *The Principles of Scientific Management*, which was published in 1911.[9] However, after 1903, Taylor no longer worked directly as a consultant. Instead, he trained a group of disciples, including Gilbreth, in the use of scientific management and he convinced employers to use its principles. With the expansion of industry in the US at the turn of the century, Taylorism soon became a popular way for large factories to overcome the remoteness between employers and employees. Taylor, who convinced these organizations that they needed an expert to oversee these strategies, otherwise the changes would be rejected by the unions, might very well have been the first change agent![10]

However, not everyone was happy with Taylorism. In 1911, the same year his book came out, Taylor was indicted by the US House of Representatives and accused of treating employees like machines. This resulted in the introduction of laws that banned the use of stopwatches by civil employees. This ban remained in place until 1949. Despite the ban, and Taylor's death in 1915, scientific management has endured throughout the years. Likewise, following the early death of Frank Gilbreth, Lillian Gilbreth continued with their work and time and motion studies have formed the basis for work analysis in a number of different areas. The legacy of early studies has had a profound effect on how work was organized and what the outcomes of this reorganization were for workers. Prior to the introduction of scientific management, organizations did not have formalized personnel or quality control departments and the role of the individual was limited to what value they could offer the organization and at what expense. This was about to change, but purely in a serendipitous way.

The human relations approach: Elton Mayo

Throughout the 1920s, Harvard Business School professor and industrial engineer, Elton Mayo, conducted studies at the *General Electric* Hawthorne plant near Chicago. Originally the studies were designed to look at the effects of illumination on employee productivity.[11] Over time, Mayo and his researchers realized that there was no clear-cut correlation between the two but they were still interested in finding out what factors did affect productivity, specifically the effects of fatigue and monotony. To do this, a group of workers was segregated in a separate area and a variety of variables, such as work schedules, including break times, hours worked and other work conditions, were manipulated in an attempt to isolate and control those that had the biggest impact on their output. Much to the amazement of Mayo and his researchers, no matter what was done, including increasing work hours, changing schedules or decreasing break times, productivity continued to rise. Contrary to the principles of scientific management, the Hawthorne studies demonstrated that money was not the sole motivator for workers. Instead, social needs, such as security and recognition and group contact were equally important motivators. Thus, quite serendipitously, Mayo had made the discovery that jobs could be redesigned so that they fulfilled these needs, which would also increase productivity. Again, this led managers to consider new ways of organizing.

It is clear from these two studies that these early theories of management could also be considered early theories of change because their goal was to change the way work was organized. Simply put, early attempts at finding new ways to manage and new ways to restructure work are still change management even if not specifically labelled as change management! The quest for us, as students of change, is to trace the trajectory of change from random strategies to a fully developed discourse of change. In order to do that, we need to take a look at the roots of this discourse to find out how the concept of change becomes an organizational imperative and we need to uncover the factors that have contributed to its development as a powerful management tool.

Making sense of classical management theories

While, at first glance, scientific management and the human relations models may appear to be very different, because the former views the worker as a machine motivated solely by money and the latter concentrates on the importance of social interaction, both approaches are actually focused on the same outcome of increasing productivity. In addition, both approaches propose a *universalist*, or 'one best way' to manage and organize approach. That means they do not recognize that there might be different ways to look at the same issue or different solutions to different problems.

At a more pragmatic level, both approaches lacked clear directions for implementation and generalizability in a variety of situations. For example, although scientific management provided clear guidelines on how work should and could be structured, it left little scope for ongoing change because once the 'best' way was discovered, there was little room for improvement; whereas the human relations approach, while recognizing the importance of addressing the needs of the workers, offered little in the way of concrete suggestions for implementing such a plan. By that we mean that although Mayo and his cohorts knew that employees valued attention and interaction, they couldn't always replicate the conditions from the *General Electric* plant. So, up until the 1950s, existing management theories offered little choice for the practising manager if they didn't fall into either of these categories. At this point, researchers started to explore the nature of work and how different systems of production affected employee motivation and productivity. Thus, we start to see the development of new ways of structuring and change in organizations.

Socio-technical systems theory

In 1951, Trist and Bamforth,[12] researchers at the Tavistock Institute in London, began an investigation into a newly mechanized coal-mining system to study the impact of this technology on mining work groups. The technique, called longwall mining, differed from traditional techniques because instead of groups of men mining 'room by room' in the underground labyrinth, an entire slice of wall was mined at once, with the aid of mechanical support systems. Because of the mechanization of the coal-mining processes, many of the previously specialized tasks carried out manually by the miners in a face-to-face environment were eliminated. That meant that traditional work groups, which relied on mutual trust and external supervision, were done away with and replaced by newly formed semi-autonomous groups, where there was little interaction amongst workers. As Trist and Bamforth discovered, the new work processes that developed from this reorganization changed both the mechanical and social structures of coal-mining work and led them to further study the relationship between technology and organizational members. The resulting *socio-technical systems theory* recognized the importance of technology on the individual and the inter-dependence between social and technology systems and contributed to the ever-growing interest in how to change organizations for peak performance and how to understand the impact this would have on worker productivity.

For our purposes, socio-technical systems theory is important to the change management discourse for several reasons. It was the first management theory to take the view that organizations operate as open systems, thereby recognizing the relationship between work systems and the environment and the interdependence between technology and structure and its impact on work groups. Socio-technical theory also provided a framework for the operationalization of the human relations approach, something that we noted was previously missing. Additionally, it set the stage for further studies of job design and new ways to approach organizational issues.

Contingency theory

The impact of technology on organizational structure and work design continued to receive considerable attention during the 1950s. A number of different theorists were studying the impact of technology on job design and employee motivation and productivity. By the 1960s, what became known as a *contingency theory* approach had replaced earlier classical approaches to the managing and structuring of organizations. The contingency approach differed from existing ways of managing because it recognized that different situations could require different solutions and that there is no one best way to fill all the requirements. Contingency theory is, therefore, based on an 'it depends' approach and it provided a theoretical base that acknowledged the importance of key variables, which had previously been ignored by people like Taylor and Mayo, such as size, technology and the environment, that affect the structure of the organization. Three key theorists emerged during this time whose classifications of technology provided the foundations for explicit job redesign strategies using a contingency theory approach.

The first, Joan Woodward, carried out a study of manufacturing firms in the UK in the late 1950s that identified technology according to the complexity and size of productions.[13] According to Woodward's classification of technology, there were three types of production: custom made (i.e. one of a kind items), mass production (i.e. assembly line) and continuous process (i.e. refineries), that would determine the structure of the organization. In the 1960s, this was followed by the work of James Thompson, who looked at levels of interdependence and environmental uncertainty in relation to the classification of task structures.[14] At around the same time, Charles Perrow was exploring the predictability and analysability of tasks in order to determine the degree of motivation. According to Perrow's analysis, jobs that use routine technologies and are highly predictable, such as assembly line work or call centre work, are more likely to lead to employee boredom[15] and therefore present the most challenges to managers, who need to find ways to relieve the tedium of the job.

Making sense of socio-technical and contingency theory approaches

The importance of contingency theory as a way to understand organizations is that it recognized that organizations are not rational entities, thereby discrediting the view that organizations can be managed by a universalist approach. By recognizing the importance of variables on structure, contingency theory provided the framework for operationalizing the objectives of the human relations approach and, at the same time, rejecting the tenets of scientific management that focused solely on economics.

Both socio-technical systems theory and contingency theory provided a solid foundation for the job design strategies and organizational development techniques that became more fully developed during the 1960s and 1970s. Job design can subsequently be understood as preliminary attempts to directly influence and change the organization by specifically focusing on changing workplace practices.

Change and job design strategies

Although Frederick Taylor had stressed the importance of *job specialization* as a means of increasing productivity and, at the same time, teaching employees to be more efficient and able to achieve higher financial rewards, by the1950s there was a growing interest in looking at other factors that motivated employees and what could be done to restructure work so that those needs could be reinforced. Following the Second World War *job enlargement* and *job rotation* were being used as job design strategies.

In 1959, Frederick Herzberg[16] conducted a study of employee attitudes in the workplace. Rather than concentrating on the technological aspects of the job, Herzberg wanted to find out what facets of their jobs made employees feel satisfied or dissatisfied with their work. Based on a survey of employees who identified key elements of work that contributed to their job satisfaction and those factors that led to job dissatisfaction, Herzberg came up with the *two factor theory* of motivation.[16] His research showed that jobs containing facets that employees identified as contributing to their satisfaction, such as increased autonomy or positive feedback, were intrinsically rewarding and served to motivate employees. However, factors such as poor working conditions or job insecurity were identified as causing dissatisfaction, but, if the working conditions were good and there was job security, these factors were not in themselves motivating, nor did they contribute to satisfaction. For example, employees who have never had to think about the threat of being laid off don't think about it but if it suddenly becomes a reality it can, for obvious reasons, cause dissatisfaction and may lead to decreased motivation. For Herzberg, the implications of this discovery were that employers needed to provide hygiene factors to eliminate dissatisfaction and intrinsic motivators to increase job satisfaction and performance. In order to do that, he suggested that jobs needed to be enriched so that they were challenging, offered increased responsibility and developed the employees' full potential. This notion of *job enrichment* was important because it showed that merely adding more tasks to existing jobs, which is known as *job enlargement*, did not address the need for intrinsically motivating jobs, it merely overcame boredom for some.

The job characteristics model

In the mid-1970s, Hackman and Oldham developed *the job characteristics model*.[17] This model provided a way to show the link between the existence of certain job characteristics, the psychological states they create and the behavioural outcomes that occur if they were in place. These 'core characteristics' of jobs included skill variety, task significance, task identification, autonomy and feedback, which were similar to the motivating facets identified by Herzberg. Hackman and Oldham then linked them to psychological states such as a sense of responsibility and meaningfulness, which in turn should lead to increased motivation, intrinsic rewards and job satisfaction. The value of Hackman and Oldham's model is that it expanded on the earlier research that started exploring the motivating potential of work and it provided a model to show how work could be designed to increase motivation.

Quality of working life

Throughout the next decade, businesses were becoming more aware of job design strategies and some of the problems associated with scientific management. With the interest in job enrichment, some of the negative effects of Taylorism were being exposed. In addition to contributing to boredom, job specialization was being blamed for feelings of worker alienation and lack of identification with the finished product. This led to the creation of the Quality of Working Life (QWL) movement, which started in Scandinavia and soon spread to the rest of Europe. QWL was seen as a way of overcoming some of these problems, while incorporating elements of sociotechnical systems theory and job enrichment.[18] One of the best-known QWL initiatives was carried out by Volvo, who introduced autonomous work groups for the production of vehicles.[19] By the 1980s, a number of change techniques that could be deemed as improving the quality of working life were being used. Some of these techniques, such as TQM, Quality Circles and Culture Change will be discussed more fully in the following chapters.

Summary

Our purpose in this section has been to highlight certain management theories, and it is based on several assumptions. First, we assume that readers will already have a good grounding in organizational theory and organizational behaviour. Therefore, it is in no way an exhaustive review of all early management theories; it is merely our objective to draw attention to the theories that we see as specifically contributing to the change management discourse. The theories we have highlighted have been selected because we feel that over time they have challenged existing work structures, identified important influences on social and work structures and paved the way for other strategies that are now fully integrated into existing change management programmes. Second, we have tried to identity points in time when researchers started linking the theories to the practice of job design. This paves the way for us to discuss in the next section the types of change that organizations engage in and the levels of change that can be implemented in organizational settings, and to cast a critical lens over how change affects individuals in those organizations.

Types of change

> I spent the day with Mitt Romney and all I got was a lesson – yet another one – in the myriad uses of the word 'change'. Curse that Barack Obama for ever having mentioned it. Everywhere you go in this wacky little state now, presidential candidates, Republican and Democratic, are talking about change: Change this, change that; agent of change; message of change; time for change; change and dynamism.
>
> (Christie Blatchford, *Globe and Mail*, January 8, 2008)

Over time, theories of change have become more sophisticated, yet there are still many simplistic elements at their core. These elements, which borrow broadly from organizational behaviour concepts, including learning theory, motivation theory, organizational culture and theories of leadership and decision-making, have been adopted and so well integrated into current change models and techniques that it is sometimes difficult to uncover the theoretical underpinnings of many of the change management techniques that are in use today. What is different from when they were stand-alone management practices is how these theories are presented and packaged, the scope of change they promise, what the change involves and how quickly it gets replaced by newer and more fashionable change management programmes.

In order to understand organizational change, it is important to remember that change comes in many forms. When we hear the term 'organizational change', our understanding of what it means depends on our past experiences with what we may have observed as a bystander. For example, at *Nova Scotia Power* change programmes were so common that the company was referred to as a serial changer and employees referred to the latest changes as the 'flavour of the month'.[20] Change also became a defining concept for the 2008 US Presidential Primaries, and, as we can see in the opening quote of this section, there was still no universal agreement on how it should be used and what it should accomplish. In organizational settings, change is often understood in terms of specific techniques, such as *Total Quality Management* (TQM). But change can also occur at a broader level and be less structured if it is unplanned or the result of uncontrollable circumstances. When this happens, organizations often use a piecemeal approach to try to manage the circumstances or they try to respond to the change as it emerges.

Broadly speaking, change can be categorized as *planned, unplanned, emergent, incremental* or *quantum*. In 1951, Lewin,[21] who will be discussed further in Chapter 3, first made the distinction of differentiating between planned change as change that an organization consciously thinks about and decides to engage in, which is designed to specifically change organizational outcomes (e.g. prescriptive techniques or *programmatic change*, such as *TQM, Balanced Scorecard, Culture Change*), versus unplanned or emergent change that the organization did not initiate or had no control over planning.

Incremental change is usually targeted at 'fixing' specific departments of the organization (e.g. restructuring a call centre to give employees more autonomy), or specific problems (e.g. university business schools who find that their enrolments for the MBA programme are dropping off might change their ways of recruiting), while *quantum change* affects the entire organization (e.g. following their emergence from bankruptcy, Air Canada restructured and changed their whole philosophy and product offering). By its very nature, planned change is likely to be either *quantum* or *incremental*, while unplanned change is more likely to be emergent.

It is worth noting that, prior to its elevation as an imperative, planned change was usually incremental and often targeted at 'fixing' specific parts of the organization. *TQM*, for example, was based on problem-solving in specific areas of the organization. It was only with the advent of change techniques, such as *Culture Change*, the *Balanced Scorecard, Six Sigma, BPR* and the *Learning Organization*, that quantum change became the norm. As well as being seen as a way to gain the commitment of all employees, quantum change also provided a way to recreate the existing organization and start out new and fresh.

Yet, despite this rhetoric about the need for change, for a number of organizations, change is not part of their strategic plan and in some cases, change is not even something that is viewed as necessary or desirable. The old adage, 'if it's not broke don't fix it', still holds true for these organizations but that isn't to say they still don't find themselves engaged in change at some point in time. What is different is that, in these cases, change is probably occurring as an unplanned response to external or internal events beyond the control of the organization that make it necessary for organization survival. We saw a good example of both types of change following the events of September 11, when, among other things, the travel industry noticed a sharp decline in business. At this point, airlines and hotels were forced to engage in unplanned and both incremental and emergent change, including lay-offs and price-chopping, as they looked for ways to respond to the crisis. At the same time, quantum changes were being put into place at airports, as new security regulations were being thought out and implemented and new staff were being hired and trained in new ways of detecting terrorism.

Ultimately the type of change an organization engages in is often dependent on forces that are both within and beyond its control. As we shall see in the upcoming chapters, planned changes are heavily influenced by a number of factors but even these can be derailed by forces that managers haven't considered. These include, but are not limited to, how the change is made sense of by organizational members and how it is 'managed'. As we shall see, even though the success rate for planned change is low, change managers remain optimistic and often oblivious to the failure of others.

Forces of change

Forces have been driving change ever since the Industrial Revolution changed the nature of work. Whether to improve efficiency or create better working conditions, productivity has been the bottom line in the organization of work and managers and consultants are continually looking for ways to improve it. Employee discontent and conflict have also become important factors that fuel the need for change. At the same time, societal and political forces, such as the fall of communism, increased competition, privatization and deregulation have all played a role.

As we mentioned in Chapter 1, since the mid 1970s there has been a rapid growth in the numbers of books and journal articles on organizational change and most companies in North America and Europe have undergone some sort of pre-packaged, programmatic change programme by 2002. These

changes have not been limited to the private sector. In Canada and the US, up to 75% of hospitals have introduced *TQM* or *BPR*.[22]

Also discussed in Chapter 1, one way to make sense of the drivers of change is to apply a sensemaking framework[23] to argue that 'change has become a conventional management practice, developed and sustained through a powerful management discourse, whose ongoing character influences the decision-making of large and small companies, profit or not-for-profit companies alike. Whether or not the adoption of a particular programme of change is the right course of action for some companies doesn't seem to matter. Decisions to implement change programmes are often based on "plausibility" rather than "accuracy" '.[24]

Today, change has come to be understood as something that is real, necessary and inevitable. For the organization, engaging in change means being on the cutting edge. For the manager, engaging in change is seen as a way of being progressive. The role of senior management is to find solutions that have clear directions and guidelines. The role of the manager is to draw upon this received knowledge that change must be managed, in order to ensure success, at the same time treating the forces of change as something out of his or her control.

This lack of clear guidance about how to manage change has forced senior managers to seek out pre-packaged solutions and it has helped to elevate programmatic approaches to the next level in the discourse of organizational change. Since the mid-1980s, the notion of programmatic change has been a recurring theme and a number of pre-packaged solutions, with an emphasis on customer service and expert knowledge to implement the change, have been developed to meet this need. Because of their popularity, techniques such as *TQM, BPR* and *Culture Change*, to name only a few, have taken on the status of management fads and fashions.[25] Yet the desire to be a 'good manager' whose company is on the cutting edge only partially explains the popularity of these fads and fashions. Another reason for the success of change models lies in the type of story that is being told, the language that is being used to transmit the stories[26] and the way the story is being transmitted.[27]

Thus, a story line that is simplistic, offers unique solutions, references mythical forces to engender a sense of uncertainty and fear, and encourages the notion of a good manager and the cutting-edge organization, will be the most attractive and have the most chance of achieving success.

Levels of change

As well as types of change, it is important to take into account the different levels within the organization where change can take place. At the broadest *organizational level*, change usually centres on restructuring and reorganizing. This can mean the introduction of new policies and rules that affect the entire organization. At this level, different strategies can be planned, such as

Business Process Re-engineering (BPR) that then gets refined and filters down to the other two levels where it becomes more specific and detailed. At the *group level*, change is aimed at altering work processes, including the introduction of new technologies to accomplish the work. In the case of BPR, this would be the stage where entire work processes would be changed by implementing *BPR* initiatives. Finally, at the *individual level*, changes attempt to alter the behaviours, attitudes and perceptions of the individuals in the organization. At this level, the organization might work on bringing the attitudes of the employees in the reengineered organization into line with the new values. This could be done by rewarding value-consistent behaviour.

Making sense of the evolution of programmatic change

As Michel Foucault, a French sociologist (Foucault, 1979) pointed out, 'A discourse draws its strength from its links to practice'.[28] Therefore, we can argue that specific change strategies, which, as we have seen, are rooted in past management theory, appear to be more appealing and influential than if there were no historical context from which to draw. In sensemaking terms, this means that change and, subsequently, specific change programmes, have become popular because they are first grounded in academic theory that comes to be accepted as truth and they are then reproduced and touted by 'experts' as plausible solutions to myriad organizational problems – whether real or perceived. Their use by other organizations makes them seem familiar and organizational decision-makers are cued to see change as necessary. As we shall see, there are a number of influences on this legitimization of change.

The business school

If not the originator, the university business school has been a major contributor to the way managers and organizations have accepted the imperative of organizational change. Over the years, business schools have tried to blend with the business environment. It has even been suggested that management education is guided by the needs of managers.[29] This means that change programmes often have their roots in academia but have gained popularity and acceptance because of how they have been marketed and sold by management gurus and consultants.

In recent years, management textbooks have been devoting entire chapters to organizational change and change techniques. By linking the discussion of change to case studies of 'real' companies that have successfully implemented these strategies, they have affirmed the need for these types of practices and they have legitimized organizational change techniques.

The popular press

The marketing of change techniques by business magazines and management 'how-to' books has also become a popular way to transmit management trends and encourage managers to engage in the practices. The offering of practical, atheoretical solutions and the conveyance of the message that certain techniques are widely and successfully being practised, has encouraged many companies to adopt such programmes as *TQM* and *BPR*.

The gurus

Once senior managers are convinced that change is both inevitable and needs to be managed, they will be open to the claims of experts, known as *business gurus*, who can help them. *A business 'guru' is someone who creates and redefines existing organizational problems for which they have pre-packaged solutions.*[30] The guru has usually started out as a consultant and has developed a model of change that has captured the attention of individual managers and companies because of its widespread use and success throughout the business community.

The elevation of the change programmes and their founders to guru status depends on several factors.[31] These can include shifts in the economy, which force the business press to find new solutions that can address these changing needs, which was the case when *Air Canada* switched strategies after their privatization, or it can include different contexts, which affect the need for change, such as *Air Canada*'s switch to *Six Sigma* as a new way of saving money.

Whatever the reasons, gurus are important because they play an enormous role in the shaping and legitimating of management consulting by making the public more aware of their ideas and by convincing organizations of the merit of a particular change technique.[32]

The consultants

Consulting firms also play a large role in the selling and implementation of change programmes. Once sold on the need to initiate widespread change, many senior managers are overwhelmed by the idea of putting them into practice. So they turn to the expertise offered by consulting firms. This is partially embedded in the idea that these unique solutions need unique guidance. As Abrahamson[33] explains, 'to sustain their images as fashion setters [management consultants] ... must develop rhetorics that describe these techniques as the forefront of management progress ... and disseminate these rhetorics back to managers before other fashion setters'.

The role of gurus, consultants and managers can be summed up as follows: management gurus have become the purveyors of change techniques, consultants their missionaries and managers their loyal followers.

Making sense of the traditional models of change

'If you aren't part of the solution, you could be part of the problem' is a phrase that has been told to employees who may have expressed concerns that their company's change initiatives might be another 'flavour of the month' and have chosen not to engage in the process. This sums up the problems associated with traditional models of change.

Today, the dominant discourse of change focuses on issues of adoption, implementation and outcomes but there are several problems with this approach and the expectations that it creates. First, there is an emphasis on the inevitability of change that promotes the idea of change for the sake of change. However, the plethora of change strategies has served to actually slow down change as employees tire of easy fixes and question their validity.[34] In addition, this can mean that change is adopted as a solution for non-existent problems! Second, the measurement of success is somewhat problematic with traditional models because the most common means of assessment is usually to see how well employees have adapted to change policies or procedures after the programme is well established. This is usually too late to correct any errors and it also makes the assumption that everyone understands and interprets company policies in the same way. Third, organizations can become divided over whose interests the change process is serving. Failure to take into account the effects that changing one part of the organization can have on employees' psychological wellbeing downplays the importance of the employee. Finally, there is a lack of sufficient longitudinal research on change. This means that little has been written about why organizations have failed. The assumption is that everyone shares similar values and understanding and the impact of those who have divergent values is ignored.[35]

Conclusion

It has been our intention in this chapter to give you an overview of some of the earlier management theories that have shaped the organizational change discourse and led to the creation of current change techniques. We have also attempted to question the taken-for-granted assumptions that are common to the discourse and show some of the problems they create. In the following chapters we will explore the most popular models of change in detail. In the next chapter, we will concentrate on Kurt Lewin's models of change and show how they were developed over time and led to the widespread introduction of *organizational development* (OD) strategies in organizations.

End of chapter questions and exercises

1 Consider a fast food restaurant and discuss how they might be using scientific management principles to standardize the work.
2 Think about your current place of employment. What types of job

design strategies could be implemented to improve employee motivation? What, if any, have already been used?

3 Describe the facets of your job that you consider to be motivating factors and those that you consider to be hygiene factors. What are some of the weaknesses of this model?

4 Using Hackman and Oldham's job characteristics model, describe some of the ways that the job of administrative assistant could be enriched.

5 What might be some of the reasons that employees might not want their jobs enriched?

6 Discuss the role of unions in job enlargement and job enrichment strategies.

7 Using the Internet, find three companies that have undergone change and describe them in terms of levels and types of change they have used. Were they successful? Why or why not? What could they have done differently?

8 Look at the business section of a recent newspaper and see how many references to change you can find. What are the similarities? What type and level of change are they offering?

9 Using the Internet, find five management 'gurus' and see what, if any, characteristics they may have in common. What conclusions can you draw from this?

10 What is the harm in changing for the sake of change? Give the pros and cons for your answer.

3 From Lewin to OD: planned approaches to change

Objectives of this chapter:

By the end of this chapter, you should:

1 Discuss the planned approach to change management
2 Understand Kurt Lewin's contribution to the field of change management
3 Be familiar with action research
4 Be familiar with field theory
5 Be familiar with the study of group dynamics
6 Understand and apply Lewin's Three-Step Model of Change
7 Discuss critically the field of Organization Development

ASDA moves into Northern Ireland [1]

On June 7, 2005 several newspapers were announcing the purchase of 12 Safeway stores in Northern Ireland. They were being purchased by *ASDA*, a leading UK supermarket chain, owned by *Wal-Mart* since 1999. Already strategically placed throughout England, Scotland and Wales, the opening of the first ever *ASDA* stores in Northern Ireland was an exciting move – at least for *ASDA*.

Some of the people of Northern Ireland were not as excited. They feared that *Wal-Mart*'s reputation for forcing the closure of smaller, locally owned grocers and retailers might impact *ASDA*'s approach in Northern Ireland. *ASDA* seemed to be doing its best to allay such fears with promises of a more competitive market for shoppers, resulting in lower prices; a significant investment in the Northern Irish economy (£30 million over two years), and the creation of 250 new jobs. They also promised to buy from local farmers and producers. The fears of residents were clearly anticipated and 'pre-empted' by the organization.

This is a significant element of successful planned change, as you'll see as you move through the chapter.

When this announcement was made, *ASDA* had 279 stores. They now have more than 340. *ASDA* has had a growth strategy since its beginning in 1965. Not only has the company grown from one store to more than 340, but what started as a mere grocery store has expanded its offerings to include books, movies, electronics, flowers, furniture, mobile phones, furniture and optical, pharmacy, photo and travel services. Additionally, *ASDA*'s policies and procedures have evolved to include issues of the environment, corporate social responsibility, and family-friendly work environments. Many would argue that *ASDA* has been an ideal model of strategic, planned organization change. Sure, it's had its hiccups along the way (product recalls, lawsuits, etc.) but its success in terms of growth is undeniable.

So, how does an organization grow in such an exponential way? The answer lies in the planning and implementation of planned change – conveniently enough, the topic of this chapter.

Of the companies in the news on Tuesday, June 7, 2005, more than 45 of them were newsworthy because of some sort of planned change – everything from mergers and acquisitions to purchases of new equipment, expansion into new markets, and new products and advertising strategies. Other news articles indicated the necessity for planned change. Seven of the articles on June 7, 2005 were part of the dynamic and highly competitive food industry. Two of these articles (*Saputo Sales* and *Bick's Pickles*) provided commentary about the current condition of the two food companies. *Saputo* was suffering from a decline in sales and *Bick's Pickles* was suffering from a controversial advertisement. Both situations would clearly serve as an impetus for change.

The other five companies were involved in major restructuring, spin-offs or acquisitions – *ASDA* purchased 12 of its competitors' stores and moved into a new market; *Agra Foodservice* purchased its rival, *Waterford Stanley*; *FPI* announced that it would spin off as a publicly traded company called *Ocean Cuisine International*; and *Premier Foods* purchased its competitor, *Marlow foods*. Change – strategic, planned change – is not a foreign concept to the food industry.

We'll use *Kraft Foods Inc.* as a case in point. *Kraft Foods*, the world's largest producer and marketer of consumer packaged goods, is not a stranger to the dynamics of the food industry and has experienced growing pains typical for a company of its size and scope.

Much of *Kraft*'s European operations have developed as a result of acquisitions, thus incorporating cultures, practices and names of the acquired companies. For example, the acquisition of *Jacobs Suchard coffee and confectionery* resulted in the name *Kraft Jacobs Suchard*. Similarly, the acquisition of *Freia Marabou* resulted in the name *Kraft Freia Marabou*. The acquisitions have resulted in fractured corporate cultures, visions and identities, thus making it difficult to drive the growth of the organization as a whole.

In an attempt to 'realign' the organization's identity and to drive growth, *Kraft Foods International* began a change process with the ultimate goal of creating 'one company' with a common vision and identity across all affiliates and regions. One of several steps in the carefully planned change process occurred in 2000. *Kraft International*, in keeping with their attempt to create a unified identity, decided to change the names of various European holdings from their combined names to the common name of *Kraft Foods*. Companies that had been born of acquisitions, some just a few years prior, were being re-named to 'bring them into the fold'. Other steps were then taken in a seemingly rational fashion over the next few years, all with the intent of creating a uniform identity for the large organization.

In 2005, *Kraft Foods* embarked on yet another strategic change initiative. On December 27, 2005, *Kraft Canada Inc.* announced that it would sell several grocery assets including well-known *Aylmer, Primo* and *Del Monte* lines. It was anticipated that the move would result in net revenues of $300 million CDN. The change, involving five manufacturing facilities and 800 *Kraft* employees, was deemed necessary for continued growth and competitiveness in the global marketplace.

As with *ASDA, Kraft Foods* is an ideal example of planned change. *Kraft International* recognized that there was a discrepancy between the actual and desired states, and carefully unrolled their major change programme designed to achieve the desired state – a common company vision and identity. Changing the names of European holdings was but one step of many in the campaign. As did *Kraft* and *ASDA*, many of the companies discussed in the news on June 7, 2005 have formal *Organizational Development* programmes and strategies. We'll move now to the theory behind such initiatives.

An introduction to planned change

History is replete with examples, like the one in the opening scenario and the others deemed newsworthy on June 7, of organizations attempting to subtly or dramatically alter their positions (culturally, competitively or otherwise). Simply stated, organizations have desired to change some facet of their organization and have taken deliberate, seemingly rational steps to accommodate this change. Unfortunately, the success rate of major change initiatives within organizations has been less than desirable. This lack of success, coupled with factors such as globalization, technology, economic instability and the resulting increased competitive pressures, has served as the catalyst for the focus on understanding what makes change work. Due to this, we have seen a stark increase in study dedicated to understanding organizational change, as noted in Chapter 1.

One of the earliest and most enduring schools of thought to emerge from the increased emphasis on understanding organizational change focused on creating prescriptive formulas for the successful implementation of change in organizations. Dubbed the *planned approach* to organizational change, this school of thought assumes that *change strategies are intentional and rational processes, that rely on analysis, forecasting and planning, thus resulting in the logical and rational implementation of change within the organization*.[2] Simply stated, the change process is intentionally initiated, carefully planned and implemented in order to achieve desired results. Although these changes can be of long or short duration, and vary greatly in scope and intensity, all have distinct beginnings and endings. They are separate and distinct from changes resulting from accidents or those that are forced on the organization, such as those caused by legislative changes or government controls.

Planned change is most often associated with the field of *Organization Development* (OD) which has evolved into a multi-billion dollar industry worldwide. OD proponents have been responsible for the creation of a multitude of universalist, prescribed change strategies, all possessing the distinct characteristics of planned change; that is, they are intentional and rational and rely on analysis, forecasting and extensive planning.

This chapter will trace the evolution of the notion of planned change, starting with its inception by Kurt Lewin. A discussion of the evolution of Lewin's work into what is now widely accepted as the field of *Organization Development* will follow. Finally, the chapter will end by taking a critical look at the discourse of planned change.

Kurt Lewin and organizational change

Kurt Lewin was born in 1890 in the village of Mogilno in what was then known as the Prussian province of Posen and is now part of Poland. His first application of psychology to the work environment was evident in a paper in 1919 on the role of the labourer in agriculture and then again in 1920 in a paper about the labourer in industry. This paper was in direct response to the work of Taylor (discussed in Chapter 2), specifically time-and-motion studies and the treatment of workers as 'parts of the machine'. Contrary to the tenets of Taylorism, Lewin felt that 'work has a "life value": a man's capacity to work gives meaning and substance to his whole existence. Accordingly, every job should sustain or enhance this "life value" '.[3] He was particularly critical of overspecialization and the resultant potential for monotony.

As identified in the previous chapter, Kurt Lewin has been described by many as an important figure in the creation and development of the field of organizational change.[4] In fact, some have even called him the creator of the planned approach to organizational change.[5] Undeniably, his concepts are so widely discussed that this is often done without recognition of their origins.[6] They have simply become part of the discourse of planned change.

Although Lewin made several significant (and often overlooked) contributions, across several different disciplines, from an organizational change perspective his most referenced and best-known contributions include *action research, field theory, group dynamics*, and his *Three-Step Change Process*. As will become evident, these contributions have had a lasting impact on the discipline of change. In fact, many more modern theories of organizational change are simply evolutions of his original ideas.

Despite the ready adoption of Lewin's work into the discourse of change, it is important to note that Lewin's contributions were not made in an effort to simplify the change process for organizations. On the contrary, much of Lewin's work was centered on the psychological study of social issues. For example, Lewin spent a considerable amount of time researching the best way to change eating habits during the Second World War. Additionally, much of his later research addressed issues of prejudice and intergroup harmony. The links to organization change strategies are not immediately evident. The following discussion will examine the evolution of Lewin's work and the links between his affinity for social issues and organization change will become more obvious.

Action research

Lewin grew up and studied during unquestionably turbulent times. The influences of dramatic world events, personal tragedy – the loss of his brother during the war and the loss of his mother in a Nazi extermination camp, and personal experiences with anti-Semitism and racism in the United States – are all evident in Lewin's work and his emphasis on research that resulted in social change.[7] As previously noted, his last few years were spent focusing on projects designed to address prejudice and intergroup harmony.[8]

As indicated by Schellenberg (1978, p.76), '[Lewin] was constantly involved in one form or another of research concerned with social problems, whether working with Margaret Mead and the National Research Council to discover the best way to change food habits during the Second World War; or analyzing the effects of group participation in decision making upon the productivity of the Harwood Manufacturing Corporation; or evaluating psychological warfare activities of the Office of Strategic Services in Washington. (He had a penchant for research geared toward social action (or, as he called it, "action research")'.

Action research, according to Lewin, was *research that was designed with action in mind*. Specifically, Lewin used action research to facilitate social change. His model of action research is cyclical and is described as follows:[9]

1   Identify a general or initial idea
2   Reconnaissance or fact-finding

3 Planning
4 Take first action step
5 Evaluate
6 Amend plan
7 Take second action step . . .

Although not specifically designed with organizations in mind, it is not difficult to see how research designed to facilitate social change might be adapted for use in organizations. The model outlined by Lewin appears logical and rational and, as such, is consistent with the discourse of organizations. In addition, it offers a 'plausible' response to the need for change. The concept of action research had such 'staying power' that it has endured and many of today's researchers engage in research activity in an effort to help clients (including organizations) enact some type of change.

Several models of action research have evolved from Lewin's conceptualization. One of the most enduring has been the one designed by French & Bell[10] whose action research model consists of '(1) a preliminary diagnosis, (2) data gathering from the client group, (3) data feedback to the client group, (4) data exploration by the client group, (5) action planning and (6) action'.[11] As you can see, this model has evolved to be even more consistent with the discourse of organizations and is designed for use by consultants to help organizations address needed changes.

Others have developed action research frameworks in similar fashions. For example, Kemmis & McTaggart[12] identify four phases of action research. They are: Planning, Acting, Observing and Reflecting. Regardless of the model, what remains consistent in all action research frameworks is the call for action. Rather than research for the sake of research, or research for the sake of new knowledge, action research is based on research for the sake of action. Applications of action research vary widely and include everything from improving the quality of classroom learning in a public education system to the successful implementation of a new computer monitoring system in an organization. Adopters of action research recognize its ability to make useful contributions to knowledge, its usefulness as a complement to more traditional forms of research, and its ability to combine action with research in a dynamic, reflective and purposeful way.

Despite action research's widespread adoption, it is not without its critics. Some argue that action research is not 'true research' and claim that it is not as rigorous as what is commonly known as scientific research. Others argue that, due to its site-specific nature (that is, it is applied to one problem at a particular organization at one point in time), results are not generalizable. They claim that what works in one organization cannot claim to work in other organizations unless it is scientifically studied, with multiple sites and circumstances.

Critics notwithstanding, action research has significantly impacted the discourse of organization change and has been readily adopted by researchers and consultants alike. Although organization consultants typically adopt a less formal approach to action research than their academic counterparts, it is action research nonetheless. That is, *it is directed toward the successful achievement of change; it includes data collection, planning, implementation and critical analysis; and it is cyclical in nature.*

Field theory

Lewin's emphasis on change led him to the study of human behaviour. Specifically, if groups or organizations are to change, then the actors within the groups would be required to change and this required an understanding of behaviour. He adopted a rather novel approach for understanding human behaviour – field theory. Although a popular concept in the physical sciences 50 years before Lewin's work, Lewin was the first to apply field theory to the notion of the individual.[13] Frustrated by traditional attempts to explain human behaviour in terms of instinct and libido (among other innate processes), Lewin believed that the individual was indeed much more complex. Specifically, Lewin saw the person as 'a complex energy field in which all behaviour could be conceived of as a change in some state of the field during a given unit of time'.[14] Just as the physical sciences had noted the need to study relationships and interactions between forces rather than studying forces in isolation, Lewin contended that behaviour is a function of the person and their environment.[15] Specifically, 'field theory postulates that a person's behaviour is derived from a totality of coexisting facts. The multitude of data from any event provides a dynamic "field" in which all facts are interdependent with all others'.[16] Accordingly, any new behaviour is the result of some change in the field.

Almost revolutionary at the time, this concept was paramount in the evolution of the study of human behaviour and change. Up until this time, much of the research on human behaviour had looked at each human subject in isolation, and failed to recognize that behaviours were not solely influenced by innate drives and needs. Lewin recognized the impact of the environment on behaviour, thus changing the way many studied behaviour and paving a new direction for the study of change.[17]

For example, an employee on an assembly line may become more productive quite suddenly. Before Lewin's work, this change in behaviour might have been attributed to the employee's needs. That translates to say that the employee decided to work harder to satisfy their own needs (more money, greater prestige, etc.). Lewin argued that this change in behaviour is not purely as a result of the employee's internal motivation but is as a result of external and internal changes. Perhaps the employee was given some input into how their job was performed and was feeling more motivated by this empowerment. Alternatively, perhaps an old command-and-control-style manager was replaced by a more democratic manager and this resulted in the employee's increased productivity.

Although more obviously a contribution to the field of behaviour research, this contribution was significant for the field of organization change. By recognizing that behaviour is the result of both internal and external forces, researchers were better able to understand the forces necessary for successful change.

Group dynamics

Field theory is an obvious precursor to the study of group dynamics. Intuitively, if one's environment has the potential to influence behaviour, then, as components of one's environment, so do the groups to which one belongs. The term 'group dynamics' first appeared in print in 1913 in an article about the functioning of groups. In it, 'Lewin and his associates saw that in a group each member recognizes the other members as persons on whom he depends to a definite degree. The group is therefore a psychologically organic whole, rather than a simple collection of individuals'.[18]

Lewin believed in a way of life that emphasized 'mutual participation and continual interaction in decision making'.[19] This was evident in his teaching style as he much preferred informal class discussions to formal lectures. 'Given this concern for democratic decision making, his interest in social action, and his own style of working with groups, it is not surprising that Kurt Lewin turned increasingly in his years in America to the study of group dynamics'.[20] This study of groups was formalized through the creation of the Research Center for Group Dynamics at MIT. In an article published in 1945 about the Center, Lewin identified four questions that he deemed essential to the understanding of group dynamics. They were as follows:[21]

1   What forces are keeping up this type of group life?
2   What type of change would be brought about by what type of action?
3   What forces would resist what changes?
4   Under what condition would a change be permanent and when will group living bend quickly back to the previous designs?

Lewin chose rather novel research methods for the study of groups and the forces of change which he called 'dynamics'. He felt that, 'the study of group life should reach beyond the level of description; the conditions of group life and the forces which bring about change or which resist change should be investigated'.[22] Rather than merely observing individuals in groups, Lewin focused his efforts on the development of group experiments, many of which focused on the notion of group change.

The goal of the Center is best summarized using Lewin's own words:

> The main task of the Center is the development of scientific methods of studying and changing group life and the development of concepts and theories of Group Dynamics. Main areas of investigations are to be:

industry, minority problems, and the relation between economics and culture.[23]

Recognition of the impact of groups on individual behaviour has been essential for the development of the field of organizational change. Essentially, Lewin's contribution has been to recognize that, 'it is futile to try to change any worker from one pattern to another unless the entire group to which he "belongs" is included in the change. Rather than disturb his relation to his group, the individual will as a rule take considerable risk, even at substantial financial sacrifice, to conform to his group. Thus the behaviour of a whole group may be more easily changed than that of a single member' (Marrow, 1969).

Lewin's Three-Step Model (1947)

It is not difficult to see how *action research, field theory*, and *group dynamics* all directly impacted Lewin's vision of societal change. In essence, Lewin viewed the group as the necessary level of study in order to understand and enact such change. He believed that groups were consistently in a state of 'quasi-stationary equilibrium'. Analogous to a river flowing, the group was in constant motion but moved in only one direction. This balance was maintained by social forces driving and resisting the flow. Only by changing the driving and resisting forces could change occur. The impact of this conceptualization is evident in the subsequent discourse of organizational change, particularly in discussions of forces for organizational change and the vast attention paid to issues of resistance to change in organizations.

Further study of the phenomenon of group change led Lewin to observe that higher levels of group performance, as a result of change, were often short-lived;[24] that is, employees returned to their original behaviours, and resulting performance levels, shortly after the change was implemented. He concluded that, in order for change to be permanent, old habits had to be discarded and new habits had to be firmly established. As a result of this, he sought a solution that would lead to permanency of change. His very well-known Three-Step Model of Change was the result.

According to Lewin, in order to effect organizational change, a three-step model should be employed. Figure 3.1 outlines the three-step model.

Unfreezing: Group members must have a 'felt need' for change and this is usually achieved through a confrontation or education during the unfreezing stage. This is not unlike the first stage of action research. In the case of a group or organization, the members must understand the need for change and must desire the change. It must be made clear why the 'old way' of doing things is no longer acceptable.

Change: This is the stage where the change actually occurs and the organization moves to the desired state. New policies, procedures, structures,

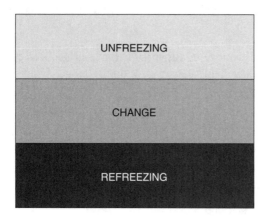

Figure 3.1 Lewin's Three-Step Model of Change.
Source: Lewin, 1947

behaviours, values, and attitudes are developed. Once again, elements of action research are evident.

Refreezing: During this stage, the changes are reinforced and supported. It is essential to ensure that organization systems are consistent with the change. For example, reward systems and social support may be used to encourage new desired behaviours.

Let's use an example to demonstrate Lewin's Three-Step Model. An organization's call centre has been receiving poor customer evaluations. The organization realizes that good customer service is essential for success in the industry and wishes to become more customer-focused. Managers conclude from survey results that customers are feeling neglected and feel that telephone representatives try to rush them off the phone, not taking their concerns seriously. Application of Lewin's Three-Step Model of Change might look like the following:

1   *Unfreezing*: Managers hold a meeting with all telephone representatives. During the meeting, customer survey results are discussed. Additionally, lost customer estimates are translated into dollars and cents so that telephone representatives can see how poor customer service results in overall poor company performance and lost jobs.

2   *Change*: After the meeting, telephone representatives are provided with customer service training that involves role-playing and group discussions. This allows the representatives to experience 'poor' service and 'good' service. Representatives are instructed to take their time with calls and to make sure they address all customer needs. A new peer support system is created whereby representatives spend 15 minutes every shift listening to other calls and providing feedback and support. Mirrors are placed on every call station so that representatives can make sure they

'end the call with a smile'. This becomes an unofficial slogan for the centre.

3   *Refreezing*: The old compensation system rewarded representatives based on the number of calls made per hour. Clearly, this old system would not support the desired changes so the compensation system is changed. Representatives are now paid on an hourly rate and bonuses are based on customer satisfaction surveys. Additionally, the employees have the opportunity to nominate each other for 'customer service guru of the week'. The honour comes with a silly hat and a certificate.

To summarize Lewin's model, organizational change requires significant organizational commitment both before and after the change. The model, unfreezing, change and refreezing, considers the organization's environment in its entirety, and recognizes the need for openness to change before it occurs and support for change once it has occurred. Curiously, although Lewin recognized these issues as early as 1947, these still remain two of the biggest oversights organizations make when attempting to implement change initiatives. Far too often, employees are asked to accept change initiatives without question or a clear understanding of the need for change and are subsequently not provided with the support and structure necessary to maintain the change.

Making sense of Lewin's work

Lewin has been hailed as 'the intellectual father of contemporary theories of applied behavioural science, action research and planned change'.[25] Clearly, he furthered our understanding of organization change in several important ways. First, Lewin was a challenger of the notion of 'man as machine'. His behaviourist position shed new light on organization change causing researchers to take pause and to recognize the worker as human with human qualities and needs. Second, Lewin introduced the notion of research as an impetus for change. The effect of this was twofold – it emphasized the necessity of careful study and planning in the change process and it introduced the notion of research for the sake of action, rather than for the sake of research. Third, Lewin drew attention to the impact of environment on behaviour, discarding the notion that all behaviour was motivated by internal drives or needs. Fourth, Lewin drew attention to the role of groups on individual and group behaviour. This is of paramount importance in today's team-based organizations. Fifth, and most certainly not final, Lewin recognized that change could only be enacted and sustained if participants felt a need for the change and were supported after the change. His contribution to the discourse of change is undeniable and remains clearly evident in the discourse of planned change.

Lewin's Three-Step Model is one of the most taught models of change in North American business schools and almost any MBA or business graduate can easily recite its edicts, often despite or without acknowledging its basis in social, emancipatory change. Moreover, many of the organizational change models developed since Lewin's work bear a resemblance to his original model. This should cause the reader to pause and consider the implications of the staying power of such a theory.

Lewin's change model, developed in 1947, was conceived during significantly different times. Critics of the continued use of Lewin's model, and not of the man himself, argue that today's more turbulent times, with the ever-changing, global and diverse business environment calls for newer, more relevant tools. Some argue that organizations simply don't have the time or luxury to 'unfreeze' or 'refreeze'. Similarly, the face of the workforce has changed significantly since the 1940s and 1950s, with the increased participation rate of women and increased diversity in the workforce, thus calling into question the relevance and applicability of behaviour research of that time. Given this, is it safe to assume that tools developed under such different circumstances will be as effective in today's business environment?

Organizational Development (OD)

The planned approach to change evolved significantly over time. Some argue that it actually evolved into and lies at the core of what is now identified as the field of Organization Development (OD) which emerged in the 1950s and 1960s.[26]

Although now a multi-billion dollar industry, and a field of study that enjoys much attention, a commonly accepted definition of OD remains elusive. Versions range from Schifo's,[27] 'OD is the ... application of behavioural science to promote system effectiveness through change' to Beckhard's,[28] 'Organizational development is an effort (1) planned, (2) organization-wide and (3) managed from the top, to (4) increase organization effectiveness and health through (5) planned interventions in the organization's "processes", using behavioural-science knowledge'. Clearly, the field of Organizational Development is cumbersome and includes a myriad theories and practices. However, it is safe to conclude that *the field focuses on people, organizations and planned change.* Much of the theory within OD stems from disciplines such as psychology, sociology, anthropology and social psychology and there is a clear commitment to the 'human factor' and organizational effectiveness.[29]

Argyris,[30] one of the pioneers of OD, explained it by stating that, 'at the heart of organizational development is the concern for the vitalizing, energizing, actualizing, activating, and renewing of organizations through technical and human resources'. Lewin's major contributions, most notably that of *action research*, are evident in this description.

French and Bell[31] later defined it as the 'long-range effort to improve an organization's problem-solving and renewal processes, particularly through a more effective and collaborative management of organization culture – with special emphasis on the culture of formal work teams – with the assistance of a change agent, or catalyst, and the use of the theory and technology of applied behavioural science, including action research'. Here, traces of *action research, field theory* and *group dynamics* are evident.

French and Bell, considered experts in OD, identified eight characteristics that differentiated OD from more traditional change interventions:[32]

1 An emphasis on group and organizational processes.
2 An emphasis on the work team as the key unit for learning more effective modes of organizational behaviour.
3 An emphasis on the collaborative management of work-team culture.
4 An emphasis on the management of the culture of the total system.
5 Attention to the management of system ramifications.
6 The use of the action research model.
7 The use of behavioural scientist-change agent.
8 A view of the change effort as an ongoing process.

French and Bell also identified some of the underlying assumptions of OD. These included:[33]

1 Assumptions about People as Individuals

   a Most individuals have drives towards personal growth and development if provided with an environment that is both supportive and challenging.
   b Most people desire to make, and are capable of making, a higher level of contribution to the attainment of organizational goals than most organizational environments will permit.

2 Assumptions about People in Groups and about Leadership

   a One of the most psychologically relevant reference groups for most people is the work group, including peers and the superior.
   b Most people wish to be accepted and to interact cooperatively with at least one small reference group.
   c For a group to optimize its effectiveness, the formal leader cannot perform all the leadership and maintenance functions in all circumstances at all times, hence group members must assist each other with effective leadership and member behaviours.
   d Suppressed feelings and attitudes adversely affect problem-solving, personal growth and job satisfaction.
   e The level of interpersonal trust, support and cooperation is much lower in most groups and organizations than is either necessary or desirable, in spite of drives towards these same qualities.
   f Solutions to most attitudinal and motivational problems in organizations are transactional.

3   Assumptions about People in Organizational Systems

    a   The interplay of the dynamics of these work teams, as conveyed by the 'linking pin' incumbents, has a powerful effect on the attitudes and behaviour of people in both groups. In particular, the leadership style and the climate of the higher team tend to get transmitted to the lower teams.

    b   Win–lose conflict strategies between people and groups, in which one comes off the triumphant winner and the other a defensive loser, while realistic and appropriate in some situations, are not optimal in the long run to the solution of most organizational problems.

    c   OD takes time and patience, and the key movers in an OD effort need to have a relatively long-range time perspective.

    d   Improved performance stemming from organization development efforts needs to be sustained by appropriate changes in the appraisal, compensation, training, staffing, task and communications systems – in short, in the total human resources system.

4   Assumptions that relate to Values in the Client Organization.

    a   Members of the system, in general, place value in collaborative effort and in the end products of the system.

    b   Value is placed on the welfare of all system members, particularly by the people having the most power over others. OD programmes are designed to improve the welfare and quality of work life for all the members of the organization.

5   Value and Belief Systems of Behavioural Scientist Change Agents

    a   Needs and aspirations of human beings are the reasons for organized effort in society.

    b   Work and life can become richer and more meaningful, and organized effort more effective and enjoyable, if feelings and sentiments are permitted to be a more legitimate part of the culture of organizations.

    c   A commitment is made to both action and research broadly conceived, which can include inquiry and examination into the nature of change processes and the effectiveness of interventions.

    d   Value is placed on the democratization of organizations or on 'power equalization'.

The field of *Organization Development* is vast and offers myriad tools, all with the promise of revitalized, more effective organizations. One of the most recent and popular prescriptions for planned organizational change is Kotter's[34] Eight-Stage Process of Creating Major Change. Kotter has achieved 'guru-like' status and book club acclaim for his work in *Leading*

Change and *The Heart of Change*. Essentially, Kotter proposes an eight-stage process and, once again, remnants of Lewin's original work are evident. He proposes the following as a recipe for effective change:

1 Establishing a Sense of Urgency
2 Creating the Guiding Coalition
3 Developing a Vision and Strategy
4 Communicating the Change Vision
5 Empowering Broad-Based Action
6 Generating Short-Term Wins
7 Consolidating Gains and Producing More Change
8 Anchoring New Approaches in the Culture.

Kotter's vision of effective change is just one example of the prescriptions available to organizations wishing to address change within the realm of OD.

Making sense of OD

Kurt Lewin's work appears to have started the long journey from *Taylorism* to OD. Management theory has come a long way from 'man as machine' as is evidenced by *action research, field theory, group dynamics, Lewin's Three-Step Change Process*, and the field of *OD* in its entirety. However, the field is not without its critics. In fact, as identified by Connor,[35] 'Not since Taylorism has a set of ideas about management and organization engendered so much controversy and commentary as organizational development (OD)'. Some of the major criticisms of the field will be discussed briefly in the paragraphs that follow.

Perhaps the most popular criticism of OD is its extensive growth into what is now a multi-billion dollar industry. The plethora of OD interventions and 'gurus' have made the field susceptible to criticism typical of such lucrative management 'hot topics'. For example, White and Wooten[36] warn that we must be cautious about the rapid growth of the OD field. They worry that the field, represented by a multitude of practitioners with varying experience from across multiple disciplines, has not managed to keep pace structurally and scientifically. They worry that a once scientific field has become something of a religious movement, and as a result, it is losing legitimacy in the scientific world.

Another criticism of OD is that the field has grown to such an extent that it has lost its original tenets – those of research for the sake of taking action for social change and recognition of the human element of change. Clearly, those were Lewin's original intentions. Although the notion of planned change, as well as Lewin's *Three-Step Model*, have endured, many OD initiatives lack any other resemblance in terms of motive and application. Instead, many appear to be top-down interventions that attempt to change the organization in the names of productivity and efficiency, with little regard to the human component.

Similarly, Edgar Schein,[37] one of the early proponents of planned change, argues that OD has become overly prescriptive and that the client focus has been lost. He argues that the plethora of 'canned' solutions now available offer an all too easy 'fix' for organizations, making it easy for consultants or change agents to prescribe a programme without first clearly understanding the issues at hand.

Finally, proponents of *radical change, emergent change* and *perpetual change* (as will be discussed in subsequent chapters) feel that *planned change* is ineffective in today's turbulent, global environment. Tom Peters, one such proponent, argues that organizations need to change constantly in order to survive. This requires more of an emphasis on continual change which can only be fostered by an organization that values innovation, risk, organization learning, and, to some extent, chaos. Clearly, this is not consistent with the prescriptive formulas commonly found in the world of OD.

Summary

This chapter was designed to take you on a journey through the early stages of the discourse of organizational change. Lewin's response to *Taylorism* and his quest to find strategies that would help to right the wrongs of society began a legacy of the study of organization change. His advocacy of planned strategies for change was adopted into mainstream organization discourse and adapted for use. From this, the field of *Organization Development* is purported to have evolved, growing into a multi-billion dollar industry full of prescriptions for change, offering organizations answers to their most current and critical ailments. Although planned change strategies are still prominent today, critics of prescriptive, universalist and static models of change claim that more dynamic, open systems and contingent models of change are required for today's dynamic, global environment.

End of chapter questions and exercises

1   Research the food companies discussed in the opening case. What has happened since they were in the news in 2005? Have other major changes occurred since then? Were they planned changes?
2   Summarize action research, field theory, and Lewin's theory of group dynamics.
3   Choose something that you believe needs changing at your university. Use Kurt Lewin's Three-Step Model to discuss how you would implement the change.
4   Visit the following Web sites: http://www.odnetwork.org/
                                       http://members.aol.com/odinst/
                                       http://www.podnetwork.org/

What can we learn about the state of the OD industry today? Is it alive and well? What are the purposes of these organizations?

5 Is there a place for OD in the organizations you are involved in? Why or why not?

6 Search a national newspaper for examples of OD. Articles may not refer to the change strategies used as OD, so look for signs of the basic tenets of OD.

4   Organizational culture and culture change

Objectives of this chapter

By the end of this chapter, you should:

1   Understand the roots of planned culture change
2   Understand the different perspectives of organizational culture
3   Understand planned culture change approaches
4   Be able to critically assess the relevant models and theories of culture and culture change.

cultural clashes

On a recent flight, two cabin attendants were overhead discussing emergency evacuation procedures. One felt that the other had been lax by only advising passengers that they should familiarize themselves with the instructions on the printed card in the seat pocket. She felt that the printed directions were confusing and passengers needed detailed verbal directions from a member of the crew. The other attendant disagreed and said that only made passengers nervous. While both attendants were following the official policies on airline safety, their interpretation of the rules varied. As it happened, each of the attendants had worked in separate airlines for the past 25 years, but the recent merger of their two airlines meant that they were being put together to work for the first time and each of them had different assumptions about how the procedures should be handled. Neither was right or wrong. This situation was a case of competing organizational cultures, grounded in different values, beliefs and assumptions. Yet, had there been a need to evacuate the aircraft, these different interpretations of the rules could have resulted in serious consequences.

What do *Scandinavian Airlines, British Airways* and *NSP* have in common? Each of these organizations reached a crisis point in the 1980s and each of them decided to implement a planned culture change to overcome their problems. Their choice of change strategy was no coincidence. In the mid-1980s, as consultants and managers started to recognize the power of culture, managing corporate culture and defining organizational values became one of the hottest management fads in the history of organizational change, despite disagreement about whether culture could actually be changed and managed, what actually constituted culture, extensive time commitments, difficulty in measuring outcomes and varying degrees of what could be deemed success. So what is organizational culture and how did planned culture change become a popular change management technique that continues to endure today?

Organizational development techniques, which have evolved from the 1970s, set the stage for change and provided the foundation for what has become a recurring theme in the discourse of change – the need by managers to continually engage in change techniques, so that the organization is viewed as being cutting edge. Increasingly, there has been a perception by mangers that they need to emphasize customer service and the use of 'expert' knowledge, through the adoption of a programmatic approach to change. Since the 1980s, the starting point for these planned changes has focused on the culture of the organization, with an emphasis on shared organizational values and beliefs acting as a 'glue' to bind together employees towards common goals. As we shall see, interest in managing organizational culture came about because of US concerns about increased competition from Japanese companies, who were producing and selling quality products that undercut similar goods being manufactured in the US. Soon this interest in Japanese management techniques spread to Europe and culture change began to be seen as a way for organizations to recreate themselves and overcome a variety of existing problems. Although managing and changing corporate culture was hugely popular in the 1980s and early 1990s, few anticipated the problems that takeovers, mergers and acquisitions would create at the end of the century, as we saw in the opening vignette.

In this chapter, we will explore the reasons for the interest in organizational culture, look at several different perspectives of organizational culture, and explore the strengths and weaknesses of planned culture change programmes.

The roots of organizational culture

Although interest in studying organizations from a cultural perspective started in the 1970s,[1] the interest in and acceptance of managing and changing culture as a management technique grew more from media attention than from academic research. Towards the end of the 1970s, it was clear that the United States was losing ground to the Japanese as the world leader in industrial power. Both business leaders and educators in the West recognized the strong competition they were facing from Japan and realized that existing Western ways of managing were no longer as effective as they had been.

In 1980, NBC, one of the major US broadcasting corporations, aired a television programme called '*If Japan Can Do it, Why Can't We*'.[2] In it, Edwards Deming, an American statistician who had gone to Japan in 1947 following the Second World War to help the Japanese find ways to regain their economic strength, and Joseph Juran, another American, were credited with the turnaround in Japanese productivity. Their methods included employing a variety of techniques that eventually came to be known as *total quality management* (TQM). Deming and Juran were relatively unknown in the US at the time but, as the crisis in organizing in North America became more pronounced, combined with feelings of disillusionment with rational models of formal organizations, educators and corporate leaders, who were keen to find out the reasons for Japan's success,[3] turned to Deming and Juran for solutions and their names soon became well known in North America as well as Japan.

It became evident that the success of Japanese companies was as much based on the technical principles of TQM as it was on the human element of creating organizations where shared values and beliefs defined the personality of the workplace. This led many US-based companies to become more people-focused and look for ways to unify employees at all levels of the organization. When *Honda* and *Toyota* opened plants in the US, it was mandatory for their employees to start each shift by standing around in a circle, holding hands and singing the company song, followed by giving the company cheer. This was considered the way to reinforce corporate values and create 'strong' cultures. Soon North American auto manufacturers, such as *Saturn*, started adopting similar strategies. They were followed by other companies, like *Wal-Mart*, where employees still start each day with callisthenics and the company cheer because Sam Walton, *Wal-Mart*'s founder, saw it being done in Korea and thought it a good way to bring together his employees:

> *Give me a W!*
> *Give me an A!*
> *Give me an L!*
> *Give me a squiggly!*
> *Give me an M!*
> *Give me an A!*
> *Give me an R!*
> *Give me a T!*
> *What's that spell?*
> *Wal-Mart!*
> *Whose Wal-Mart is it?*
> *It's my Wal-Mart!*

Who's number one?
The customer! Always![4]

Other large organizations, such as *IBM* and *Disney*, were also being singled out as exemplars of companies with successful cultures. This snowball effect led consultants to look for prescriptive ways to manage culture change. Thus, we can see how a need for increased productivity and effectiveness led consultants to focus on organizational culture. All this is part of the sensemaking process. As managers and consultants look for plausible ways to solve their problems, they draw on past experiences and look to see what other organizations in similar situations are doing. That means that many organizations that engage in planned culture change do so because they have read about similar organizations having successful outcomes with culture change. In the case of *Nova Scotia Power*, an electrical utility in Eastern Canada, their president was strongly influenced by the successes experienced by *Kansai Power* in Japan and *Florida Power and Light*. He believed that by changing the culture of the organization, he could increase its effectiveness. This tied in nicely with the research into Japanese management styles, which revealed a connection between organizational culture and organizational effectiveness.[5] By mimicking and reproducing what seems to work for others, managers and consultants reinforce the need for culture change, which in turn increases its popularity and subsequently reinforces the belief that change is good and culture change is really good because others are also engaged in it. This cycle will then continue until a new change technique comes along.

Culture and culture change

The techniques being used in Japan also meshed nicely with Western developments in the *Organizational Development* and *Quality of Working Life* movements of the 1970s. Interest in creating organizations that had 'strong' cultures spread quickly to the UK and the rest of Europe. By the early 1980s, *Business Week*[6] had done a cover story on Japanese management techniques and organizational culture.

On the academic side, in 1981, a management scholar, William Ouchi, drawing on experiences taken from Japanese firms, proposed his 'Theory Z'. This was a culture change programme that merged Japanese management practices ('Type J'), with American cultural realities ('Type A') and led to the development of a range of theories of organizational culture, including planned culture changes and the expansion of *Total Quality Management* techniques into North America industries. Soon a number of best-selling books that showcased studies of Japanese culture and lessons to the US were appearing,[7] including Peters & Waterman's *In Search of Excellence*, and management consultants were designing strategies for changing culture. The endurance of culture change as a change technique lies in its ability to mesh nicely with other change programmes, such as *TQM, Balanced Scorecard, Six*

Sigma and others. Culture change can either be the direct focus of the change or it can be a secondary outcome of another change programme, as we shall see.

Making sense of organizational culture

So what is organizational culture? Disagreement over what culture is, how it should be studied and whether or not it can be changed or managed, has led to 'conceptual chaos' as even today nobody can seem to agree on a single definition of culture. Part of the reason for this lack of consensus has been attributed to the failure by researchers to read or acknowledge each other's work[8] and partially to the multitude of definitions of culture. For example, by the mid-1980s, when interest in culture was at an all-time high, there were 73 words from 58 sources to describe organizational culture.[9] These words, which included values, beliefs, language and norms, raised a number of questions about how culture is understood in organizational settings, including whether or not it can be changed. In the following sections, we will highlight the key cultural definitions and perspectives. By unravelling some of the confusion surrounding the definitions of culture we can start to make sense of the problems of understanding culture change as a planned change strategy and highlight some of the disagreements between practitioners and academics.

Because there are so many different ways to approach the study of culture, let's start with some universally agreed-upon understandings of organizational culture. We know that organizational culture is rooted in anthropology. It has been described as *the 'social glue' that hold together organizations.*[10] *Culture represents the organizations values and beliefs and it guides organizational behaviour. In short, culture represents 'the way things are done' in the organization.*[11] From a sensemaking perspective, organizational culture provides members with a sensemaking device for symbols and events that take place in the organization.[12] From these definitions of culture, we can begin to understand that it has a very powerful influence and we can start to see how culture could influence organizational success. But, as we shall see, this will depend which cultural perspective we take.

Cultural perspectives

One of the most fundamental disagreements about defining organizational culture stems from whether or not culture is understood as something tangible that can be managed and changed, or something that reflects the various beliefs and values members bring with them to the organization. In the first instance, which is the view of management consultants, culture is understood as something an organization 'has'; a variable that can be manipulated or changed in order to achieve organizational effectiveness. It is this perspective that has shaped the 'cultural excellence' literature,[13] which will be discussed in detail in the next section. In the second instance, culture is more complex and subtle and is seen as 'root metaphor' for conceptualizing what an organization 'is'.[14] Culture understood this way views it as the 'collective personality' of the organizational members and, therefore, not something that can be easily manipulated or changed. Academics can be divided on which perspective reflects their thinking. They can also be divided on what constitutes culture, what levels exist and what they mean, as we shall see in the next sections.

Schein's 'Iceberg' Model of Culture: *McDonald's* is a good example of a company that works hard to portray its corporate culture. Based on the entrepreneurial and family values of its founder, Ray Kroc, his vision has been translated into tangible artefacts, such as 'the golden arches', Ronald McDonald and the 'Big Mac', and slogans like 'I'm lovin' it' provide powerful cues to its customers about what they can expect from a *McDonald's* experience that sets it apart from other fast food establishments. Indeed, *McDonald's* have built a culture based on standardization, which has contributed to its success at home and abroad. For example, Americans travelling abroad often seek out *McDonald's* because they know what to expect. Likewise, for their overseas customers, *McDonald's* represents a piece of American culture that they might not otherwise experience.

It is generally agreed that Edgar Schein invented the term 'corporate culture'[15] and it is his multi-level model of culture, first developed in the mid-1980s,[16] that is the most enduring and widely reproduced in management texts, making it the model of culture that most students have familiarity with.

According to Schein, culture is apparent at three levels in the organization. At the first level, culture is visible to organizational insiders and outsiders through organizational artefacts. These can range from the pens and coffee mugs, to corporate logos and slogans, such as *McDonald's* 'I'm lovin' it'. The similarity of *McDonald's* restaurants around the world, from design to food, is a part of their cultural blueprint and helps them relay their culture at the most basic level.

At the middle level, culture involves the expression of culture through stories, myths and rituals that are often expressed in mission statements. Everyone knows the story of Ray Kroc, the founder of *McDonald's*, who started out as a milkshake machine salesperson, to become the owner of the largest fast food chain in history. Likewise, companies like *Mary Kay Cosmetics* and *Southwest Airlines* have annual employee recognition programmes that award employees with outstanding gifts, like the famous *Mary Kay* pink Cadillac!

At the deepest level of the model, the transmission of culture is done unconsciously or beneath the surface. According to Schein, basic assumptions help to formulate organizational values, and these become 'shared assumptions' that serve to guide how organizational members interact with each other. Over time and through socialization, the values are passed on and taught to new organizational members as the correct way to do things. Culture at this level is intangible but it has a profound influence on how it is enacted and becomes visible at the other two levels. For example, professionalism is a basic assumption at the airline that is sometimes mistaken for aloofness in employee behaviour; whereas entrepreneurship and customer service were basic assumptions of the airlines that merged with them, which resulted in behaviour that was perceived as friendly. Thus, when the employees of the airlines were assimilated into one airline, there were conflicting values and assumptions about how they should behave and how airline policies should be followed, as we saw.

According to Schein, culture is something that is learned and evolves with new experiences. While he recognizes that culture is the most difficult element of the organization to change, he also believes that it can be changed *if* the learning dynamics of the (culture) process are understood. Furthermore, Schein believes that culture can help deal with difficult events and organizational uncertainty, but whether or not they translate into action depends on how deeply these values are ingrained within the organizational membership. In this sense, we can assume that Schein believes culture is a variable to be manipulated.

Schein's model is valuable because it was one of the first scholarly studies that provided the link between scholarly activity and practical applicability. Moreover, the model provided rationales for failures with planned culture changes. The discrepancies in behaviour and understanding between levels two and three also provided a partial explanation for the inability of organizations to create unifying cultures. For example, basic assumptions offer an explanation for the difference between behaviour that is incongruent with stated organizational values. On the negative side, Schein has failed to take into account the impact of issues of identity on the creation of culture. In particular, gender is ignored.

A Rules Perspective of Culture: Another way of defining *culture is to think of it as the enactment of organizational rules.* According to Mills & Murgatroyd,[17] organizations are composed of a series of both formal and informal rules. How members of the organization choose to make sense of and enact those rules reflects the culture of the organization. We saw this reflection of 'how things are' rather than 'how things should be' in the opening case of *Air Canada*, whereby each flight attendant had their own interpretation of the safety procedures, even though they were formally stated in the company's official policy. This perspective is grounded in the notion that organizations are structured around a configuration of rules. Some are formal rules, such as workplace policies and regulations that provide guidelines and structure employee behaviour. Others can be informal rules, which are not explicitly stated in organizational manuals but arise out of practice and custom and usually represent the values and assumptions of organizational members. Casual dress days or seating arrangements in the workplace are some examples of these kinds of rules, but, as we shall see later, informal rules can also be influenced by our prejudices and can have serious consequences for those affected by them. Thus informal rules are equally important in guiding behaviour and transmitting culture.

The strength of this approach is that it also takes into account that culture is the result of basic assumptions that are the basis for both informal rules and how the rules are understood. It also offers an explanation for how cultures become gendered, which will be discussed in a later chapter. Organizational culture as an outcome of organizational rules recognizes that culture, like personality, is fairly stable over time and cannot be easily managed. Despite rules being in place for how employees should behave, how they choose to behave and what guides their behaviour is more complex and not accounted for in this model.

Martin's Perspectives of Culture: In a recent interview, Joanne Martin, a management professor at Stanford University, describes culture as the working environment of the organization.[18] Martin, who has written extensively in the area of cultural studies,[19] looks at organizational culture from different perspectives. Instead of seeing culture as something that holds the organization together, she suggests that organizational cultures are not all necessarily unifying. Instead, several different cultures can be in existence in the same organization. According to Martin, any definition of culture needs to take into account the possibility of competing subcultures that are a fact of life in the workplace. In this vein, Martin initially suggested three perspectives of culture. She argues that, rather than being representative of a single culture in an organization, the perspectives provide ways to make sense of cultures in an organization. They are how we as onlookers frame our understanding of what culture is and how it operates and how it looks at a particular point in time. Thus, the previous definitions of culture that we have seen fit within the different perspectives and Martin's perspectives are ways of categorizing the different viewpoints of culture.

The Integrative Perspective: This is most similar to Schein's model of culture, which assumes that the culture is clear, that members share in an organization-wide consensus and that all cultural manifestations are interpreted consistently and reinforce common themes. *McDonald's* would be an example of an integrative culture. *The Differentiation perspective* sees organizations as a set of subcultures that perceive organization-wide consensus as a 'suspicious concept'. The premise of this approach is that it is the group, not the organization, that shares beliefs and values. The focus is on the difference in power and conflicts of interest between groups (subcultures). Any consensus will be within the groups. However, what benefits one group may be at the expense of another group. Mills and Murgatroyd's rules perspective of culture would fit best into the differentiated perspective and we can see how this was enacted at *NSP*, where different geographic and departmental areas have competing subcultures. Finally, *The Fragmented perspective* sees culture as ambiguous and constantly changing. There is a low level of interdependence and little or no stability in what is going on, except maybe the language that is being used. Companies that outsource their work might have fragmented cultures because there is little interaction between employees. For example, call centres that provide customer service for several different credit card companies would have fragmented cultures because there would be very little interaction with the credit card company itself and there would be further fragmentation between employees within the call centre, depending on whom they were representing.

From theory to practice

In the previous section we have looked at how the interest in organizational culture began and the differences in opinion as to what corporate culture is and if it can be managed. Obviously, the predominant view held by both management consultants and many academics is that culture is indeed something tangible that can be isolated and changed and in so doing will lead to a more effective organization. As we said earlier, culture change has endured as a change technique because there are a number of ways culture can be changed. Organizations like *NSP, Scandinavian Airways* and *British Airways* have implemented specific change programmes that target organizational values and the underlying belief system, so that the focus is directly on changing the culture. Other organizations, such as *Barclays, British Petroleum* and *General Electric* have implemented other change techniques (re-engineering, learning organization strategies, Balanced Scorecard, TQM, etc.) where culture change is an expected outcome but not the primary focus. Still other companies inherit a changing culture because of merger or acquisition, which we saw in the opening vignette of *Air Canada*, and then have to learn how to manage the new culture. In the next section we shall look at some examples of planned culture change.

Planned culture change

> 'This is not just about restructuring our balance sheet,' Robert Milton, Air Canada's chief executive, said today in announcing the application for protection under the Companies' Creditors Arrangement Act, roughly equivalent to a Chapter 11 filing in the United States. 'The business model is broken and it must be fixed without burning any more furniture', Mr. Milton said. 'Air Canada and our people need to embrace a culture change and a new way of doing business.'[20]

In 1982, two important books were published that provided the impetus for organizational change to take off as a change management tool in North America. First, Terrance Deal and Allan Kennedy released *Corporate*

Cultures, which clearly laid out the key elements of corporate culture and provided a template for what managers needed to be aware of in order to change or manage their existing cultures. There were:

- *The business environment* – the orientation of organizations within this environment leads to specific cultural styles.
- *Values* – made up of the key beliefs and concepts shared by an organization's employees. Successful managers are clear about these values and their managers publicly reinforce them.
- *Heroes* – personifications of the organization's values, achievers who provide role models for success within the company. (. . .) Heroes have vision and go against the existing order if necessary in order to achieve that vision.
- *Rites and rituals* – ceremonies and routine behavioural rituals reinforce the culture.
- *The cultural network* – the carrier of stories and gossip which spread information about valued behaviour and 'heroic myths' around the organization.[21]

At the same time Tom Peters and Robert Waterman, management consultants with *McKinsey*, published the bestseller *In Search of Excellence*.[22] This book, which in 2002 *Forbes Magazine* voted as 'the most influential business book in the last 20 years',[23] highlights 43 'best run' US companies. These were selected because of the innovative management techniques they used during the period between 1961 and 1980 and the 'excellence' they achieved in terms of productivity and employee satisfaction. The companies ranged from small to large and crossed a wide spectrum of industries, including *Disney, 3M, McDonald's* and *Stan's Market* – a regional grocery chain. But their success was based on one commonality – the use of eight management principles, which helped them create and maintain strong organizational cultures. These principles, according to Peters and Waterman, needed to be adhered to in order to create and maintain strong (i.e. integrated) organizational cultures:

- *Managing ambiguity and paradox* – being prepared for uncertainty and having a plan of action.
- *A bias for action* – effective decision-making.
- *Close to the customer* – maintaining good, strong customer relations and listening to what they have to say.
- *Autonomy and entrepreneurship* – being innovative and giving employees responsibility.
- *Productivity through people* – making use of your employees and keeping them happy.
- *Hands-on, value-driven* – good management values to guide actions.
- *Stick to the knitting* – doing what you know and do best.
- *Simple form, lean staff* – no need for a complex organizational structure.[24]

By showing what needed to be done and how to do it, both Deal and Kennedy and Peters and Waterman were able to 'sell' culture change as a management technique. The popularity of both books catapulted them and their ideas into the popular media. In turn, their ideas served as the foundation for numerous pre-packaged culture change programmes offered by consultants. As we shall see in the next section, there are a number of common elements across these programmes but the outcomes do vary because of factors that are not always as controllable as managers might like. We shall take a look at some of the 'successful' changes and some of the 'unsuccessful' ones and see what conclusions we might make.

Successful planned culture change

Scandinavian Airlines: Moments of Truth

In 1981 *Scandinavian Airlines* (*SAS*) had posted a loss of eight million dollars and the CEO, Jan Carlzon, knew he had to do something about it before the airline filed for bankruptcy. He decided that the airline was too technically oriented and needed to be more customer-focused. Carlzon decided to implement a programme called 'Moments of Truth' (MoT)[25] in order to change the interactions between employees and customers. 'Moments of Truth' are 'critical incidents that exemplify the cohesive and adaptive qualities of an organization as expressed in some particular task or action'.[26] For example, the cancellation of a flight is a moment of truth and, depending on how it is handled by the airline agent, the customer can have a good or a bad experience. According to Carlzon, MoT can occur when least expected but can have a huge impact on customer impressions. By making employees aware of these moments, and by giving them training about how to respond proactively in such situations, both the employee and the customer can feel good about the experience. Carlzon personally oversaw the culture change and over time, the MoT campaign not only changed the culture of SAS but also made them profitable at a time when other airlines were losing money. Soon other airlines were looking to them for ways to overcome similar deficits and Jan Carlzon went on to write a book about the culture change and the foreword was provided by Tom Peters!

British Airways: Putting People First

At the same time that *SAS* was facing financial disaster, *British Airways*, Britain's Flag Carrier, was also in a precarious position. A series of factors, including the acquisition of a number of smaller regional airlines combined with employee apathy, created a culture where poor customer service was the norm. With the privatization of *BA* in 1979, the company had reached a crisis point. The 1981 appointment of Lord King, a successful businessperson, signalled the beginning of *BA*'s turnaround. Concerned with the airline's poor public image and financial predicament, King named Colin Marshall as a senior executive. Marshall, who had previously been President of *Avis Rent a Car*, was very aware of the importance of good customer service and influenced by what others in the travel industry, including *SAS*, were doing to deal with similar problems. He decided to introduce a programme called 'Putting People First', which was managed by a consulting firm in the Netherlands. Like 'Moments of Truth' PPF was designed to change the culture of *BA* by making employees aware of exploring their own interpersonal relationships and then transferring that knowledge to how they interacted with customers. The programme was a huge success with employees and between 1983 and 1985 all 40,000 *BA* employees went through the PPF programme. In 1985, in order to reinforce the new culture at *BA*, the company unveiled new colours and logos and introduced employee excellence awards. By 1990, employees and management agreed that the culture had seen successful changes.[27]

Making sense of successful change

Much has been written about what it takes to change the culture of the organization. It is generally agreed that, in order to make change happen, certain ingredients are necessary. As we see above, both *Scandinavian Airlines* and *British Airways* were experiencing similar problems with customer service and both realized that they had to do something quickly to turn around their businesses, otherwise they would be bankrupt. In addition, both airlines had strong leaders, who were committed to turning the culture around, both had very clear ideas about how they were going to do it and both recognized the need to involve employees in the process and give them autonomy to do their jobs.

We can agree that there are key ingredients that should to be in place for successful change to occur. These include defining a common set of organizational values that are consistent with individuals' values; involving both management and employees in the change process (i.e. getting their input on how to recognize 'Moments of Truth' and identify potential solutions); finding a committed leader of change; managing storytelling that reinforces the new values (i.e. how Jan Carlzon turned the airline around);

rewarding employees who behave in a way that is consistent with the new values (i.e. employee excellence awards); hiring employees whose values are consistent with the new culture and retaining employees so that the new culture is not forgotten. However, even if these steps are taken, they do not always guarantee the success of planned culture change, as we shall see.

Unsuccessful culture change

Culture change at Nova Scotia Power

In 1987, Louis Comeau, President of *Nova Scotia Power* (*NSP*), conducted an employee attitude survey. The results indicated that employee morale was low and employees were unhappy with a paternalistic style of leadership. In an attempt to find a way to humanize the company and to put more emphasis on the employee, Comeau decided to change the corporate culture of *NSP*. His decision was not made randomly. In the US, a culture change at *Florida Power and Light* was being used as an exemplar in the business literature and in Japan changes made by *Kansai Power* also influenced their decision. Closer to home, the local telecommunications provider and the government-run liquor agency were also engaged in planned culture changes. Comeau made the decision to hire the same firm that was facilitating the changes in the local companies and a hired consultant to set about implementing a pre-packaged culture change at *NSP*. The first step in the process was to help the company define four values and their purpose was to provide guidelines for day-to-day employee behaviour. This was done at the senior management level in conjunction with the consultant. The second step was to provide a four-day training seminar for senior managers, followed by a one-day training session, using facilitators selected from the four-day sessions, for the remaining 1,800 employees. The third step was to make sure that the values were 'visible'. This was done by introducing a number of tangible artefacts, such as pens with the values printed on them, and coffee mugs that said, 'we value our environment', and posters of the values on office walls. In addition, events were held and stories that exemplified the values were spread through annual reports and periodic bulletins. The company expected to see evidence of a changing culture within three years and pockets of resistance to the proposed changes were also anticipated. However, they were unprepared for the first act of resistance, which resulted from the discrepancy in training times for management and other employees. Many employees, especially in isolated and strongly union-ized industrial areas, announced they would not lend their support to something they felt they were not included in. Quickly, the company expanded the four-day training sessions to include all supervisory and management staff and all union executives. This cooptation of the union reinforced their acceptance of the culture change. The next act of resistance was related to issues of power and trust. For some managers the idea of giving up power and having to 'manage' in a more participa-tive way instilled fear. At the same time, a number of employees were mistrustful of management's motives and didn't feel they really believed in what they were doing. This was more difficult to resolve and, in some cases, those who didn't support the change quit the company, while others paid lip service to the changes. Finally, the issue of whose values and interests were being served became more important than the values themselves in some cases. That is, many managers felt that the value of 'employee' had taken precedence over the other three values. Four years after the culture change was introduced, *NSP* was privatized and it was decided that the values no longer reflected the goals of the company. Today, when you mention the planned culture change to employees at *NSP*, most don't know what you are talking about, yet the culture did change, but maybe not the way *NSP* anticipated. What went wrong and could anything have been done differently?

Making sense of unsuccessful change

At first glance, the culture change at *NSP* seems to have all the key ingredients necessary for successful change. Like *SAS* and *BA*, they had a leader who was committed to change; he looked to similar organizations to see what change initiatives they had used; he hired a consultant to introduce a pre-packaged change programme that had been successful in other organizations. A set of corporate values had been defined and had eventually been offered to all employees. And cultural artefacts, stories and rewards were used to reinforce the new values. Yet, *NSP* faced strong pockets of resistance, including from management. Why was this change less successful?

Sensemaking helps us explain employees' reaction to *NSP*'s four values. Even though employees were involved in the change process, all but a select few executives were involved in selecting the four values. This did not create a culture of inclusiveness; rather it appeared to contradict the valuing of 'the employee'. Secondly, there was no clear direction for how the values were supposed to be enacted, so employees were uncertain about what they were expected to do to 'value the province'. Unlike 'Moments of Truth' or 'Putting

People First', there was nothing that could help them define their actions. Thirdly, managers were inconsistent in how they managed the culture change, with some openly disagreeing with the values. Finally, a longstanding mistrust of management, especially in certain geographical areas that were heavily unionized, led many to question their motives in bringing about change. This could also have been fuelled by the perception that there was no apparent crisis that had precipitated the change (other than the President's desire to improve morale), so many felt that no action was necessary.

Pre-packaged change programmes

> *This same applies to my approach to outside consultants . . . To me it cannot be anything other than sensible and responsible to bring a ship's pilot on board when you are steering your vessel into new and dangerous waters!*
>
> (Jan Carlzon, 1989: 38–9)

Jan Carlzon's turnaround of the culture of *Scandinavian Airlines* provided a template for how culture could be managed in customer service organizations. Yet, he did not do this alone. Both *SAS* and *British Airways* hired consulting firms to manage their culture changes. And eventually culture change became a staple of consulting firms, who were anxious for a piece of the business and wanting to be able to offer the latest management fad. With varying degrees of expertise, consultants started to create their own culture change packages, often diluting or simplifying existing programmes and implementing them in haphazard ways.

For example, *NSP* hired a consultant based on a pre-packaged culture change solution that she had 'successfully' sold to other local businesses and government agencies. Although it was an amalgam of the key cultural ingredients of values, artefacts and training sessions, it provided minimal support and follow-up after the initial training sessions. Also, rather than customizing the values to meet the needs of each organization, the consultant used the same values for each company she worked with, regardless of their needs.[28] This standardization of culture change and overreliance on the views of the consultant can be problematic because it fails to take into account individual and organizational differences and the sensemaking of those involved in the change process.

Conclusion

Pilkington Building Products

For *Pilkington Building Products*, Six Sigma is not seen as a major change or culture-change programme but as an addition to day-to-day operating excellence. *Pilkington* will progressively train more Six Sigma black belts and green and yellow belts throughout the group. As their projects begin to deliver at the same level as the first wave, it may just be, as with Tim Jenkinson and the first wave of black belts, that they all find themselves doing things differently. That means that an already excellently performing business could find that it has shifted up several gears in performance and culture via Six Sigma without appearing to try.[29]

Like all change techniques, planned culture change can be categorized as a management technique that followed the ebb and flow of the popularity associated with management fads and fashions. Although, as we mentioned at the beginning of this chapter, culture change is still an important element of more current change techniques, it no longer takes centre stage as a 'stand-alone' management tool. Instead, organizations like *Pilkington's* are now using Six Sigma and Balanced Scorecards to reposition themselves and they are, either consciously or unconsciously, changing the culture of the organization. Others, like the airline in the opening vignette, are forging new cultures because the merging of employees from different organizations means they have to find common ground.

Firms that have engaged in culture change clearly believe that culture is something tangible that can be managed; however, both the successes and failures in the above case studies show us that organizational culture is not that concrete and fixed and that outcomes of planned interventions are dependent on the collective 'personality' of what an organization 'is'. Whereas desired behaviours, such as responding to customer needs in a particular way, can be reinforced, there is only a true change in the culture of the organization when employees are wholeheartedly engaged with and believe in the values. Thus, it is our belief that culture change can certainly be achieved but the new culture may not be the one the organization is striving for, unless it reflects the values, beliefs and assumptions of all those involved.

End of chapter questions and exercises

1 How might *Air Canada* have created a more unifying culture? What are some problems that companies might encounter when they merge or acquire different organizations?
2 Do you believe that culture is something that an organization 'is' or something an organization 'has'? Explain your answer.
3 Do you think culture can be planned and changed? What might be some of the pitfalls that an organization thinking of changing its culture might

encounter and what might they do to prevent problems before they start the change?

4 Why were the culture changes at *SAS* and *BA* successful? What, if anything, could they have done differently?

5 How important do you think the role of the leader is in planned culture change? Explain your answer with examples of what a leader should be doing to facilitate change.

6 What should the role of employees be in planned culture change? How might they get involved?

7 Why was the culture change at *NSP* not successful? What, if anything, could they have done differently?

8 Describe the culture of your organization according to Schein's model of culture. Give examples of beliefs, values, assumptions, artefacts, rituals etc.

9 Describe the culture of your university. What sets it apart from other universities? Describe some formal and informal rules that exist. How do you see these enacted? Is there resistance and how does it look?

10 Using the Internet, find three organizations, each in a different country, and categorize them according to Joanne Martin's three perspectives.

11 Using the Internet, look up three of the companies that Peters and Waterman exemplified in their book, *In Search of Excellence*, and describe their current culture.

5 Organizational learning, the learning organization and appreciative inquiry

Objectives of this chapter

By the end of this chapter, students should be able to:

1 Understand what is meant by organizational learning
2 Understand the roots of organizational learning
3 Understand what is meant by the learning organization
4 Understand the differences between organizational learning and the learning organization
5 Understand what is meant by appreciative inquiry
6 Understand the roots of appreciative inquiry
7 Understand the strengths and limitations of each approach

British Petroleum creates a learning organization

In 1987, *British Petroleum* (*BP*) employed 129,000 employees and was in financial difficulty because of its unfocused performance, increased costs, excessive spending and the geographic spread of its oil fields. Yet ten years later, it had become one of the world's most profitable oil companies and had decreased its employee numbers by more than half. What happened? John Browne, the former head of BP, credits the company's turnaround to the 1995 creation of a learning organization. In a 1997 interview with the *Harvard Business Review*, Browne claimed, 'learning was at the heart of a company's ability to adapt to a rapidly changing environment'. Explaining that knowledge comes from a variety of sources, Browne decided to make use of the advancements in technology to enhance teamwork and performance. In 1996, after setting up a computer network throughout the organization, consultants were hired to teach employees how to become effective members of 'virtual team networks' by sharing their knowledge quickly and easily.

Eventually, because of the popularity of these networks, membership was offered to external partner organizations. Through restructuring, new technology, training (including ways to work cooperatively and ways for managers to set targets that helped employees achieve goals) BP had created a learning organization environment and was able to promote the value of 'competitive performance' and subsequently increase revenue and flatten the organizational structure.[1]

Organizational learning in a Canadian Hospital

Hope Hospital is a regional medical facility located in Eastern Canada that provides health care for women and children. The present facility is a result of the merger of a maternity hospital and a tertiary pediatric facility. In 1995, prior to the merger, the education department introduced Peter Senge's five principles of the learning organization as resources for the creation of a learning organization. In addition to their own staff, a team training initiative was developed, with the help of several external consultants, to create a customized version of the learning organization approach in order to foster team-building and the evolution of 'high performing teams'. At this stage organizational learning was a term that was not clearly defined or understood throughout the health centre; rather, leadership pointed to various workplace initiatives as a concrete action that proved learning was supported.

By 1998, the organizational learning and development department at *Hope Hospital* was a vibrant department, with 18 full-time staff members who had input into organization wide policies and programmes. However, for employees who were expecting to see elements of an empowered workplace, the changes associated with workplace democracy were not happening.

Frustration with the slow pace of change within the organization and the continuing issues of inequality and lack of respect created tension between the espoused values of organizational learning and the reality of the *Hope Hospital* workplace, adding to the level of workplace stress. By 1999, employee' demands for more democratic team decision-making and power-sharing within the organization were met with resistance by the senior team. The tension this created between the director of the education department and the rest of the organizational leadership led to a call for a departmental review. Two years later, the entire department was, 'devolved'. The staff in the department lost their positions and the education department ceased to exist.

In retrospect, former departmental members agree that there were some indicators that structurally the department was in trouble. After the devolution of the department it became clear that, although the language of organizational learning was heard throughout the organization, the commitment to this concept, and the meanings it conveyed, were not shared outside of the learning and organizational development department.[2]

In the previous chapter, we saw how a focus on organizational values was used to change the culture of organizations. In this chapter, we will look at two management strategies – organizational learning and appreciative inquiry – that arose from the learning literature and were developed as change management strategies in the 1990s. *Organizational learning is most often described as a heuristic, or prescriptive device, used to explain quantifiable learning activities, which creates an environment that focuses on incorporating principles of learning to enhance employee involvement in organizational goal achievement. The learning organization, therefore, has become a metaphor of a type of organization that engages in organizational learning techniques.*[3] As we see with *British Petroleum*, the need for learning organizations was fuelled by an interest in globalization and the new economy, so that organizational learning became a common *strategy of alignment* (see Chapter 11) for organizations that wanted to remain competitive. At the same time, fostering a learning culture was also a desired outcome of creating a learning organization.

With the second *strategy of appreciative inquiry*, the focus is also on learning but in this case it is learning that relies on retrospection and is grounded in plausibility. By understanding what has worked in the past, organizations choose to focus on these positive elements and build on the strengths of their past successes to create a competitive organization. Whereas a learning organization builds on the knowledge and involvement of its employees in the learning process, appreciative inquiry concentrates on the success of past experiences and tries to build on them for the future.

As we shall see, however, both strategies draw upon principles of learning to further develop employee expertise in order to create an organization that is continually improving. Both of these techniques follow a paradigm shift in strategic management away from 'hard' approaches used in such change programmes as re-engineering, towards softer, more humanistic HR management techniques that increase employee involvement. Both attempt to enlist workers' intellectual assets and cooperation in the labour process. In this chapter, our objective is to explore the issues surrounding these concepts, including their theoretical roots and strengths and limitations.

Organizational learning

Making sense of multiple meanings of organizational learning

The idea of organizational learning is not new but there is a lot of disagreement within the organizational learning literature about what it is. Basically, this lack of consensus arises from the inability of researchers to find a shared meaning about what activities constitute learning and who gets to participate in the learning process. As early as 1969, Herbert Simon described *organizational learning as a process whereby individuals develop insights and take structural and other actions to overcome organizational problems.*[4] These two events (developing insights and structural actions) reflect different meanings of learning and do not necessarily take place at the same time,[5] which is where some of the confusion arises. As we saw in the case of *Hope Hospital*, visible structural changes took place but there was little understanding on what would constitute organizational learning and this led to the devolution of the department. What was unclear was not knowing what activities had to take place in order for the employees to recognize concrete examples of learning. Simon's definition of organizational learning, therefore, raises questions about what constitutes learning, including when and how it takes place, whether organizational learning is the same as individual learning and even if an organization is capable of learning and if so what is being learned.

In 1974, Harvard University professor Chris Argyris and MIT professor Donald Schon broadened the definition of *organizational learning 'as a process of detecting and correcting error'.*[6] But they refined the concept by separating learning into single and double loop learning, whereby double loop learning represents what takes place in organizational learning.[7] While *single loop learning is a fairly common and simple process that occurs when organizations detect and correct something that inhibits learning, double loop learning occurs when organizations change the underlying structures and policies in order to facilitate the learning process.* As we saw in the case of *British Petroleum*, John Browne recognized that in order to remain competitive, the company needed to change the underlying structure at *BP* to create an environment allowing employees to develop their technological skills. By setting up the 'virtual network teams', double loop or organizational learning was taking place for those within those networks.

Currently, organizational learning is described in management texts as a way for an organization 'to acquire, disseminate and apply knowledge for its survival and success'.[8] Although learning is centred around problem-solving, it primarily involves only those individuals whose paid work is seen as adding knowledge to the organization. Specifically, workers whose jobs require certain skills that assist the organization in increasing its competitive advantage are the most likely to participate in continuous learning initiatives. This has led to the creation of *communities of practice*, which are *'informal groups bound together by shared expertise and passion for an activity or interest' and are ways that organizations share knowledge.*[9] The limitation of these communities is that participation is often restricted to those employees who have something that contributes directly to the growth of the organization.

From theory to practice

Today, organizational learning has become synonymous with activities that lead to successful outcomes. In general, the organizational learning literature places a great deal of emphasis on the 'potential' individuals have to learn and the means, through 'empowerment' and changing leadership style, they have to achieve these goals. Yet, as we saw in the case of *Hope Hospital*, many organizations are unsure of how to translate the theories into practice and companies that promote organizational learning often fail to achieve what they promise because of either a lack of a clear-cut process or a piecemeal approach to the change initiative.

The learning organization

In 1987, Peter Senge, a professor at MIT and a protégé of Jay Forrester, an expert in *systems theory*, joined a weekly study group that focused on learning organizations. At the same time, a senior executive of *Royal/Dutch Shell* (*Shell Oil*), who specialized in *scenario planning*, spent a sabbatical at Harvard.[10] By 1989, influenced by these factors, Senge had started to work on his book *The Fifth Discipline*[11] and subsequently heading up the Center for Organizational Learning at MIT.

The Fifth Discipline became a bestseller and established Senge as one of the leading management gurus of the last century. The five disciplines are based on:

- shared visions (having a long-term view of how things should be)
- mental models (uncovering our assumptions and their influence on our behaviour)
- team learning (working as a team)
- personal mastery (continuous individual learning)
- systems thinking (linking all the elements together).

These were derived from a variety of sources but their strength was that they provided concrete guidelines for how to create an organization that could deal with the challenges of increased competition and globalization or with the dissatisfaction of existing organizational development techniques. In 1995, *Shell Oil*, under the direction of Senge, introduced a four-year organizational learning programme, using the five disciplines, and the creation of learning organizations started to gain momentum as a change technique. This elevated organizational learning from its academic theoretical roots to a cutting-edge management fad that led to the proliferation of 'learning organizations' worldwide.

Distinguishing the terms

> . . . organizations where people continually expand their capacity to create the results they truly desire, where new and expansive patterns of thinking are nurtured, where collective aspiration is set free, and where people are continually learning to see the whole together.
>
> (Senge, 1994)

In the past, the terms organizational learning and the learning organization were often used interchangeably. While some suggest that there is little difference, it is now recognized that they are separate and distinct concepts and the literature for each tends to target the audience for whom it is being written. Those writing from a learning organization perspective are most often academics or consultants working in a management consulting role where the focus is on a prescriptive approach, on how an organization should be constructed and how organizational learning should be understood. At its most basic, the *learning organization is a broad term used to describe any organization that employs various learning principles as a means of coping with current challenges.* The notion of the learning organization is a relatively intangible concept that signals a specific organizational direction[12] and it typically describes the physical space where learning is facilitated so that its members can continually transform the organization.[13] We see this in the above definition of the learning organization. Learning organizations create an environment that fosters learning through strategies that promote growth and develop activities, which can help address organizational problems stemming from globalization and increased competition. Generally speaking, the learning organization emphasizes the importance of continuous individual and team-based learning and on developing and refining work-related problem-solving skills. It also emphasizes trust, empowerment and sharing as necessary ingredients for successful outcomes, while stressing the importance of community and the creation of more humanistic workplaces. But, as we shall see a bit later, because the strategic choice and the approach to understanding the learning organization is dependent on key decision-makers, a lack of clear direction sometimes makes it difficult to see how these goals will be accomplished, which was the case with *Hope Hospital*. In the next section, we will explore these different approaches.

Making sense of the learning organization literature

Since the mid-1960s, researchers have been studying ways organizations attempt to adapt the behaviour of their employees in order to help them achieve the goals of the organization. Evidence of the success of the learning organization can be seen in the number of articles and books published about the topic and the number of scholarly journals dedicated solely to it. During the entire decade of the 1980s, for example, there were more academic publications in the area of management learning than in any other management area.[14] The number of companies that have implemented and endorsed learning organization concepts continues to grow, yet the actual techniques used to create a learning organization remain oblique and are open to a variety of interpretations. One thing is certain, however: over time, the concept of a learning organization has come to be viewed as a necessary element to humanization of the workplace.

Cyert's[15] work on standard operating procedures and organizational rules provided an early prototype of how a learning organization could be structured in order to achieve the organization's goals; Argyris and Schon's concept of double loop learning offered a way for managers to link the learning loops directly to both incremental and radical organizational change; and, as we saw, Senge was greatly influenced by systems theory. Over time, these theories have been refined and reworked into three separate perspectives of the learning organization.

The learning organization from a technical perspective

The first is known as the *technical perspective. This approach views a learning organization as one where specific variables are manipulated so that performance is enhanced, through the acquisition of the knowledge or skills necessary to accomplish the task.*[16] Researchers in this area, such as Senge, have fairly explicit and narrowly defined rules concerning what learning entails. In general, it is believed that isolating and controlling certain traits will lead to better performance and thus create successful learning organizations. This is the most popular approach among practitioners and consultants because the increased emphasis on competition makes it an appealing way to manipulate certain elements of the organization that will influence employee behaviour and ultimately help them to gain competitive advantage.[17] This is the rationale that John Browne used at *British Petroleum* when he introduced the computer networking system, which encouraged employees to share knowledge in order to increase competitiveness, and it has certainly been used to great advantage by companies that utilize elements of TQM and re-engineering to enhance employee performance and increase effectiveness.

Limitations of the technical perspective

Despite its widespread use, there have been concerns by some critics with the technical approach to organizational learning. Specifically, the emphasis on measurement and productivity narrowly focuses the concept of learning, and this focus is usually on what is necessary to help achieve organizational goals, which can minimize the role and voice of the employee. The technical process tends to ignore the influence of politics and individual sensemaking and assumes that organizations and the people within them are rational entities. The political influences on behaviour that can get in the way of learning are downplayed with the assumption that a shared meaning of experiences exists and resistance to suggested plans of action is not an issue in the learning process. Clearly, this is often not the case, as we saw at *Hope Hospital*, where senior management resisted the politicized notion of team-based decision-making and power-sharing, leading to the eventual devolution of the organizational development unit. Although some proponents, like Senge (1994), suggest that politics can be treated as a variable that can be controlled or eliminated through open dialogue, we would argue that it is the sensemaking of those in power which controls the goal setting and actions of the organization and the nature of politics should not be ignored.

The learning organization from a social perspective

By the early 1990s, as the deficits of the technical perspective became more obvious, the social perspective was becoming a more dominant form of creating learning organizations. Politics and the irrationality of individuals were finally accepted as important influences on workplace behaviour so that the influence of social interactions on workplace outcomes began to be recognized as a way of making sense of learning in organizations. *The social perspective of a learning organization stresses the importance of understanding organizational learning as a series of interrelated actions of individuals towards the creation of a collective mind, where shared meaning drives the learning process.* In this approach, an understanding of the *process* of organizational learning is more important than seeking out a universal and prescriptive approach.[18] Proponents of this approach recognize that learning is only validated by the meaning given to it by organizational members which often occurs through the informal exchange of information, such as stories and rituals. This lack of exchange may help to explain why *Hope Hospital* failed to create a learning organization.

The learning organization and the socio-cultural perspective

The third perspective of the learning organization builds on the previous social perspective. In this instance learning is framed from *a socio-cultural perspective where the organization is thought of as a cultural metaphor, which focuses on the meaning that is assigned to actions in order to make sense of outcomes, rather than the skills and knowledge the organization needs to accomplish its goals and strategies.* This sensemaking approach[19] sees culture as something an organization 'is', rather than something an organization 'has'.[20] Thus organizational variables, such as skills, cannot be manipulated. Instead, learning organizations are understood as organizations that either possess or do not possess cultures that contribute to and support the learning process. The key in this approach is learning from past experience.[21] For example, a new employee in *McDonald's* may be paired with a more experienced employee so that she or he becomes socialized into the organization and assimilates the culture.

Whatever the perspective, the idea of creating learning organizations has shifted the focus away from an emphasis on efficiency and effectiveness, predominant in techniques such as TQM and re-engineering, towards a focus on people and communities of learning but, despite this, organizational learning and learning organizations have received much criticism, which is mainly concerned with its exploitation of employees. We shall look at some of these criticisms and the paradoxes they present in the next section.

Making sense of the organizational learning literature

Despite an emphasis on collective action, it has been argued that learning organizations are detrimental to the majority of employees because the principles of organizational learning are non-democratic, controlling and can violate workers' rights and privacy.[22] In a 1993 article in the *Harvard Business Review*, David Garvin claimed that 'the only learning that is useful to managers is measurable learning',[23] while Barbara Townley claims that human resources management practices are designed to make workers more governable.[24] The learning organization is no exception to these practices.

Because learning organizations tend to focus on jobs that generate knowledge considered important in helping the organization accomplish its goals and maintain its competitive edge, jobs that don't contribute to this objective are ignored and employees in them are not normally part of the decision-making process. What is being contributed and what its value is to the organization are key determinants of participation in the learning organization.

Types of knowledge

What type of knowledge is central to the learning organization? Despite an emphasis on community learning, empowerment and open dialogue, the organizational learning literature has been accused of too narrowly defining learning, which limits the generation of knowledge to reflect the interests of those whose goals are to be achieved.[25] Subsequently, it fails to give the same weight to the input and decision-making of non-managerial workers or those in knowledge-reliant positions. This limits the participation and contribution of the majority of employees to a select few and may disqualify many of them from actively participating in the learning process.[26]

Consider the employee who works in a call centre. He or she is not paid to be creative or to contribute to the decision-making process. In fact, the call centre employee's job is so heavily scripted that any deviation from the script tends to be frowned upon because it can cut into the time that has been predetermined for each call. It is rare to find a call centre employee who is willing to engage in small talk because they know they are being monitored and failure to resolve the customer's concerns or to close the sale may result in punishments that can range from dismissal to 'coaching' from a team leader.

What is contributed

In the same call centre, managers and supervisors are constantly looking for ways to increase sales, while at the same time training and motivating employees. Whether it is through new job design strategies or ways to train employees to be more effective, the knowledge of management employees is valued whereas non-management employees are expected to absorb that knowledge, not necessarily contribute to it.

In this way, prior experience, emotions and memories are often ignored in the understanding of what constitutes valued knowledge. This exclusion from the learning process has potential negative psychological consequences for employees and the devaluation of their knowledge may cause the organization to overlook important skills that could be beneficial to the organization. For employees in the call centre industry, where jobs are technology-based, there is little chance for generating knowledge through creativity or innovation.

Issues of control and privacy

While empowerment and emancipation are allegedly the central building blocks of the learning organization, it has been suggested that these principles actually hinder the emancipation of workers.[27] One of the two main criticisms of organizational learning is that it is often used as a management tool to modify undesirable employee behaviour.

The second is that the principles of learning organizations invade the privacy of workers' beliefs and values, under the guise of concern with their wellbeing and advancement of workplace learning through open dialogue. As part of what Senge calls *critical self reflection*, workers in learning organizations are asked to share their innermost thoughts, in order to break down existing negative beliefs, which might be holding them back from being more creative. Practices such as sensitivity training force employees to share intensely private information with others in the name of personal development. But, in reality, it is the organization's goals that are of primary concern. These types of practices suggest that organizational learning is nothing more than an attempt to control the culture of the workplace and it leaves employees vulnerable to disciplinary action should their visions differ from those that the organization is trying to promote.

The future of organizational learning research

The different views of what constitutes organizational learning and the learning organization have led to confusion over a universally acceptable model of organizational learning. Some of the criticism centres around the suggestion that organizational learning is too oblique and does not provide a useful prescriptive approach that offers measurable outcomes for practitioners. We can certainly see that this was the case at *Hope Hospital*. Individuals did not know what they were supposed to be doing to create this learning environment and employees were waiting to see results. Like many organizations, *Hope Hospital* borrowed from some of the elements of organizational learning principles but they failed to initiate change because they didn't have a clear idea of how to proceed.

This leaves us with the question 'is organizational learning offering anything new, or is it nothing more that the repackaging of existing organizational development techniques designed to rectify current organization problems'? We would suggest that what is different is the increased focus on learning. Whether or not it is possible to create a learning organization is another issue. The idea of the learning organization is premised on the notion that shared understanding is a part of learning. Yet, this has not always proven the case when we look at some of the organizational outcomes that have resulted from different interpretations of the same experience. In order to improve and expand on the existing literature, it has been suggested that researchers need to seek out new ways to make the organization truly empowering to all employees[28] and to pay attention to the type of employee who is best suited to a learning organization.[29]

Appreciative inquiry

> I would like to commend you more particularly for your methodology of Appreciative Inquiry and to thank you for introducing it to the United Nations. Without this, it would have been very difficult, perhaps even impossible, to constructively engage so many leaders of business, civil society, and government. (Kofi Annan, writing on behalf of the Global Compact of the UN[30])

Appreciative inquiry (AI), developed in the 1980s by David Cooperrider and Suresh Shrivastva,[31] is a change technique that is different from the others. Simply put, it is about finding the best in people and discovering what works best in an organization and then focusing on building and celebrating these successes. Unlike other change management techniques that seek to problem-solve, AI explores the positive events that have taken place in an organization and looks for the strengths of its employees and uses them to build on what is good for the organization. For example, an organization normally will follow a process whereby they identify a problem and perform an analysis of the potential causes of that problem and then look for possible solutions. AI is suggesting something different. Instead of making sense of 'organizations as problems to be solved', AI sees 'organizations as mysteries to be embraced' and 'envisioning what it might be' and should be (see below),[32] instead of what it is. In conjunction with this new strategy, proponents of AI believe that over time the culture of the organization will change as it builds on its positive elements and no longer focuses on problem-solving.

The appreciative inquiry model

There are several steps to successfully implementing AI. According to Cooperrider and Shrivasta,[33] the inquiry should be a proactive and collaborative process. If these characteristics are in place, the model can then be operationalized using the '4-D Model'. This model shows how the AI gets participants involved in the inquiry process, which takes them from the inquiry stage to the implementation stage. The elements of the 4-D process involve:

- Discovering: trying to uncover the strengths of individuals and the organization
- Dreaming: envisioning what might be
- Design: planning on what could be
- Destiny: sustaining what has been achieved.

What does this look like in practice and what types of organizations have used AI? It is safe to say that AI has become a very popular change management technique with a wide range of industries. These range from schools to forestry and a number of them involve not-for-profit organizations and religious groups. For example, AI gained legitimacy when the United Nations Leaders Summit chose it as the methodology for their 1994 meetings. This summit, which was part of the UN Global Compact, had over 1,400 organizational members at the time, including companies such as *Hewlett Packard, Starbucks* and *BP* (who we saw had earlier used learning organization principles), so its impact in management circles was huge. The success of AI with the Global Compact was followed by an unprecedented partnering of the UN Global Compact with the Academy of Management, who worked together on the next forum.[34] Today, the *AI Commons* has a website[35] sponsored by *Case Western Reserve University*, where Cooperrider and Shrivastva are on faculty. The site 'shares academic resources and practical tools' related to AI and invites people and organizations to share their success stories. It is of interest to note that AI seems to be particularly popular with a number of not-for-profit and religious organizations.

For example, in 2004, Susan Star Paddock wrote a book about the Catholic Church's use of AI. In an attempt to shift the focus away from the sex scandals that were plaguing the church, Paddock, as a psychotherapist and practising Catholic, saw AI as a way to help the Church concentrate on its successes and develop them. At the same time, the Anglican Church in Canada was using Diane Whitney and Amanda Trosten-Bloom's 2003 book on AI (Gergen & Whitney, 1996)[36] to help them move forward with changes in the diocese by seeing AI as a 'paradigm of hope'.[37]

> ### AI and the Catholic Church
>
> In 2002, I became deeply concerned about the health of my spiritual home, the Catholic Church. Widespread media coverage of the sex abuse cases led me to realize that the Church was at a choice point. We could pursue the usual course of finding out 'what's wrong with our Church' or we could use the energy created by the crisis for an inquiry into what is right with our Church. We could begin to have conversations to share what we think the 'life-giving forces' of the Church might be.[38]

It is interesting to note that AI appeals to organizations that one wouldn't normally associate with overtly undertaking planned organizational change techniques. Perhaps the somewhat mystical qualities of AI, with its emphasis on human and organizational growth and potential, make it seem like a plausible change technique for mainstream religions but does that make it less appealing to organizations, such as manufacturing, that need to show measurable outcomes? While these types of industries tend to use TQM initiatives such as quality circles or continuous learning are they any different from using the 4-D model? Let us look at some of these issues.

Making sense of appreciative inquiry

Two main concerns with AI initially come to mind when reviewing the literature. The first is to question whether or not it really is any different from other change techniques and the second is to wonder that if it does not focus on problems, does that mean that they don't exist? Is AI just using the same tools as other techniques, only packaging them differently, or does it truly offer something new? While we agree that AI is appealing because it takes a proactive and optimistic approach to change by concentrating on the positive, does ignoring problems and focusing on what works help the organization? In the case of the Catholic Church, one of the reasons they turned to AI was to shift the attention away from the negative publicity of the sex scandals they were experiencing and concentrate on what was good within the Church and build on that. However, that did not make the problem of the sex scandals disappear and it could still be argued that the decision to use AI followed the traditional problem-solving, solution-seeking format. The definition of organizational change is the need to change from one state to a more desired state, which is usually brought about either by a crisis or a perceived need that change is necessary for the wellbeing of the organization. Thus, it could be argued that change itself is a form of problem-solving and AI is a solution to that problem. Ultimately, the popularity of AI cannot be denied. Psychologically, participants in AI believe that what they are doing makes a difference and they believe that they are given autonomy to move the organization, and themselves, forward. If this meets with the values and objectives of the organization, then it can hardly be considered bad.

Conclusion

In this chapter we have looked at some current and popular change techniques that take an indirect approach to changing organizational culture. Rather than concentrating on organizational values as a change technique, both organizational learning and appreciative inquiry create an environment that fosters a culture or learning and expansion of strengths for the betterment of the organization. While each technique focuses on different ways to nourish this culture and bring about change, each one is more people- than process-oriented. As we saw, in the first instance, principles of organizational learning are used to create learning organizations, through continuous improvement and the nurturing of a learning culture by developing the skills and knowledge of the employees, whereas, in the second instance, appreciative inquiry overturns existing cultures by shifting the focus away from problem-solving to appreciating what has worked well in the past and transferring that knowledge to the future, without looking back.

End of chapter questions and exercises

1   From the perspective of management, what are some of the strengths of implementing organizational learning principles in an organization?
2   What are some of the drawbacks, from an employee perspective, of creating a learning organization?
3   How might an organization overcome some of the potential pitfalls of creating a learning organization?
4   Compare the benefits of introducing appreciative inquiry into an organization versus creating a learning organization. What are the potential strengths and weaknesses of appreciative inquiry?
5   What might *Hope Hospital* have done differently when they decided to create a learning organization?
6   Why was *BP* more successful than *Hope Hospital* in creating a learning organization?
7   From an employee perspective, how would you feel if your organization introduced learning organization principles and excluded you from the process because they did not see your knowledge as valuable? What

psychological effects would this have on you and how might this affect your work performance and motivation?

8 Compare and contrast learning organization principles with appreciative inquiry. What are the differences and what are the similarities? Which would you be more comfortable using and why?

9 Using the Internet, look up the websites of three call centres, each in a different country. How do they portray the role of the employee? Are there any differences across countries? Are there any signs of organizational learning principles and what are they?

10 Using the Internet, find three organizations that have successfully created learning organizations. What factors contributed to their success?

11 Using the Internet, find three organizations that have used appreciative inquiry. What are the similarities among the three organizations? What are the differences? What conclusions can you draw from this?

6 The quality movement – TQM and business process re-engineering

Objectives of this chapter:

By the end of this chapter, you should:

1 Be familiar with the history of the quality movement
2 Understand what is meant by Total Quality Management
3 Be familiar with Deming's quality theories
4 Be able to discuss critically Total Quality Management
5 Understand what is meant by Business Process Re-engineering

---

The big three auto makers in the news

On Tuesday, June 7, 2005 *Daimler-Chrysler, Ford* and *General Motors* were all in the news. It seemed that the 'Big Three' were all newsworthy for different reasons.

Daimler-Chrysler (a company formed in 1998 with the merger of *Daimler-Benz* and *Chrysler Corporation*) was experiencing a loss in sales of the Mercedes, but above average growth in their other divisions. The merger of the two companies would ultimately be deemed a failure and they would be separated in 2007.

Ford 'rescued' one of its main suppliers, *Visteon*, in May of 2005, by acquiring 24 plants and more than 17,000 unionized workers in the glass, powertrain and chassis manufacturing divisions from the troubled company. The announcement in the news on June 7 was one of massive restructuring of the *Visteon* acquisitions. The article notes that this restructuring effectively places *Ford* in a position to compete directly with *General Motors*.

The news about *General Motors* on this day announced innovative new sales strategies and new automobile models. Both were deemed necessary in order to remain competitive in the tough automobile market.

Interestingly, all three of these companies were instrumental in the quality movement of the 1980s. In fact, all three adopted *Total Quality Management (TQM)* and *Business Process Re-engineering (BPR)* at some point in their history. Some speculate that Ford was the first of the Big Three to investigate the quality movement when it sent hundreds of its employees to Japan to study manufacturing methods in the early 1980s. This study concluded that Japanese organizations were more efficient in every part of the manufacturing process, and this success was attributed to how well Japanese employees worked together. This new philosophy wasn't consistent with *Ford*'s then emphasis on military precision in manufacturing. In 1981, Ford hired Deming – known as the number one expert in quality management – as a consultant in their quality efforts.

Remnants of the quality movement can still be seen in each of the Big Three. For example, *Ford* requires all of its suppliers to achieve Q1 status – a quality standard – if they wish to continue to supply Ford. Similarly, *GM* has collaborated with the *United Auto Workers* to form the UAM-GM Quality Network. Finally, *Saturn* (a division of *GM*) received an award in 1994 from the National Business Process Re-engineering Conference for 'its efforts to reinvigorate U.S. manufacturing through its leadership and exemplary practice of Business Process Re-engineering (BPR), thereby demonstrating management commitment, total team effort, innovation and perseverance that will inspire others to similar achievement'.[1]

Despite the adoption of what were heralded as the Holy Grails of success by management gurus of the 1980s, and the continued application of some of the quality principles, all three auto makers have continued to adopt newly emerging change strategies, and the need for change seems to be as strong as ever, as demonstrated by the news articles in July of 2005.

The 1980s saw a huge movement in manufacturing efforts towards quality in North America. Hundreds of organizations, including the Big Three auto makers noted above, jumped on the quality bandwagon and adopted change techniques that embraced the notion of quality manufacturing. In the late 1970s and early 1980s, the best-known and most frequently adopted change schema was Total Quality Management (TQM). Following on the heels of this now infamous change strategy was the Business Process Re-engineering (BPR) era. Both of these will be discussed in this chapter. It is interesting, however, to note where the quality movement came from, as its history provides us with insight into the impetus for change.

The history of the quality movement

At the centre of this history is a man by the name of W. Edwards Deming. Although not solely responsible for the quality movement, his name is most often associated with it. Other notables include Philip Crosby, Armand V. Feigenbaum, Kaoru Ishikawa, Joseph M. Juran and Tom Peters.[2] Although worthy of discussion, examination of all of the major players in the quality game is beyond the scope of this text. Instead, we'll concentrate on the work of Deming, with an understanding that the others were also instrumental in the quality movement. It behooves the scholar truly interested in quality management to dig a bit deeper into the contributions of each of these men. Figure 6.1 provides a brief introduction to each of these pioneers of the quality movement.

On January 14, 1952, an American statistician by the name of W. Edwards Deming delivered an address in Tokyo at a meeting of industrial executives.

Quality Pioneer	Contribution
Philip Crosby	• Closely associated with the concept of zero defects, created in 1961. • Quality management is all about prevention. • Companies need to adopt a quality 'vaccine' – determination, education and implementation. • Crosby's 14 steps to quality improvement.
Armand V. Feigenbaum	• Top-quality expert for *GE* in 1944. • Author of *Total Quality Control* in 1951. It is now in its fourth edition. • Feigenbaum's three steps to quality and four deadly sins.
Kaoru Ishikawa	• Foremost figure in Japan in terms of quality control until his death in 1989. • First to use the term 'total quality control'. • He identified seven quality tools that could be used by any worker – Pareto charts, cause–effect diagrams, histograms, check sheets, scatter diagrams, flowcharts and control charts. • Responsible for the creation of quality control circles.
Joseph M. Juran	• During his career he was the quality manager at *Western Electric Company*, a government administrator and a professor of engineering. • He began consulting in 1950. • Lectured and consulted in Japan. • Managing for quality involves three processes – quality planning, quality control and quality improvement.
Tom Peters	• Major bestseller – *In Search of Excellence* Peters & Waterman, 1982 • Peters provides nine aspects of excellent companies and a 45-step prescription for the transformation of organizations.

Figure 6.1 Pioneers of the quality movement.

Source: Adapted from Brocka & Brocka, 1992

The meeting was sponsored by Nihon Kezai and the Union of Japanese Scientists and Engineers. In the address, Deming made the claim that the use of simple statistical techniques could lead to organizational success. He suggested that the statistical control of quality, in all stages of production, would lead to the most economic way of producing the most useful goods and services. The American Marketing Association published some excerpts from the speech in the *Journal of Marketing* in 1953.[3] It appears that the Japanese were listening – the Americans were not.

After the Second World War, Japan was focused on rebuilding its social and economic infrastructure. Before the war, most Japanese products were considered 'junk' and they desperately wanted to shed this image. They knew a new image was critical for the country's success. They sought the advice of American statisticians, engineers and manufacturing gurus. W. Edwards Deming, brought in from the United States, was one of the most influential of these specialists. He gave numerous speeches, workshops and did a considerable amount of consulting. Following Deming's focus on quality, the customer, workforce empowerment and planning, Japan rose from the ashes to become a benchmark in excellence.[4] The success of what had been termed 'Total Quality Control' was being celebrated and was spreading throughout Japan. Deming was a well-respected, even revered, figure. In fact, a Japanese annual national quality award was named in his honour – the Deming Prize. This award has been given out every year since its inception in 1950.

By the 1970s, Japanese manufacturers were claiming huge international success and were winning markets formerly supplied by American and European companies. By the 1980s, Japanese manufacturing was seen as a threat on a global scale in terms of industrial competitiveness.

So where were the American manufacturers? After the war, the United States was seen as the world's dominant supplier.[5] The Americans were manufacturing 'fast and furiously' and markets seemed to open up for them as never before. Industry in the United States was focused on mass production – producing as much as possible for as little as possible. The problem with this was that quality, employee motivation and customer satisfaction suffered as a result. These fundamentals of Japanese manufacturing at the time, as stimulated by Deming, were simply missing in the American model.

When international markets and global manufacturing dominance were threatened by the Japanese, the Americans began to be concerned and to take a harder look at what was happening. Closer inspection revealed that the Japanese were able to produce quality products and meet customer needs while still remaining economically competitive. How was this possible?

In 1980, NBC broadcast a White Paper entitled 'If Japan Can, Why Can't We?'. This documentary has been credited with jump-starting the quality revolution in North America. It also served as a formal introduction of W. Edwards Deming to North American managers as a quality master, despite his own attempts in the 1950s to spread the quality message throughout the

United States. It seems that now North American managers were ready to listen. This was the springboard for companies like *Ford* to begin their TQM journey. After 1980, TQM spread rapidly through the US.[6]

What is Total Quality Management?

So far, we have seen how a change in emphasis from mass production to quality production, through an emphasis on people and teamwork, helped the Japanese gain industrial dominance. We have hinted that the tenets of TQM come from an American statistician who deemed total quality as central to organizational success. But what *is* TQM?

Total Quality Management is best described by looking at the three words in its name. The first word, 'total', tells us that this method is organization-wide, encompassing all systems, policies, procedures and functional units. The second word, the one most associated with TQM, tells us that the method focuses on quality – quality products, services, systems and organizational outcomes (including costs, market share and growth). Finally, the word 'management' tells us that this method involves the control of people and processes. To summarize, *TQM is an organization-wide method of managing people and processes, to ensure the continuous delivery of quality products and services.* Although not overtly stated in this definition, the delivery of quality products and services implies an evaluation of quality by customers, thus placing customers at the centre of TQM.

The concept of TQM has evolved into a strategy for change, based on Deming's philosophy. Most proponents of this type of change recommend strategy based on Deming's now famous 14 points for quality management and his 7 deadly diseases. Deming published these in his 1982 book, *Out of the Crisis*.

Deming's 14 points [7]

1   Create a constancy of purpose towards improvement of product and service – Deming emphasized that continuous improvement will help the company to become competitive, to stay in business and to provide jobs. He also stressed that this type of constancy of purpose requires strategic planning.
2   Adopt a quality philosophy – Deming argued that a new economic age was dawning and that companies must accept the challenge, learn their new responsibilities and lead the change.
3   Cease dependence on mass inspection – Many firms were relying on mass inspection for quality control prior to TQM. Deming said this would no longer be acceptable and that quality must be built into the product from the very beginning.
4   End the practice of purchasing at the lowest price – Deming advocated reducing the number of suppliers and eliminating the 'lowest price wins'

philosophy. He felt organizations should develop relationships built on loyalty and trust with their suppliers.

5   Improve constantly and forever – This point reinforces the idea of continuous improvement through continuous change. Here began the philosophy that organizations could not stand still and that change was inevitable. Deming suggested that processes must continuously be evaluated and improved.

6   Institute training on the job – Employees were key to quality. Deming encouraged firms to make people part of the quality process. He stressed that people were not costs that should be minimized whenever possible. Instead, they should be engaged in the process of continuous improvement and that investment in people should lead to higher quality, lower costs and better overall firm performance.

7   Institute leadership – The aim of management should be to help the people and the machines to do a better job. Leadership was emphasized as more of a supporting position than traditionally thought.

8   Drive out fear – The goal here is to rid the organization of mechanisms that created fear. These included coercive management styles, punitive mechanisms and company-wide beliefs that it wasn't OK to fail. Deming claimed that people couldn't work effectively if they were afraid of making mistakes.

9   Break down barriers between departments – In order for the organization to function as an effective system, barriers had to be removed between departments. He argued that cross-functional communications were essential for quality.

10 Eliminate slogans, exhortations and targets for the workforce asking for zero defects and new levels of productivity – The argument here was that most of the causes of low quality came from the system – not the people. Slogans and targets aimed at people only caused adversarial relationships. Deming felt that quotas and management by objectives could both be replaced with good leadership.

11 Eliminate numerical goals for hourly workers – Quotas merely rob the employee of pride of workmanship. If the goals are centred on numbers of output, quality is almost sure to suffer.

12 Remove barriers to worker pride – Abolish merit pay and management by objective.

13 Institute a programme of education and self-improvement – Deming felt that continuous training, growth of workers and pride in oneself were essential for quality management.

14 Put everybody to work to accomplish the transformation – Deming argued that the transformation was everybody's job.

Deming's 7 deadly diseases[8]

1   Lack of constancy of purpose – As stated above, everyone in the organization has to focus on quality. Everything anyone does should be guided by this.
2   Emphasis on short-term profits – The organization must focus on long-term success. Investing in research and development, training and customer satisfaction may cost in the short term but will provide gains in the long term.
3   Evaluation by performance, merit rating or annual review of performances – These only get in the way of creating quality products and services. If you ask an employee to create a certain number of widgets in a certain amount of time, and you base rewards on the achievement of this goal, quality will suffer and fear will build. Moreover, a focus on the individual will destroy teamwork.
4   Mobility of management – Deming was worried about the constant movement of managers. He worried that managers were seen as easily transferable and argued that managers needed to spend considerable time and energy in any one organization to truly understand it.
5   Running a company on visible figures alone – Return on investment, share prices and profitability don't tell the whole story. Pay attention to customer satisfaction numbers, employee satisfaction and turnover, and other 'invisible' figures.
6   Excessive medical costs for employee healthcare – Deming was calling for transformation of the American Healthcare system.
7   Excessive costs of warranty – If TQM is administered properly, warranty costs should drop. Don't focus on providing great warranties – focus on producing quality.

Interestingly, Deming did not use the term Total Quality Management. In fact, the origin of the term is debated. Despite claims to the contrary, the American Society for Quality (ASQ) claims that the term was first used by the US Naval Air Systems Command to describe their Japanese style management system for quality.[9]

Despite disagreement about where the term came from, quality management initiatives soon became known as Total Quality Management and Total Quality Management became big business. Although statistics vary from study to study, some estimate that as many as 67 per cent of American organizations had adopted some sort of TQM strategy by 1995.[10] Between January 1994 and February 1996, 1,078 articles were published on TQM.[11] Additionally, a search under business and investing books at Amazon.com today results in more than 7,500 books, and a Google search of TQM consultants turns up hundreds of organizations committed to selling the TQM dream. Finally, not only does the Deming Prize still exist and is highly revered in 2008, but other awards based on the Deming Prize have been established.

For example, the Malcolm Baldrige National Quality Award was established in 1988 and the Presidential Award for Quality was established in 1989. Private US companies are eligible for the former, and public sector organizations are eligible for the latter. These awards are not only prestigious awards for excellence in quality management, but the criteria used for judging are also used internally as 'benchmarks' for many organizations.

Making sense of TQM

The International Organization for Standardization (ISO), established in 1947, defines TQM as 'a management approach for an organization, centered on quality, based on the participation of all its members and aiming at long-term success through customer satisfaction, and benefits to all members of the organization and to society'.[12] This appears promising and pledges to deliver all that an organization could want – long-term success that benefits all members of the organization as well as society. Who wouldn't want to participate?

Unfortunately, the fantasy was better than the reality. Statistics suggest that more than 75 per cent of TQM initiatives failed.[13] Reasons for this high failure rate vary from poor adoption of TQM elements to improperly diagnosed organizational problems and the subsequent adoption of the wrong solution (i.e. TQM). Advocates of the contingency approach to change argue that TQM's emphasis on the 'one best way' is its biggest problem and the source of much of the aforementioned failure. Simply stated, TQM isn't the right answer for all organizational problems. However, this was often overlooked as TQM was touted as the solution to all organizational ills.

TQM has also been criticized as having detrimental effects on organization members – something that is often overlooked in the quest for the better bottom line. For example, TQM is accused of creating more stressful work environments for employees by setting them up in no-win situations. Take the middle manager as an example. According to Deming's 14 points, middle managers are supposed to empower lower-level employees and to let them know it is OK to fail. However, ultimately, the manager is responsible for the success of the unit – and success is measured by total quality output and customer satisfaction. This places the manager in a no-win situation and one that threatens their levels of power and control.

Another criticism of TQM is that the emphasis on job enrichment and employee involvement most often translates into more work for the same pay. Employees are given more tasks and responsibilities without any additional compensation. In addition, this employee empowerment often takes the form of minor administrative duties – such as scheduling lunch breaks or vacations – and very often has nothing to do with the quality initiative.[14] Employees can see these attempts at empowerment for what they are, which creates more ill will than good.

Despite the disappointing failure rate of TQM and the above-noted criticisms, some organizations claim huge successes. Examples include *3M, FedEx,* the 'Big Three' auto makers, and *Ben and Jerry's*. Books and articles have been written that outline exactly how TQM was a success in these companies.

In summarizing our discussion of TQM, we cannot suggest that TQM is the answer to all. In fact, huge failure rates indicate that the opposite is true. However, we cannot conclude that TQM can't work either, for some organizations claim TQM success. What we can conclude is that TQM is one change strategy that may work for some companies. Proper problem diagnosis, application of TQM within the context of the organization and self-regulating mechanisms appear to be essential for success with TQM.

What we can say about TQM is that it led to a fundamental shift in philosophy within the North American business environment. Figure 6.2 outlines this shift.

This new philosophy impacted every part of the organization. Take 'Customers know what they want', for example. This fundamental shift in philosophy would be felt throughout the organization. Now, manufacturing, marketing, customer service, and research and development had a brand-new task – identifying and satisfying the needs of the customer. This philosophy can be seen in many of the change strategies that followed TQM. Business Process Re-engineering was next to emerge.

Business Process Re-engineering (BPR)

Just as TQM was in the 1980s, BPR was hailed as the biggest business innovation of the 1990s. As a result of globalization, political realignments, the rapid advance of IT and dismal success rate of TQM, companies were

Old Philosophy	New Philosophy
Profits are number one.	Quality is number one – it leads to productivity, customer satisfaction, hence competitiveness, market share, return on investment, and profitability.
Improving quality will raise costs, thereby making firms non-competitive	Improvements in quality will reduce rework and scrap, and will lessen the costs of warranties.
Employees are a cost burden – pay as little as possible and lay off when necessary.	Employees are partners with management. During economic downturn, management will work with employees to chart a new course. Lay-offs will be 'shared'.
Long-term investment is a loser for management because success isn't seen until they have moved on.	Long-term investment is important and should be rewarded.
Customers don't know what they want.	Customers know what they want.
Top management must portray an image of wealth and success.	Top management should be seen as 'part of the team'. Corporate egalitarianism is increasing in popularity.

Figure 6.2 Old and new business philosophy.

Source: Adapted from Anschutz, 1995

looking for a new strategy for change. BPR, often referred to as radical change, process obliteration, and/or revolutionary, seemed to be the answer. Consultants, methodologies, techniques and tools flooded the marketplace. Between January 1994 and February 1995, 1,264 articles were published on re-engineering[15] and, by 1994, 70 per cent of the largest US corporations had undergone re-engineering.[16]

So what is BPR?

BPR harks back to the days of Frederick Taylor and the birth of Scientific Management (late 19th century). Taylor suggested that all processes could be broken down and studied at the most minute level. This would result in learning the 'one best way' to do any task. He suggested a very mechanical separation of planning and work – managers would plan and workers would work, according to the 'one best way' described.

In 1990, echoes of this could be heard in Michael Hammer's contention that much of the work being done in organizations did not add value to the customer and was, as a result, wasteful. He suggested that work processes of the entire organization be studied carefully and radically redesigned in order to reduce costs, improve quality and service, and shorten cycle times.

In their 1993 book, *Re-engineering the Corporation: A Manifesto for Business Revolution*, Hammer and Champy defined BRP as '*The fundamental rethinking and radical redesign of business processes to achieve dramatic improvements in critical contemporary measures of performance, such as cost, quality, service, and speed*'. As you can see, BRP was still touting the quality tenets of TQM, but was suggesting radical transformation instead of incremental and continuous change.

Moreover, BPR focuses on processes – usually small, interdependent sets of roles, people and tasks created to provide some sort of service or product. For example, there may be two or three people in an organization who are responsible for ordering parts. These people provide a service to those in manufacturing. BPR advocates that the single process of ordering parts should be analysed and radically transformed so that it is done in the most efficient way. Similarly, those on an assembly line follow a process that allows them to provide a quality product to those who are next on the assembly line. Studies should be conducted to determine the 'best' way to complete each process in the assembly line. According to BPR, each process in the entire organization should undergo such scrutiny so as to achieve high measures of performance in terms of cost, quality, service and speed. After that is accomplished, BPR should be pushed to the input and output levels; that is, suppliers and customers alike should be engaged in the re-engineering process.

BPR isn't for the faint at heart, as it attempts to radically change everything from management (style, values and measures), to people (jobs, skills and culture), to information technology and organizational structure.[17] Virtually nothing remains untouched and the organization is radically changed.

Although BPR advocates the 'one best way', BPR itself doesn't offer such a solution. Instead, BPR is made up of a toolbox full of techniques that can be used to analyse and radically alter organizational processes. These tools fit into the following categories:[18]

- Project management (PERT, Gantt)
- Problem-solving and diagnosis (cognitive mapping)
- Customer requirement analysis (benchmarking, focus groups)
- Process capture and modelling (flowcharting)
- Process measurement (activity-based costing, time–motion study)
- Process prototyping and simulation (role-playing)
- IS systems analysis and design (software re-engineering)
- Business planning (value chain analysis)
- Creative thinking (out-of-box thinking)
- Organizational analysis and design (employee attitude assessment, team-building techniques)
- Change management (assumption surfacing)

Making sense of BPR

As with TQM, the reality of BPR wasn't as good as the fantasy. Statistics tell us that failure rates were as high as those for TQM – somewhere between 60 per cent and 85 per cent.[19] However, these numbers may be somewhat skewed due to the fact that many (most) adopters of BPR were companies on the brink of disaster who were attempting to cut costs and return to profitability. This negative starting point doesn't bode well for any change strategy.

There are, however, some critiques of BPR that mustn't be overlooked. The biggest criticism of BPR is the separation of the work from the workers; that is, BPR suggests that a small design team should design the work of many. Often, this team is external to the organization and is brought to the organization in a consulting relationship. Picture this: a team of people that have never met you before come in and tell you how best to do your job. Although they have watched you and 'measured' your job, they have never actually done your job. However, they are somehow able to tell you how best to do your job and that the way you have been doing it is not the best way. You can see how this might upset and anger some employees – thus causing stress and job dissatisfaction. In addition, one could safely argue that an outside consultant may not always know enough about the intricacies and human factors associated with a job – thus, are not able to determine the 'best' way to do the job.

Another criticism of BPR is the tendency towards encouraging short-term thinking in top executives.[20] This, in turn, has a negative impact on long-term results. You see, with re-engineering, the firm focuses on reducing redundancies and eliminating processes that do not add value today. Typically, this re-engineering results in job losses and a fall in turnover, and the elimination of processes that might be of value in different times. The short-term gain (measured as improved profitability) is rewarded and touted as 'success', while long-term costs (in terms of stress, absence due to sick leave, fall in turnover, loss of intellectual capital etc.) are rarely measured.

Because of the high failure rates, BPR fell out of favour in the mid-to-late 1990s with many managers.[21] However, the Cutter Consortium reports that as many as 83 per cent of organizations were using BPR in 2002.[22] It appears that BPR has made a bit of a comeback.

Summary

The quality movement had a huge impact on global businesses. The promotion of the 'one best way' philosophy, coupled with the notion of producing the best-quality product or service, using the most efficient methods, generally sums up the 1980s and early 1990s. Although both TQM and BPR had some successes, success was not the norm. Despite this, there are some lessons that can be learned by the quality movement. These lessons, coupled with new strategies, became the bedrock of change strategies to come. Six Sigma and the Balanced Scorecard were the next to emerge.

End of chapter questions and exercises

1   Do an Internet search on any of the quality pioneers in Figure 6.1. Make notes on their contribution to the quality movement. Prepare a short presentation for the class.
2   Using the business section of a national newspaper, look for evidence of TQM or BPR initiatives. The articles may not state that the organizations are using TQM or BPR overtly. Look for clues based on the main tenets of each change strategy.
3   Although many of the examples used in this chapter were from a manufacturing viewpoint, both TQM and BPR are also used in non-manufacturing, services and not-for-profit organizations. What would TQM look like if it were implemented at your university?
4   Compare and contrast TQM and BPR. Some argue that BPR is merely an adaptation of TQM. What do you think of this?
5   Do an Internet search of the Big Three auto makers. Identify elements of TQM and BPR that still remain.
6   Research three of the BPR tools listed in this chapter. Prepare a short explanation of each of the three for your classmates. Explain what they are and how they might be used.
7   Visit the American Society of Quality website – http://www.asq.org – and prepare a short summary of your findings.
8   In a small group, discuss the human implications of the quality movement. How can these be reconciled? Prepare a report that will be presented to your class.

7 A measure of change: Six Sigma and the Balanced Scorecard

Objectives of this chapter:

By the end of this chapter, you should:

1 Be familiar with the stages of the Balanced Scorecard
2 Be familiar with the multiple perspectives of the Balanced Scorecard
3 Understand what is meant by Six Sigma
4 Be familiar with the Six Sigma Method
5 Understand how individuals make sense of the Balanced Scorecard and Six Sigma approaches to change management

Measuring Change at *General Electric*: From Balanced Scorecard to Six Sigma

In the early 1990s, Jack Welch, the chief executive officer (CEO) of *General Electric* (*GE*), adopted a new approach to managing change and efficiency – the Balanced Scorecard (BSC). Developed by Robert S. Kaplan and David P. Norton,[1] BSC combines concern with financial outcomes with that of the human factor in performance outcomes, and involves measurement of key elements of the financial, customer, internal process and learning/growth aspects of a company.[2] *GE* was well placed to adopt this kind of approach. It is credited with developing a prototype of BSC as early as the 1950s when it adopted a system of non-financial measurements.[3]

Announcing the introduction of BSC and the general goals of the company, Welch singled out customer satisfaction as priority number one. Next, all the company's business units were required to reduce inventory levels and increase inventory turns. Third, the company sights were set on global presence through new product development. Fourth, all managers were to be focused on ensuring that, in terms of sales and profit, *GE* was to achieve and maintain first or second place in whatever business it operated in.

Following the implementation of BSC results were encouraging, although with varying levels of success across plants.[4] Nonetheless, when he retired as CEO of *General Electric* in 2001 Jack Welch credited BSC and Six Sigma as important change programmes that had seen the company's market capitalization go from US $13 billion in 1981 (when Welch was appointed as CEO) to US $500 billion in the year prior to his stepping down.[5]

Six Sigma, a programme designed to systematically improve processes by eliminating defects, was introduced at *GE* in the mid-1990s. Reportedly Jack Welch 'went nuts' over the programme, telling his senior management team that adopting Six Sigma was 'the company's most ambitious undertaking ever'.[6] By 2004, *GE* was claiming that Six Sigma had driven operating margins to 18.9 per cent from 14.8 per cent four years earlier.[7] This fuelled a number of other companies to follow *GE*'s lead, including more than twenty-five per cent of Fortune 200 companies, and many of our featured companies in Chapter 1.

The Balanced Scorecard and Six Sigma are similar in their focus on measurement, their roots in the quality movement[8] (see Chapter 6), and their phenomenal influence on multi-national companies. Companies that adopted BSC and Six Sigma include several from our featured companies. Those adopting BSC, as we saw from our opening vignette, include *General Electric*, but also *Chrysler, Ford, IBM, UPS*, and the *Walt Disney Company*. Those adopting Six Sigma include *Abbott, Apple, Bank of America, Boeing, Bombardier, Bristol-Myers, Citigroup, Ford, General Electric, Home Depot, Honda, IBM, Kodak, Nokia, Nortel, Raytheon, Samsung, Saputo, Sony*, and *Starwood Hotel & Resorts*. In the latter case, *Starwood* became – in 2001 – the first company in the hospitality industry to adopt the Six Sigma approach. In language that is almost identical to that of *GE*'s Jack Welch, Barry S. Sternlicht, *Starwood*'s CEO, called his company's launch of Six Sigma 'one of the most important strategic initiatives since the formation of [the] company'.[9] The process was successful and six years later *Starwood* was still claiming that Six Sigma was increasing the company's 'financial performance by improving the quality and consistency of [*Starwood*'s] guests' experiences as well as [their] internal customers'.[10] For *Starwood*, Six Sigma 'provides the framework and tools [needed] to create a consistently superior guest experience at all properties while dramatically improving the bottom line'.[11] Similar success stories are told by other leading companies.[12]

Nonetheless, there are those, including quality guru Joseph Juran, who feel that Six Sigma has been overly hyped and offers nothing new beyond a basic version of quality improvement.[13] Worse yet, a study of 58 large companies that adopted Six Sigma found that 91 per cent trailed the S&P 500 since.[14] The report argued that Six Sigma 'is narrowly designed to fix an existing process, allowing little room for new ideas or an entirely different approach'. It overly utilizes the skills and talents of its employees to reduce the defects of existing products rather than developing new ones. It can be seen as contributing to an 'inward-looking culture' that can kill off initiative by trying to overly manage, predict or timetable events.[15]

So what are the Balanced Scorecard and Six Sigma? What are the strengths and weaknesses of each method? Birkenshaw and Mol's (2006) study of management innovation provides a useful way of exploring these two approaches. They argue that management innovation (by which they mean changes in the process of *managing*), goes through four stages: (1) dissatisfaction with the status quo; (2) inspiration from other sources; (3) invention; and (4) validation. However, they also refer to the fact that following these stages the innovation is then diffused to other organizations.

The Balanced Scorecard

Stage one

In the late 1980s, Art Schneiderman, the manager at *Analog Devices*, was dissatisfied by the attention being paid to the nonfinancial indicators of company performance. So when he was asked by his CEO 'to develop a quality improvement process for the company's manufacturing',[16] Schneiderman began collecting data not only on financial measures but also on nonfinancial measures of performance.

Stage two

Arguably, much of Schneiderman's efforts to collect and measure both sets of data were influenced by his background in his previous company, where he had worked on continuous improvement techniques.

Stage three

At the monthly business meetings, Schneiderman placed the nonfinancial data first on the agenda, ahead of the financial data. However, there was resistance from his boss – CEO Jerry Fishman – who insisted every time that the presentation of the data be reversed, with financial measures taking precedence in the ensuing discussions. Eventually, Fishman confronted Schneiderman and warned him to find a way to compromise or they would do it Fishman's way. The problem was seemingly solved through an unexpected source – a television commercial for candy, which emphasized the combination of two different products (peanut butter and chocolate) to provide the unique flavour. The advertisement inspired Schneiderman to combine the financial and nonfinancial data in a single monthly report and this came to form the basis of the Balanced Scorecard approach.

Stage four

By combining nonfinancial with financial metrics and showing how they are linked to overall performance Schneiderman won acceptance from his boss and his fellow managers, thus achieving the all-important internal validation. External validation followed when Professor Robert Kaplan of the Harvard Business School began studying *Analog* for a case that he was developing. In his teaching case, Kaplan highlighted Schneiderman's 'corporate scorecard'.[17] In a subsequent article in the *Harvard Business Review*, Kaplan discussed the potential for the scorecard to be used across various companies and industries.

Stage five

Schneiderman's 'corporate scoreboard', despite some external validation, might have run its course at *Analog Devices* before dying out if it wasn't for the fact that Kaplan teamed up with David P. Norton to develop the concept into a book that codified and generalized Schneiderman's approach into the 'Balanced Scorecard'.[18] Several other books and a host of consulting and other bodies have sprung up since.[19]

An outline of the Balanced Scorecard approach

The Balanced Scorecard is a method for developing strategic objectives through the measurement of key financial, structural and process factors linked to organizational performance critical to its success.

There are various arguments for adopting a BSC approach including continuous quality improvement, better management structures and systems of communication, higher and continuous levels of data collection and knowledge, and strategy development. As one group of BSC consultants put it, the Balanced Scorecard 'helps create a management structure that clarifies the direction the company needs to go, communicate that direction, align everyone's work to support those goals and ultimately perform more efficiently and be more competitive in their market'.[20] The same consulting group argues that: 'Only 5% of the workforce understands their company strategy; [that] only 25% of managers have incentives linked to strategy, 60% of organizations don't link budgets to strategy [and] 86% of executive teams spend less than one hour per month discussing strategy'.[21]

It is argued that through use of a comprehensive scorecard approach the performance measurements that are developed help employees to clarify what is important in achieving company goals. In the process, the measurement tools (i.e. the scorecards) as well as the associated processes (i.e. the factors that are measured and the way they are measured) provide the company with a useful way of developing consistent and up-to-date data on performance outcomes. They also provide information on the links between selected organizational behaviours and performance outcomes.

The four perspectives

The BSC approach consists of four 'perspectives' that constitute the core of what are to be measured. These perspectives are financial, customer, internal and learning/growth.

The term 'perspectives', however, needs to be understood as standing for two, sometimes conflicting, factors. On the one hand, the term refers to the interests of core stakeholders, such as shareholders (financial), customers (customer), and to a lesser extent managers (internal) and employees (learning/growth). On the other hand, the term also refers to elements of an overall strategy that consist of a focus on such things as profitability and risk (financial), customer needs and requirements (customer), operational factors that are crucial to the achievement of the company's strategic objectives (internal), and employee competencies, potential, expectations and satisfaction (learning/growth). These perspectives form a framework for developing measures of required performance that arise out of the company's strategic direction.

The financial perspective: This perspective needs to be balanced to provide a view of both the company's current financial performance (e.g. through measures of cash flow, liquidity, daily sales, accounts receivable, orders in the pipeline), and its future trends (e.g. measured through investment in Research & Development as a ratio to sales or profit, market segment, sales from new products). It is suggested that successful companies would be those that continually evaluate and improve their metrics to predict short-term and long-term success; know the true costs of its processes and products and/or services; link financial measures to key success factors, and use a few central statistics to measure overall company performance.[22]

It has been argued that the financial perspective needs to be adjusted for not-for-profit organizations, such as hospitals and government agencies, that are not used to giving priority to (financial) shareholders, nor being primarily concerned with profitability.[23] The health care industry in North America, for example, has been slow compared to other industries to embrace BSC. Ironically, Canadian hospitals, which are on the whole government-funded, seem to have been faster to adopt BSC than their US counterparts,[24] many of whom are profit-oriented. However, results have been mixed at best, with some commentators suggesting that the failure rate was due to lack of management commitment and technical know-how,[25] while others have argued that the method is totally inappropriate and counter-productive to health care.[26] Based on study of several hospitals in the Midwest of the United States, one argument for the successful implementation of BSC in the health care industry is to change the focus of the perspectives from (financial) shareholders and customers to 'key stakeholder groups, such as patients and their families, employers, health plans (insurers), physicians, employees, administrators, shareholders (when the health care organization is a for-profit entity), communities and regulators'.[27] Similarly, it has been argued that the BSC framework, as developed for the private sector, would not work for government agencies where 'citizen satisfaction/support' rather than profitability is the top priority.[28] Again the solution is a reframing of the perspectives to take these priorities into account. It is the overall strategy that is important rather than the specific character of the perspectives. The perspectives need to be modified in the not-for-profit sector to take into account different strategic outcomes.

The customer perspective: This perspective is about finding a way of adequately predicting customer behaviour through such things as measures of customer opinions and perceptions of existing and potential products/services; gains and losses of customers across different market segments; market share; surveys of customer satisfaction; and price and quality information on key competitors.[29] As we have seen above, this focus may need to be changed in not-for-profit organizations where the main 'consumer' of the product or service may be a student (university), patient (hospital), welfare recipient (social work agency), aggrieved citizen (police), or any number of other stakeholders. In such cases, the metrics have to be aligned with the needs of the specific consumers in pursuit of strategic goals. A hospital, for example, might measure such things as patient and other users' perceptions of quality of care but also judge the balance between care and cost structures by assessing levels of satisfaction at different cost levels. In the latter case, a good example could be the use of hospital beds. Apart from obvious health issues and risks, adequate measures of such things as comparable recovery rates of hospitalized versus non-hospitalized patients could help identify whether extra time spent in a hospital bed justifies the expenditure. In one study of the successful implementation of BSC in US hospitals, the benefits of BSC most cited by senior hospital administrators included the development of consensus around a clear strategy; an improvement of the credibility of managers with their boards; a (four perspectives) framework for decision making; helping employees to better understand the value of their work and its relationship to the overall strategy; a 'depoliticization' of the budget process (as employees gain a clearer understanding of strategic needs and decision making); greater accountability (especially when linked to incentive plans); and the enablement of learning and continuous improvement through the ability to compare results to predictions.[30]

The internal perspective: This is about finding effective ways of controlling the organization's production and/or operational 'processes to produce reliable and consistent products and services'.[31] Here the focus is on finding adequate measures of those processes such as, for example, cycle times, production and/or service delivery time, productivity, and key purchases of supplies. It may also involve identifying and measuring key processes in each department and unit of the organization; correlating performance measures with customer metrics (e.g. satisfaction); establishing benchmarks based on customer requirements; developing a safety index to reduce accidents and production hold-ups; and promoting a preventative 'approach to achieving quality products and services'.[32]

The learning & growth perspective: This requires a focus on building and refining an organizational infrastructure for skills and knowledge development, and an effective workplace culture or climate. Typical measures include improvement of knowledge levels through training and education; overall company-relevant certification levels (i.e. degrees, certificates, professional accreditations, internal certifications); workplace satisfaction levels and workplace climate; and the generation of new ideas leading to improved productivity.

Implementing BSC

The *Balance Scorecard Institute* has developed a series of outline steps for implementing BSC. Their 'Nine Steps To Success' is as follows:

1   Assess the organization's *mission* and *vision*. Prepare a *change management plan*. Conduct a series of workshops to identify key messages and their transmission throughout the organization and to relevant external agencies.
2   Identify and develop *strategic results, themes and perspectives* through workshop discussions of customer needs and the central value of the organization.
3   Build *strategic objectives* categorized by *perspectives* that are linked to cause and effect relationships (*strategic maps*) for each *strategic theme*.
4   Merge each of the strategic maps to form a single company-wide, or master, strategic map 'that shows how the organization creates value for its customers and stakeholders'.
5   Develop *performance measures* for each company-wide *strategic objective* by identifying leading and lagging measures, establishing baseline and benchmarking data, and expected targets and thresholds.

6   Develop *strategic initiatives* to support the strategic objectives. Assign ownership of performance measures and strategic initiatives and in ways that build *accountability*.

7   Begin the implementation stage by applying performance measurement software and ensuring that ensuing information is directed to carefully designated people at the right time.

8   Translate the organizational level scorecard (Tier 1) into business unit or support unit scorecards (Tier 2), and then to team and individual scorecards (Tier 3). Develop performance measures for all objectives at all levels of the company and emphasize results and strategies throughout.

9   Evaluate the completed scorecard.

Six Sigma

The story of the 'invention' of Six Sigma is an interesting one because of the complexity of factors involved, in particular the number of myths that surround the case. There are various stories about the invention of Six Sigma. One prominent story has it that in the mid-1980s Bill Smith, a key member of the Communications Division of *Motorola*, was concerned about a growing number of complaints that were hitting the company through warranty claims. This led Smith to search for new quality measures and in the process to develop Six Sigma.[33] In another story the development of Six Sigma begins in the early 1980s with the CEO of *Motorola*, Bob Galvin, a 'very ardent pursuer of excellence in quality',[34] who devised a strategy to 'achieve tenfold reduction in product-failure levels in five years'.[35] In yet another story, by Marjorie Hook, Bill Smith's daughter, it is suggested that Smith, always concerned with high levels of quality, developed a prototype of Six Sigma prior to joining *Motorola* but that it was at *Motorola* that he was able to put it into practice.[36] According to Hook, her father was 'thrilled that a good thing was happening to *Motorola* and that Six Sigma had made such a difference. He drafted Six Sigma long before . . . Bob Galvin ever took it on board. So, for him [Smith], it was the culmination of so many years of work and trying to change the way people think about things. He finally had some phenomenal success at *Motorola* and he was getting great recognition for it'.[37] Other stories credit Mikel Harry,[38] Allan Larson,[39] and George Fisher,[40] with the development of Six Sigma. All *Motorola* employees, Harry was an engineer with a statistics background, Larson an internal Six Sigma consultant, and Fisher the head of the company's communications sector. Harry, it is claimed, developed Six Sigma as a result of studies of variance in the company's work processes;[41] Larson is credited with making the concept more widely known by introducing it to other major companies, including *GE* and *Allied Signal*;[42] and Fisher is seen as providing the leadership, if not the inspiration, that shepherded the development of Six Sigma. Finally, continuous quality guru Joseph Juran argues that Six Sigma is really 'a basic version of quality improvement' whose roots are to be found in the work of the American Society for Quality (ASQ), in their issuance of certificates for reliability engineers.[43] Juran describes Six Sigma as 'a goal' which focuses on the reduction of defects to a minuscule level but does credit *Motorola*'s CEO Bob Galvin with its development.[44]

So we might ask, who did develop Six Sigma and what were the steps involved? According to Alan Ramias, a former *Motorola* employee who participated in and observed the various processes, the answer is 'all of the above'.[45] Certainly, Six Sigma was developed against a background of widespread continuous process and quality improvement projects; it was developed at *Motorola*; and Smith, Galvin, Harry, Larson, Fisher and others were all involved. Drawing on Ramias' account the following stages are suggested:

Stage one

In the mid-1980s, *Motorola* felt compelled to examine and change many of their techniques and tools in the face of a severe downturn in the memory chip market due to powerful Japanese competition. They were also under serious pressure from large customers, including *Ford*, who were demanding greater quality and on-time performance. This helped to shift thinking inside the company from 'quality' per se towards cycle time as 'managers began to recognize that some of the quality problems were due to wait times, inventory management, and other issues related to long-cycle times'.[46]

Stage two

In the early 1980s, *Motorola* was involved in a quality circles programme called participative management. A series of training products – aimed at factory production workers, technicians and engineers – were developed to support the programme. According to Ramias, with a focus on defects, these training programmes would form the basis of much of Six Sigma's methodology. In the meantime, and in the face of growing market pressures, the company bought in a consultant – Geary Rummler – to develop analytic tools for process improvement, especially cycle time improvement. The problem, as Ramias sees it, was that Rummler's process improvement programme, or OPS, was 'aimed at business processes and management teams, while the quality programs were aimed at product design and manufacturing employees' and no-one was linking the two to develop a coherent approach.[47]

Stage three

Enter the various players. Ramias concedes that Smith played an influential role by writing and circulating a technical paper setting forth what he called Six Sigma, which did 'influence the thinking of many people to move away from the narrow focus on defects to the concept of process capability'. However, he adds that it would be wrong to say that Smith single-handedly invented Six Sigma but rather it should be seen as the efforts of various people and processes. Those contributors include Edwards Deming and Joseph Juran's pioneering work on quality improvement, Geary Rummler's OPS programme at *Motorola*, Mikel Harry's work as a quality training instructor, then head of *Motorola's* Six Sigma academy, George Fisher's leadership of the communications section (where Smith worked) and later as CEO during the crucial development of Six Sigma, and Alan Larson's consulting work, which brought Six Sigma to wider audiences.

Stage four

Validation of the new method came from the fact that Six Sigma was an amalgam of already accepted practices within *Motorola* and the fact that it quickly became associated by those in charge – Fisher, Galvin – with an effective way of reducing cycle times and meeting customer needs. If Smith can be said to have played an important role at stage three, Harry, Fisher and Galvin played an important role at stage four. What also played a role, but perhaps more in retrospect than at the time, was the fact that *Motorola* won the coveted *Malcolm Baldrige Quality Award* in 1988, which quickly became associated with Six Sigma. As Marjorie Hook expresses it, 'winning the Baldrige Award stands out as a career high point in her father's [Bill Smith's] life. He was thrilled that a good thing was happening to *Motorola* and that Six Sigma had made such a difference'.[48] Interestingly, Ramias contends that Six Sigma had only been introduced at *Motorola* in 1987 and it was far too early for the results to be felt and widely known by 1988, so the Award was much more likely for a range of long-established efforts.[49] Nonetheless, regardless of the actual truth of the matter, the Baldrige Award did serve not only to validate Six Sigma but also to facilitate its dissemination.

Stage five

Regardless of the actual reason for *Motorola's* Baldrige Award, it provided a platform for *Motorola* employees to sell the idea of Six Sigma; one of the conditions of the Baldrige Award is that 'winners agree to share their quality program with anyone who is interested'.[50] According to Marjorie Hook, since *Motorola* was the first company to win, others were eager to learn more about Six Sigma: 'That's one of the primary reasons Six Sigma became so widely known'.[51] In the process, her father, Bill Smith, 'got to spend the last few years of his life traveling around, teaching and introducing Six Sigma to people'.[52] Thus, Smith, along with Larson, can be seen having played an important role in the dissemination of Six Sigma, and that dissemination sometimes came in an unusual form, as in Smith's depiction in the occasional Dilbert comic strip! Like BSC, a host of books and consulting associations have sprung up to propagate the idea and methods of Six Sigma.[53]

An outline of the Six Sigma method

Six Sigma is a set of practices that combines statistical techniques and management training to improve organizational processes – of cost minimization, schedule adherence, high product quality and customer satisfaction – specifically through the elimination of defects.

The Six Sigma method has become very important to organizations that have to compete with increasingly globalized competition and customers that have come to expect high degrees of quality, delivery and service. Dealing with defects is, of course, nothing new but Six Sigma comes with a strategy and set of statistical methods for reducing the level of defects to 0.00034 per cent or 3.4 mistakes per million opportunities, and applying that standard not only to manufactured products but to any process that is critical to organizational outcomes. As the American Society for Quality argues, a 99 per cent accuracy rate can sometimes be fatal if you consider that it could mean 200,000 wrongly prescribed drug prescriptions every year; two unsafe airport landings every day; 5,000 incorrect surgical procedures every week; 20,000 lost items of mail per hour; power outages seven hours every month; and fifty dropped newborn babies every day.[54]

The level of accuracy promised by Six Sigma is a likely contributor to the fact that the Central Intelligence Agency (CIA) and the Department of Homeland Security are thought to have adopted it in their fight against terrorism.[55] Why? National Intelligence agencies receive countless pieces of information in a given period that have to be processed and decisions made on them. However, the sheer volume of information often makes effective decision making difficult and highly problematic. For example, an intercepted telephone call containing a threat to blow up the New York Stock Exchange could be anything from a hoax to a joke between friends, a misheard communication, or an actual terrorist plan. On its own it is clear that a CIA agent would be inclined to investigate further but what if the message was one of a quarter of a million pieces of information received? In the latter case agents would have to make relatively quick decisions that weighed taking all threats seriously against the sheer volume of information, limited resources and the percentage of likely false leads. While it is important to act on good information it is also important to discard bad information because such data 'paralyze decision makers further up the line'.[56] Thus, arguably, if the CIA and Homeland Security were to achieve Six Sigma levels of accuracy that would lead to only one bad decision per 294,000 pieces of information.[57] According to Mickel Harry, one of the founders of Six Sigma, this level of attainment would be 'a quantum difference' that would make the United States 1,800 times safer.[58]

Discussion around the use of Six Sigma in the fight against terrorism also raises some interesting questions about the method's viability. To begin with, the Six Sigma level of accuracy is, as pointed out by Joseph Juran (see above), a goal – a target, not a guarantee. It requires considerable training and commitment to come close to the realization of such accuracy. Commenting on the CIA, Homeland Security and Six Sigma, Michael Dell (CEO, *Dell Computers*) contends that it would take years for US intelligence agencies to fully implement a Six Sigma programme and attaining the required level of accuracy is possible but far from certain.[59] Elizabeth Keim, ASQ President, has pointed out that Six Sigma is 'lousy at fixing rare and random problems' and the fight against terrorism could well fit that category. Nonetheless, as she argues, much of what counts as 'the war against terrorism' involves innumerable routine and mundane tasks that are the stuff of Six Sigma.

Despite its high profile with US intelligence agencies and its touted success at companies such as *GE*, there are indications that fewer that 15 per cent of Fortune 1000 companies are using Six Sigma in any significant way.[60] Dan Burham, CEO of Raytheon, argues that it doesn't work without the commitment of an 'obsessive, compulsive' CEO like Jack Welch, and companies that introduce Six Sigma need to stick it out for at least five years or they will likely lose all progress.[61] Nonetheless, supporters of Six Sigma continue to argue that, at the very least, coherent strategies to reduce defects to 0.00034 per cent lead to massive improvements even if Six Sigma is not achieved.

The meaning of Six Sigma

We have referred at length to the goal of improving processes by reducing defects to 0.00034 per cent or 3.4 per one million opportunities. But what do 'processes', 'defects', and 'Six Sigma' refer to? In Six Sigma thinking, the primary goal is to improve customer satisfaction by reducing and eliminating defects. A defect is seen as 'nonconformity of a product or service to its specifications'[62] in 'any aspect of customer satisfaction: high product quality, schedule adherence, [or] cost minimization'.[63] In Six Sigma 'everything is a process. All processes have inherent variability. Data is used to understand the variability and drive process improvement decisions'.[64] The Six Sigma philosophy of process improvement, customer satisfaction and defect reduction is based on a 'statistical thinking' paradigm[65] and refers to the Greek letter sigma that is used to symbolize the standard deviation in statistical equations.[66] Thus, for example, in a normal distribution we might find 68 per cent of our measures within one standard deviation, or one sigma, 95.5 per cent would likely fall within two standard deviations, and 99.7 per cent at three standard deviations, through to 99.99966 per cent at six standard deviations or six sigma.[67]

Implementing Six Sigma

In addition to the development or adaptation of a number of statistical tools for analysing defect levels, Six Sigma involves two different five-part processes, one for improving existing processes, and another for developing new products or services. Each task involves the development of quality improvement teams who are responsible for identifying the process, defining the defect and developing/applying the corresponding measures.[68]

Improving existing processes involves definition (D), measurement (M), analysis (A), improvement (I) and control (C) – or DMAIC. Usually when a specific project is launched customer satisfaction goals have been established at the organizational level and broken down into subgoals that include cycle times, costs and defect analysis. Following this, the *first step* involves defining the process improvement goals to match customer needs and the organization's strategy, establishing baselines and benchmarks for the process to be implemented, breaking the process into manageable subprocesses – complete with their own subgoals, establishing the infrastructure for attaining the goals, and assessing the cultural and structural changes necessary for success.[69]

In the *second step* the improvement team, having identified those aspects of the process that need to be understood for purposes of measurement,[70] collect relevant data for future comparison through such things as baselining and benchmarking.

In *step three* the team analyses the data to understand trends, patterns, causal relationships and root causes. In *step four* the team then sets out to improve on the existing process through various methods, including experimental design, modelling, tolerancing and robust design – a variety of methodologies for developing objective measures of the existing and projected processes. This sets everything up for *step five*, where the team then sets out to control the process by ensuring that any variances are corrected before they result in defects.[71]

Developing new products and services involves an almost identical set of steps, including definition (D), measurement (M) and analysis (A) but then includes design (D) and verification (V) – or DMADV. For all practical purposes the definition stage is the same as for DMAIC but measurement involves identifying factors that are critical to qualities and measuring 'product capabilities, production process capability, and risk assessment',[72] and analysis is used to develop alternative process designs to select the best design. This leads to the design stage where the details are developed and optimized, ready for the verification stage where the design is tested and verified through pilot runs, before being handed over to the team who will be responsible for overseeing the process.

Improvement teams

We have mentioned process improvement teams but who or what do they consist of? Actually these teams are a key part of the Six Sigma process and constitute a large part of the process and its potential success. These teams consist of people who have been trained and certified in one or more quality functions: Six Sigma has played an important role in the professionalization of quality functions and roles.[73] *Executive leaders*, drawn from the top management team, establish the vision, empower and resource others to develop various projects. *Champions*, also drawn from top management, oversee and coordinate Six Sigma implementation across the organization. *Master Black Belts* – following the language of the martial arts – are in-house expert coaches who are employed specifically on Six Sigma, integrating projects across the organization, assisting *Champions* and guiding the work of *Black Belts* and *Green Belts*. *Black Belts* are staff who are trained and certified to oversee and execute Six Sigma projects. *Green Belts* are employees who have also undergone a level of training to work on Six Sigma implementation, under the guidance of *Black Belts*.[74] Unlike *Black Belts* who work full-time on Six Sigma, *Green Belts* have other job responsibilities.[75]

Making sense of BSC and Six Sigma

As we have demonstrated throughout this chapter, the Balanced Scorecard and Six Sigma are widespread, acclaimed, but also controversial change strategies. On the face of it, it could be thought that, unlike other change strategies, BSC and Six Sigma, with their focus on measurement and 'hard' data, have little to say about behaviour at work. Indeed, their added emphasis on training and concern with processes adds to the illusion of scientific study and objective analysis. However, both approaches have important implications for the behaviour, structure and culture of an organization. We have already alluded to several of these factors throughout this chapter.

To begin with, both programmes develop strong frameworks for directing the strategies and associated behaviours of all employees of an organization – from top to bottom. In the Balanced Scorecard all employees are focused on strategic thinking through the lens of four key perspectives. In Six Sigma strategy is viewed through the lens of defects, various statistical techniques and methods for reducing defects. Employees are not simply trained in the new methods but in ways of thinking about every aspect of the company. This is bound to have its impact on behaviour and the culture of the organization. For example, supporters suggest that even where BSC and Six Sigma are not fully attained the attempts to implement them encourage employees to focus on the strategic goals of the organization.[76] Critics argue that BSC and Six Sigma have a powerful influence on an organization's culture, because 'The mindset that is needed, the capabilities that are needed, the whole culture that is needed [for BSC or Six Sigma] are fundamentally different' from that required for a culture of innovation: 'The more you hardwire a company [in this way, the more] it is going to hurt breakthrough innovation'.[77] Others critics argue that BSC and Six Sigma not only provide a tool for measurement but also a way of making sense of corporate strategy. These methods shift attention from intangible assets to those that can be measured. In some ways this can be a very important way of focusing workplace behaviour but it can ignore many of the non-measurable factors that constitute the cultures of an organization, such as values, beliefs, symbols, systems of communication, and inter-relationships that may contribute to the strength of the organization.[78] It can be argued that BSC encourages rigid behaviour, forcing indicators into one of four perspectives, leaving little room for 'cross perspectives'.[79] At the very least, the factors that make BSC and Six Sigma effective in one context may make them ineffective in another. For example, we already saw that Six Sigma is very good for routine tasks but not good for situations involving rare and random problems.

Six Sigma and *Home Depot*[80]

For a time Six Sigma appears to be the big success story at *Home Depot* under the leadership of CEO Robert Nardelli, whose mantra 'facts are friendly' summed up his approach to management. Six Sigma was focused on streamlining the check-out process. Soaring profits seemed to confirm the value of Six Sigma. However, contrary to expectations, employee morale was dropping dramatically through irritation with constant data measurement and associated paperwork that reduced attention to customers. Customer satisfaction also began to fall, as evidenced in an American Customer Satisfaction index for 2005, which showed *Home Depot* falling from first to last among major retailers. Nardelli was ousted in 2007 and his successor Frank Blake has since curtailed some of the Six Sigma activities and given store managers more leeway to make their own decisions. This is a story that has been repeated across a number of companies, including *3M* and *Young & Rubicam*. So are BSC and Six Sigma past their sell life? Yes, according to Tom Davenport, professor of management at Babson College: 'Process management is a good thing [but] it always has to be leavened a bit with a focus on innovation and [customer relationships]'. They are effective change programmes where the focus is on quality, cost-cutting and improving profitability. However, where innovation is the driving force of a company 'companies are increasingly confronting the side-effects of a Six Sigma culture'. Finally, in the opinion of *Raytheon* consultant Robert Carter, while the popularity of Six Sigma (and by implication BSC) endures, its notion of a corporate cure-all is subsiding. Once a company has gone through a process of requisite belt-tightening, 'the strategic needs of a business change'.

Change and the change management approach

What is interesting about the development of change programmes is the sensemaking processes they also go through. As we have seen in our discussion of the stages that BSC and Six Sigma went through in their formulation, much of the process depends on how various managers and key employees work to make sense of things. It is not a simple process of identifying a problem and applying the appropriate method to deal with it. The first stage involves some dissatisfaction with the status quo, or some 'shock' to the system, such as increased competitions and dwindling market sales.[81] However, it is not as simple as a clear dissatisfaction. Someone, usually a senior manager, has to first decide that there *is* a problem and then define what that problem is: in the process the problem becomes 'enacted', which means that it begins to be seen as a problem by other people.[82] As we have seen from the development of BSC and Six Sigma, problem identification and enactment often depends on several key actors, as do the solutions and diffusion of ideas. Thus, inspirations for new methods draw very much on cues from existing and dominant ways of working. We can see this particularly well with the invention of Six Sigma, which relied heavily on a dominant ongoing sense of the need for quality improvement, reinforced through networks of people across various companies that provided a social sense of the situation. Not surprisingly, those more readily associated with the 'invention' of BSC and Six Sigma came from the ranks of those social networks. Indeed, it is the very existence of social networks around a dominant ongoing sense that facilitated the validation of distribution of BSC and Six Sigma. By the diffusion stage, as we have seen in earlier chapters, organizations are more ready to accept something not simply because it is seen to work but also and especially because it is popular. It has formed part of an ongoing sense of what is important across major companies. However, this may help to push the limits of a new change programme as companies – like *3M* and *Home Depot* – begin to find that the new methods may not work for them or disrupts other important ways of thinking (e.g. innovation). In other words, at some point, BSC and Six Sigma (and other change methods) may themselves cause shocks to the system and force a rethink. Finally, as the various debates around BSC and Six Sigma demonstrate, the extent to which these methods can be seen as successful or not also depends up to a point on the sense that is made of the outcomes.

If the company has a financially successful year following the introduction of BSC or Six Sigma that will likely influence how those methods are viewed. If, on the other hand, the company experiences losses that could have a negative association with BSC and Six Sigma. It is up to employees and senior managers alike to understand that an important aspect of any method is the embedded sense that is contained within it and what continued sense is made of it. Change methods as well as change are reliant on the management of sensemaking.

End of chapter questions and exercises

1   Use an Internet and library search to find one company that 'success-fully' and one that 'unsuccessfully' implemented the Balanced Scorecard method. Where possible try to find companies from Figure 1.1. Also try to find material that provides fairly detailed information. Make a list of the pros and cons involved in implementing the Balanced Scorecard. What does this tells you about the strengths and weaknesses of the Balanced Scorecard approach?

2   Use an Internet and library search to find one company that 'success-fully' and one that 'unsuccessfully' implemented Six Sigma. Where possible try to find companies from Figure 1.1. Also try to find material that provides fairly detailed information. Make a list of the pros and cons involved in implementing Six Sigma. What does this tell you about the strengths and weaknesses of the Six Sigma approach?

3   Using the sensemaking framework (Table 1.1) in Chapter 1, write short notes, with examples, on how each of the four companies researched for questions 1 and 2 above uses the eight sensemaking properties to develop, explain and/or present their account of the Balanced Scorecard or Six Sigma.

4   What similarities can you find in the way each strategy of implementing or failing to implement BSC or Six Sigma is made plausible? What can we learn from this?

5   What are some of the differences in the way each implementation strategy is made plausible? What can we learn from this?

6   Make notes on how key managers are presented in the accounts of implementing BSC or Six Sigma. What is the role of identity construc-tion in these accounts both for the managers and for others? What can we learn from this?

7   What 'pressures' to change can you identify in each company case? What pressures, if any, are similar across all four companies? What, if any, are different? What can we learn from this?

8   Using the Birkenshaw & Mol (2006) study of management innovation, find an example of a company that developed either BSC or Six Sigma (they can be the same ones that you studied for question 1 or 2) and explain how they went through the five stages.

9 Using examples of companies that have implemented BSC, discuss the strengths and weaknesses of the four perspectives.

10 Using examples of companies that have implemented Six Sigma, discuss the strengths and weaknesses of either the DMADV or the DMAIC method.

8 Leading change

Objectives of this chapter

By the end of this chapter, you should:

1 Understand the role of leadership in terms of organizational success
2 Be familiar with trait-based theories of leadership
3 Be familiar with behavioural theories of leadership
4 Be familiar with contingency theories of leadership
5 Understand the differences between transactional and transformational leadership
6 Understand and be able to discuss critically various contemporary theories of leadership
7 Be familiar with strategies for overcoming resistance to change
8 Be familiar with the concept of 'leading from the middle'.

HealthSouth CEO faces 36 Criminal Charges [1]

On June 7, 2005, the newspapers were marking the start of the 21-day trial of Richard Scrushy, founder and CEO of *HealthSouth Corporation*. The charges included conspiracy, securities fraud, mail fraud and a charge for filing false financials that fell under the fairly new Sarbanes-Oxley Act (established in 2002). This act was minted to force companies to strengthen their internal controls. The act also mandated penalties for CEOs who make or sign false financials. This was the government's first attempt to charge someone under the Sarbanes-Oxley and the campaign was highly publicized.

Mr. Scrushy claims that he was never involved and that his top subordinates were trying to pin the fraudulent acts on him to lessen their own punishments. Five senior executives with *HealthSouth* plead guilty to lesser charges and agreed to testify against their former boss in plea-bargain arrangements. Only one received a short jail term while the others were sentenced to home detention or probation.

According to an article in *The Wall Street Journal* on June 29, the case fell apart because the government could not prove that Mr. Scrushy was involved. The fact that fraud had occurred was blatantly obvious, claimed several of the jurors. However, what was not obvious was Scrushy's involvement. After tearing apart the reputations of many of the senior executives who testified against Mr. Scrushy (for issues such as excessive drinking, extra-marital affairs, violent tempers and bouts of depression), the jury was left with the testimony of five discredited witnesses as the prosecution's sole case. It wasn't enough and Mr. Scrushy was acquitted of all 36 criminal charges.

However, Mr. Scrushy's problems were not over. He still faced three perjury charges, one charge of obstruction of justice and a civil suit by the SEC. On June 30, 2006, Mr. Scrushy was found guilty of six charges of bribery, conspiracy and mail fraud. He was sentenced to seven years in prison in June 2007.

Before the charges were brought against him in 2005, Mr. Scrushy was considered a shining example of the American Dream. He started as a gas-station attendant at age 17, newly married with a baby on the way. He later earned a degree in respiratory therapy and headed up *HealthSouth* in 1984. According to *The Wall Street Journal*, 'Barely a decade later . . . Mr. Scrushy was running the biggest provider of rehabilitative services and outpatients surgery in the country.'[279] He was definitely considered a great leader who was adept at leading change. Under his leadership *HealthSouth* grew and changed considerably to become a Fortune 500 company.

So what happened? How did such a shining example of seemingly good leadership end up in such a disaster? At the end of this story, we are left with a man who was once considered a great leader, able to grow and change what was once a small organization into an empire, being sentenced to seven years in jail and five other senior leaders who had been publicly discredited and convicted of criminal involvement. Without a doubt, Mr. Scrushy and his colleagues once fitted the 'ideals' of leadership. They were variously described as charismatic, energetic, intelligent, ambitious and aggressive at one time or another. They seemed to fit the requirements of leadership outlined in numerous theories of leadership. No doubt you'll recognize a few of these attributes as the chapter takes you through the most popular of these theories. Given this, are current theories of leadership and strategies of leading

change enough? How do we avoid such leadership disasters? These are
questions to ponder as you read the following chapter.

Theories of leadership have existed for as long as there have been leaders and
are as varied as the leaders themselves. The emphasis has traditionally been
on what makes a leader great. That is, how do we find a great leader, what do
we look for, and how will we know a great leader when we see one? The oldest
of these theories are known as trait-based theories. These were followed by
behavioural theories, and, eventually, contingency theories. All three will be
discussed briefly later in the chapter. The goal of this chapter is not to make
you intimately familiar with the various leadership theories that fall under
these categories but to give you more of a general overview as an introduction
to the topic of leading change.

   Many of the leadership theories discussed in this chapter make two
important assumptions of which you should be aware. The first is that leadership actually matters and the second is that leadership happens at the top of
an organization. In this chapter, we will address these assumptions, as we
try to make sense of the challenges of leading change. We'll start with the
first assumption – that leaders actually matter. In the second half of this
chapter we will address specific tools for leading change, discuss the challenge
of resistance to change and question whether change actually has to be led
from the top.

A look inside today's companies – the leadership factor

June 7, 2005 was a busy day for business leaders. More than 71 of them were
mentioned in *The Times* of London, *The New York Times* and Canada's *Globe
and Mail*. Of the 71 leaders, 67 were men and only four were women. These
figures indicate a definite problem, but we'll save that discussion for the Gender
and Diversity chapter.

   The business leaders mentioned were named for various reasons; several
were newly appointed into positions often linked to leadership (i.e. CEOs,
CFOs and presidents) or were named as leaders spearheading a new venture,
takeover or merger, while others were on trial (as in the case of Mr. Scrushy),
being 'taken to task' by the organization's board of directors or shareholders,
or being dismissed. It appears that a change in leadership is very newsworthy
indeed. Similarly, it appears that most of what happens within an organization is somehow attributed to those in senior leadership positions. This
observation is due in part to the fact that of the 76 leaders mentioned,
the vast majority held CEO, CFO or presidential positions. When good
things were happening, the CEO was often interviewed or credited with the
accomplishment. Similarly, when bad things were happening, it was the
CEO who was being questioned, charged or dismissed (also as in the case of

Mr. Scrushy). Very rarely are more junior people in the organization questioned about their perceptions of or contributions to what was happening. Can we surmise from this that they have little or no impact on the activities of the companies? Are the successes and failures of organizations due only to the efforts/behaviours of senior leaders? These questions will be addressed in the following chapter.

It is also interesting to note the abundance of articles discussing the appointment of new senior leaders. Each one lauds the accomplishments of the leader and tries to convince the reader that the choice was a good one. It makes sense that they'd do that – nobody wants to publicize the appointment of a bad leader or admit to have chosen one! What is perhaps most useful for the purposes of this chapter is to look at which accomplishments are deemed to have made the individuals appropriate for a leadership role. This helps us to make sense of what the criteria were in each case. For example, on June 7, 2005, Susan E.C. Mey was named as the new President and Chairman of the Board of *Kodak Canada Inc.*[2] The news article talks about her past accomplishments in terms of her previous experience and five-year term with *Kodak*. It talks specifically about her role as General Counsel for *Kodak* and *The T. Eaton Company*, her experience as a business owner and her qualifications to practise law in Canada and Hong Kong. Her personal attributes and characteristics are not mentioned.

This news article generates some interesting questions; are personal traits and characteristics not important? Is experience in similar senior leadership positions a prerequisite for leading *Kodak Canada*? Does this make her a good leader? And, finally, is a law degree important for the position of CEO?

A similar analysis of other new senior leader appointment announcements is quite revealing. Rarely are personal characteristics mentioned. Most of the 'justification' is based on previous leadership experience and professional credentials. This illuminates the research-practitioner gap in its extreme as you will soon see as you move through the chapter.

Do leaders matter?

The assumption has been made for many a decade that the success of an organization depends in large part on the efficacy of the leader. This is consistent with the analysis of newspaper articles outlined in the opening vignette. We can see the consequences of this assumption even today. For example, it is quite common to witness the firing of a coach when a baseball team is performing badly. Similarly, it is not unusual for organizations with falling stock prices to fire the CEO. They do this to 'fix the problem' and alleviate the fears of stockholders. The flip side of this is also true. Steve Jobs, Lee Iacocca and Bill Gates are household names and their leadership styles have been studied and documented so that we might all learn from them and become successful leaders. Additionally, the lucrative compensation packages commonly associated with senior organizational leaders must be indicative of something! Unless they were seen as making significant contributions to the organizations in their roles as leaders, these lofty wages would not be seen as appropriate.

Rarely do we see people questioning whether the success of the organization would have occurred without that particular leader. Perhaps it is the followers who were responsible for the success! As noted in the opening vignette, we never seem to ask the followers. A notable exception to this dearth of research is Jeffrey Pfeffer,[3] who, in 1976, published an article that questioned the concept of leadership, the link between leadership and organizational performance and leader selection processes. He argued that there are at least three reasons why the observable effects of leaders on organizations might actually be small: (1) leaders are selected and only certain, limited styles of behaviour might be chosen, excluding many other potential behaviours; (2) the discretion and behaviours of leaders are constrained by their positions; and (3) leaders can realistically only affect a few of the variables that impact organizational performance. He makes a strong argument against the plethora of studies using the uncontested assumption that leadership matters.

Drawing on the work of Pfeffer, James Phills Jr., in an article in *Leader to Leader* (2005), contends that, in order for leadership to matter, two assumptions have to be made. The first is that leaders can and do influence the performance of organizations. The second is that this influence is intentional rather than accidental. He uses Steve Jobs, founder and CEO of *Apple Computer*, to conclude that more needs to be done to determine whether leadership matters.[4] Researchers need to study more than organizational success and leadership styles to ascertain whether leadership matters. They need to be able to link intentional acts of leadership, subsequent influence and performance outcomes.

A few scholars have since taken up the challenge proffered by Pfeffer and have done studies that attempt to measure leadership effectiveness. The general consensus is that yes, leaders probably do matter.[5] However, not all of these studies have addressed the challenges set out by Phills; that is, intentionality and direct causality are usually not both addressed. The issue remains open for debate. However, the assumption that leadership matters still dominates most leadership research and public opinion.

Now that we have concluded that leadership 'might matter', we'll move on to a discussion of leadership theories that rely on the assumption that leadership does matter, and of their contributions and limitations.

Traditional theories of leadership

Trait-based theories of leadership

The oldest theories of leadership focused on the traits of the leaders. *These theories were based on the belief that leaders are born rather than created.* To determine what made great leaders, people commonly believed to *be* 'great leaders' were held up as examples and their traits or characteristics examined. From here, it was concluded that the characteristics shared by those 'great leaders' were what made them great. As you can imagine, this eliminated a lot of potential 'great leaders'. Most notable was the exclusion of feminine traits – those traits commonly shared by women. As most of the ideals held up as great examples were men due to the beliefs and roles of the times, feminine traits were not recognized as being those that contributed to great leadership. Others were eliminated for different reasons. For example, it was once believed that height was an indicator of greatness as a leader. This suggested that those of shorter stature could not be great leaders. Followers of Napoleon would not agree!

As trait theory evolved, most physical attributes were eliminated as sources of 'greatness' and less tangible traits were examined. Instead, personality, social and intellectual attributes were credited with differentiating leaders from non-leaders. Once again, the use of 'notable leaders' was used to formulate such theories. Attributes common to more modern trait theories of leadership include charisma, courage, decisiveness, ambition, cognitive intelligence and integrity.

Trait-based theories, sometimes called competency-based theories today, are not without their critics. There are certain assumptions that have to be believed in order for trait-based theories to remain true. These assumptions include the assumption that all great leaders have most traits (or competencies) in common. Despite research contending that great leaders possess certain traits, few would agree with this assumption. In today's global business environment, it would be hard to say that all great business leaders fit a general mould. Certainly, the traits of Bill Gates and Mother Teresa do not fit a specific mould. Although they may have a few traits in common, they are significantly different in both leadership styles and personal traits.

Another criticism is that, because we associate great leaders with certain traits, we then identify someone who has these traits as being a good leader – regardless of whether they make a difference in the organization or not. Basically, we are perpetuating the stereotypes about what makes great leaders. You can see the conundrum.

Trait theories are not rendered completely useless by the criticisms noted above. In fact, they have gained in popularity in recent years as useful for determining 'potential' for leadership success. In other words, organizations are looking for traits commonly associated with leadership greatness in new recruits. They recognize that possession of certain traits doesn't guarantee success as a leader, but that these traits may enhance the recruit's chances of becoming a great leader. Again, it is important that these traits not be used in an exclusionary way. Much of what we know about 'great leaders' comes from a fairly homogeneous group.

Behavioural theories of leadership

Behavioural theories of leadership are based on the belief that leaders are not great because of who they are, but rather what they do. Theories based on this assumption began to appear in the 1940s and 1950s, and were based on surveys asking subordinates to rate their supervisors. Conclusions were drawn based on subordinates' beliefs about what greatness looked like, subsequent turnover and job satisfaction. The *Ohio State University* and *University of Michigan* studies are the most notable of these studies. These studies resulted in dichotomous characterizations of behaviours – those that are task-oriented and those that are people-oriented (often given other names). Task-oriented leaders focus more on telling people what to do and how to do it, structure, rules and peak performance. People-oriented leaders tend to focus more on respect, communication, relationships with people, and socio-emotional support. The two styles, task-oriented and people-oriented, are independent of each other. This suggests that people can possess one, both or none of these leadership styles.

The *Ohio State University* study found that employee turnover was lower and job satisfaction higher when a people-oriented style was used. It also indicated that these leaders received higher ratings from their superiors and had higher-performing work groups. The *Michigan* studies also found that leaders with a more people-oriented leadership style had more productive work groups.

One major criticism of this approach is that it assumes 'one best way' and is rather prescriptive in nature. It implies that if a leader behaves in a particular way, leadership success is guaranteed. The belief that such a claim is too bold to make and that different situations require different leadership styles led to the development of contingency theories of leadership.

Another criticism is similar to the one discussed in terms of trait-based theories. Behavioural approaches use existing leaders to determine what makes a great leader. This severely limits the range of behaviours associated with successful leadership. Once again, behaviours commonly associated with groups underrepresented in the existing leadership pool would be overlooked. If we use a gendered or homogeneous pool of leaders to determine which behaviours make great leaders, we are merely perpetuating stereotypes and biases.

More recently, behavioural theories have been seen as merely part of the leadership equation; that is, leadership behaviours, coupled with leadership traits and situational factors must be considered to ensure good leadership. This brings us to contingency theories of leadership.

Contingency theories of leadership

Contingency theories of leadership are less prescriptive than trait and behavioural leadership theories, but are prescriptive nonetheless. *They propose that the best leadership style can only be determined when the situation (task) and the followers (willingness, training, independence etc.) are considered.* These theories contend that certain situations and certain follower types require certain leadership styles.

The best-known of these theories are *Fiedler's Contingency Theory of Leadership* and the *Path Goal Theory of Leadership*. Fiedler's model uses the categorizations of task- and relationship-motivated styles of leadership and examines the conditions under which each should be adopted.

Path Goal Theory also stipulates when each leadership style is most appropriate, but does so using four different leadership styles: Directive, Supportive, Participative and Achievement-Oriented. In deciding which style is best, the characteristics of the followers and the demands of the tasks are considered. Although both are interesting models, it is beyond the scope of this chapter to delve much further into each of these theories.

Although interesting, these theories make some assumptions that could be problematic. For example, these theories assume that leaders can simply change their leadership styles as required or that, as a situation changes, a more appropriate leader with a certain leadership style can be inserted. Neither of these could be accomplished easily. However, all is not lost. Using these theories, hiring a leader, based on leadership styles, may be advantageous if the task and follower variables are known. However, as either of these changes, leadership may become problematic.

As leadership scholarship grew and evolved, scholars recognized the need for leadership theories that specifically addressed organizational change. Practitioners were looking for leaders who could 'transform' their organizations – radically altering their destinies. These theories that specifically address leading change are discussed in the following section.

Leading change

Now we have come to the 'how-to' section of the chapter – not that it will be quite that easy. Unfortunately, there isn't one best way to lead change (contrary to what some theorists may say). Instead of one easy, step-by-step guide to leading change, this section will present several options to you. It is the authors' hope that through critical examinations and evaluations of several theories/methods, you will be better able to deal with leading change in your own life. You see, it will be up to you to decide which might work best given your own situation. We'll begin with a very well-known and variously accepted leadership theory – transformational leadership. You can see by its very name that it is a leadership theory focused on transformation (or change).

Transformational leadership

James MacGregor Burns[6] is credited with identifying two types of political leadership in his 1978 book, *Leadership*: *transactional and transformational*.

Transactional leadership occurs when one person takes the initiative to approach another for the purposes of exchanging something. Think of it as the relationship between a boss and a subordinate. The boss asks for labour in return for wages. With transactional leadership, the emphasis is on efficient exchange (i.e. low-cost), minimizing resistance to the exchange and maximizing performance outcomes. This is a very traditional and conservative conceptualization of leadership. The theories of leadership discussed so far (trait, behavioural and contingency) focus on this type of leadership.

It is the second type of leadership described by Burns that we are most interested in here. Transformational leadership, although defined in 1978, gained its fame and popularity much later when Bass further developed the notion of transformational leadership in his 1985 book, *Leadership and Performance Beyond Expectations*,[7] where he applied the concepts to organizational leadership.[8] According to Bass, *transformational leaders transcend short-term exchanges and goals by heightening followers' awareness about 'big picture' organizational goals and issues.* Not only are these 'big picture' goals the new focus, but so are higher-order intrinsic needs of both the leader and the followers. The goal is transformation of the organization through transformation of the followers. Avolio and Bass further developed this conceptualization of transformational leader in 1999.[9] They contend that transformational leadership is accomplished through four elements, described in Figure 8.1.

Transformational leadership theories have enjoyed relative success and continuous development among organizational researchers. New models have been developed to deal with the contention that Bass and Avolio's suggested characteristics are too broad and relatively undefined,[10] making them difficult to apply. For example, Alimo-Metcalf and Alban-Metcalf[11] developed a nine-factor, transformational leadership structure. They contend that an effective transformational leader can be described as having the following characteristics:[12]

- a genuine concern for others

Charisma/Inspiration – Developing a vision, engendering pride, respect and trust; creating high expectations, modelling appropriate behaviour.

Intellectual Stimulation – Continually challenging followers with new ideas and approaches; using symbols to focus efforts.

Individualized Consideration – Giving personal attention to followers, giving them respect and responsibility.

Contingent Reward – Rewarding followers for conformity with performance targets.

Figure 8.1 Transformational leadership.[13]

- integrity, trustworthiness, honesty and openness
- is accessible and approachable
- is an inspirational networker and promoter
- is decisive and has determination and self-confidence
- has political sensitivity and skills.

Additionally, Alimo-Metcalf and Alban-Metcalf contend that an effective transformational leader should engage in the following:[14]

- empowering and developing potential in others
- clarifying boundaries and involving others in decisions
- encouraging critical and strategic thinking.

Although transformational theory has made a significant impact on leadership research and has enjoyed empirical success,[15] it is not without its own issues. The first is one that has been discussed earlier in the chapter. Much of the transformational leadership literature exalts the virtues of various leaders considered to fit the transformational mould. For example, Pierre Trudeau (former Prime Minister of Canada), Bill Gates, Gandhi and Martin Luther King have all, at some point, been held up as shining examples of transformational leaders. Once again, we run the risk of defining transformational leaders by the leaders themselves, creating an exclusive club that fails to consider the characteristics of underrepresented groups.

A second problem is identified by Leavy and Wilson.[16] They found that the actions of transformational leaders were significantly constrained by contextual factors like technology, industry structure, the international trading environment, national public policy and social and cultural transformation.[17] These constraints severely limited the actions of the transformational leaders, thus hindering their success. This is an important point – with any theories of change leadership or 'how-to guides', the context within which the change is happening could play a significant role in the success or failure of the endeavour. The same is true with the next theory of leading change.

Kanter's change masters

In 1983, Rosabeth Moss Kanter, a professor at Harvard Business School, developed a theory of organizational change in her book, *The Change Masters*. She contends that effective organizational change must be led by 'Change Masters'. Defined as, '*those people and organizations adept at the art of anticipating the need for, and of leading, productive change*',[18] change masters *question old assumptions and beliefs, focus on the 'big picture', think creatively, and exploit opportunities for change.*[19] In 1989, Kanter further developed her notion of change masters, using the 'business athlete' metaphor.[20] Figure 8.2 describes Kanter's business athletes.

If we look at Kanter's conception of a change master, we see a combination of all three of the more traditional leadership theories. We see the trait-based leadership theories in her description of this change master. Although not explicit, it is readily apparent that the change master must be charismatic, influential, humble and self-motivated. The behavioural leadership theory characteristics are probably the most prevalent. We see evidence of this in all seven of the points in Figure 8.2 The change master must build relationships, use influence, work with others, be willing to learn, have a process focus, be able to find synergies and form alliances and practise humility. Contingency theory elements can be found in Kanter's assertions that the change master

---

- They must *learn to operate without the might of the hierarchy behind them.* The crutch of authority must be thrown away and replaced by their own personal ability to make relationships, use influence, and work with others to achieve results. Business athletes stand – and run – on their own two feet, rather than being propelled automatically by the power of their position, just as a member of any athletic team is revered not for wearing the uniform but for his or her own performance.

- Business athletes must *know how to 'compete' in a way that enhances rather than undercuts cooperation.* They must be oriented to achieving the highest standard of excellence rather than to wiping out the competition.

- Business athletes must *operate with the highest ethical standards.* While business ethics have always been important from a social and moral point of view, they also become pragmatic requirements in the corporate Olympics. The doing-more-with-less strategies place an even greater premium on trust than did the adversarial-protective business practices of the traditional corporation.

- Business athletes must *have a dose of humility* sprinkled on their basic self-confidence, a humility that says that there are always new things to learn. Just as other kinds of athletes must be willing to learn, willing to accept the guidance of coaches, constantly in training, and always alert to the possibility of an improvement in their techniques, so must business athletes be willing to learn.

- Business athletes must *develop a process focus* – a respect for the process of implementation as well as the substance of what is implemented. They need to be aware that how things are done is every bit as important as what is done.

- Business athletes must *be multifaceted and ambidextrous,* able to work across functions and business units to find synergies that multiply value, able to form alliances when opportune but to cut ties when necessary, able to swim equally effectively in the mainstream and the newstreams. There is no room for narrow or rigid people in the new business environment.

- Business athletes must *gain satisfaction from results* and be willing to stake their won rewards on them. The accomplishment itself is really the only standard for the business athlete.

Figure 8.2 Kanter's business athletes.

Source: Kanter, R.M. (1989) *When Giants Learn to Dance: Mastering the Challenges of Strategy, Management and Careers in the 1990s,* Unwin Hyman, London, pp.361–64.

must know when to build alliances and when to cut ties, must be able to build relationships when necessary and must be process-focused so as to understand what is happening and why. These points all suggest that the change master must be nimble and aware; that is, they must be able to adapt their leadership as required by the situation.

So, you ask, what is new about Kanter's theory of change leadership? Well, it certainly makes the assumption that the leader is important and it also seems to indicate that leadership needs to happen from the top. What makes it different is twofold. First, despite the fact that leadership is happening from the top, it assumes more of a team effort, where the leader learns from others, is willing to take advice and emphasizes charismatic and referent sources of power rather than the more traditional legitimate or position-based power. The leader, in this case, is followed because people want to follow them – not because they have to.

The second point of departure of this change leadership theory is the emphasis on ethics, trust and non-adversarial relationships. It requires this both within the organization and among competitors. Instead of a win–lose relationship in the marketplace, Kanter suggests that a focus on excellence is more appropriate and conducive to success than a 'wipe-out-the-competition' strategy.

As with any theory, it is not without its issues. Although perhaps appropriate for long-term, incremental change, the processes, relationships and strategies outlined by Kanter would probably not be conducive to rapid or radical change. Teamwork, trust relationships and referent sources of power all take time.

Additionally, when choosing a leader, how are the traits and behaviours outlined by Kanter identified? One might assume that Mr. Scrushy, introduced in the opening vignette, possessed some of these same characteristics. The theory isn't as cut and dried as presented. Although it sounds straightforward, it fails to address the minute details and isn't so much of a 'how-to' as a general theory. Additionally, it doesn't address some of the issues identified by many of the contingency theories. For example, context is not mentioned. The needs and characteristics of the followers are not considered, nor is the nature of the change at hand.

Despite these shortcomings, Kanter's concept of change masters has made a significant impact. It provides leaders-to-be with a more modern view of leadership that takes into consideration the need to build relationships based on teamwork and trust. It is more consistent with today's psychological contract of employment than the old 'command and control' styles of leadership.

Tipping point leadership

Another leadership theory to have made a significant impact in recent years is Tipping Point Leadership, conceived by W. Chan Kim and Renée Mauborgne and published in the popular *Harvard Business Review* in 2003.[21] Much like older leadership theories, Tipping Point Leadership is based on the style used by a notable figure, deemed to have been a great leader. In this case, the theory is based on William Bratton's turnaround of the *New York Police Department* (*NYPD*). Bratton was appointed as police commissioner to the *NYPD* in 1994. At the time, the department was having major difficulties and the crime rate in New York had skyrocketed. In less than two years, Bratton turned the department around and New York City was heralded as the safest large city in the nation. This was the fifth successful turnaround of a police department for Bratton. It is no wonder that his style of change leadership was of interest to researchers.

Kim and Mauborgne studied Bratton's leadership successes. They soon realized that he was able to lead the police departments through successful change despite the four major hurdles they had identified in earlier research. They contend that change is often hindered by four hurdles faced by managers. They are, an embeddedness of the status quo, limited resources, demotivated staff and opposition from people with divergent invested interests. They were amazed that Bratton was able to overcome all of these hurdles in a very short period of time. His methods became central to their work on leading change.[22] Their own words describe the theory best:

> The theory of tipping points, which has its roots in epidemiology, is well known; it hinges on the insight that in any organization, once the beliefs and energies of a critical mass of people are engaged, conversion to a new idea will spread like an epidemic, bringing about fundamental change very quickly. The theory suggests that such a movement can be unleashed only by agents who make unforgettable and unarguable calls for change, who concentrate their resources on what really matters, who mobilize the commitment of the organization's key players, and who succeed in silencing the most vocal naysayers.[23]

Kim and Mauborgne developed a theory of change leadership that promises to bring about 'rapid, dramatic and lasting change with limited resources'.[24] They suggest that this can be accomplished by overcoming the four most common hurdles faced by those wishing to lead change. A short description of these hurdles and some helpful hints are provided below.

The Cognitive Hurdle: According to Kim and Mauborgne, many change initiatives fail because those charged with carrying out the change simply don't see the reason for change. Simply stating, 'change needs to happen' isn't enough. People need to come face to face with the problem. This means putting managers in front of customers and operational problems. For example, when Bratton was charged with turning around the New York City Transit Police, he discovered that none of the staff officers rode the subway. In order to make sure the need for change was 'in their face', he insisted that all transit police officials, including himself, use the subway to work and all meetings. The problems became very real to the officers quite quickly.

Kim and Mauborgne suggest similar tactics for leaders wishing to enact rapid change. This translates into very real experiences, with very real customers and front-line workers, for managers and higher-ups who may not truly understand the need for change.

The Resource Hurdle: After the need for change becomes apparent (by overcoming the cognitive hurdle), the next challenge is that of resources. Very rarely do organizations possess the resources they need to actualize the change. Kim and Mauborgne contend that most managers when faced with resource constraints do one of two things – they either ratchet down their expectations of change and accept mediocrity, or they begin a lengthy and often unsuccessful battle for more resources with shareholders and bankers. What is interesting about Bratton is he was able to achieve large-scale change without additional resources. According to Tipping Point theory, extra resources are not required. Great leaders of change, like Bratton, merely concentrate resources where they are needed and where the payoffs are the greatest.

Careful analysis of police procedures led to the conclusion that a lot of policing time was wasted by processing arrests. It took almost 16 hours for a police officer to book a suspect and file the appropriate paperwork. Clearly, this was not a great use of police hours. After making some adjustments, Bratton was able to cut processing time to one hour. Now he had 15 police hours to redistribute to where it was most needed.

The Motivational Hurdle: Overcoming this hurdle is crucial to success. Employees must not only understand the need for change and have the resources to make the change, they must want to make the change. Bratton's strategy was to identify the individuals with the most influence in the organization – not based only on positional power but based on influence, ability to persuade and the ability to block access to resources. He likened them to the kingpins in bowling, 'When you hit them just right, all the pins topple over'.[25] After identifying the 'kingpins', Bratton's strategy was to put them in the spotlight, giving them responsibility for change, making them accountable for change within their own departments and requiring that they report on their success and failures publicly. Hand in hand with this strategy was the use of specific goals and targets. In essence, Bratton was making monumental change possible and manageable through the use of smaller-scale goals.

The Political Hurdle: Very often in organizations, attempts to lead change are stymied by competing interests. This is the essence of the political hurdle. As change becomes more probable and imminent, those opposed to the change due to the impacts of the change on their own interests typically become more vocal and will fight harder to protect their interests. Bratton's strategy, and the one advocated by Kim and Mauborgne, is to identify the potential naysayers and to silence them early in the change process. This sounds ominous and is reminiscent of something from the *Godfather* movies. However, the intent here is not as dark as it may at first appear. Although Bratton wasn't against dismissing those vehemently opposed to the change, he also developed strategies for getting internal and external support by building powerful coalitions. Those who were not part of these powerful coalitions were isolated by their resistance to the change. This significantly reduced the power of the voices of resistance.

This theory is among the first to address the challenges that occur when organizational members resist the change, although the resistance to change literature is certainly not new. The following section will deal with this important issue.

Overcoming resistance to change

Resistance to change has been an important area of inquiry for decades. In fact, the importance placed on this issue might lead one to believe that resistance is inevitable when change is being implemented. Newer research indicates that this isn't always so. On the contrary, some people embrace change and become bored and uninterested if change isn't imminent! Some researchers argue that the younger generations of workers (after the baby-boomers) are more used to a constant rate of change, are more adept at change and actually expect to be moving forward constantly. Despite this, resistance to change can and does occur – just not all the time by everybody. Given that resistance to change can be a very real problem for those leading change, we'll look at some of the causes of resistance and ways to overcome them.

Patrick Connor and Linda Lake argue that:

> People tend to resist change or alterations of the status quo. This resistance is broader than simple opposition to a particular change; more widespread than a particular group's or individual's refusal to accept a specific change. There is simply the wish in most people to maintain the consistency and comfort that the status quo holds. This generalized resistance to change stems from a variety of sources. We have categorized these causes or sources into three groups: Barriers to understanding, barriers to acceptance, and barriers to acting.[26]

Although their theory of resistance is one of the many that seem to indicate all people will resist change all of the time, their framework is still quite helpful. It creates a framework for understanding why resistance may be happening, when it does, in fact, happen. A brief description of each of the groups follows.

Barriers to understanding

This occurs when followers, or targets as Connor and Lake call them, do not understand the need for change, the details of the change and/or how the change might impact the individual. This barrier may be the result of poor communication from those leading the change, intellect or language use.

Barriers to acceptance

This happens when followers simply refuse to accept the change and usually occurs when the follower is feeling threatened by the change in some way. They might fear a loss of power, a threat to their self-confidence or they may simply resist change because it takes them out of their 'comfort zone'.

Barriers to acting

Sometimes the resistance to change occurs because followers are simply not equipped to make the changes. They may not possess the skills, abilities or resources required. Other reasons for this barrier to change include habit and convention, called organizational inertia by Connor and Lake.

By understanding the underlying causes of resistance, leaders are better equipped to overcome them. Once they move past the belief that people are negative, stubborn or 'not team players' to see what's really causing the resistance, they can address the issues and facilitate the change. Given the barriers just explained, here are some tips for reducing resistance to change:

- Communicate well and communicate often – People need to understand what is happening, why it is happening and how it will impact them. This means that an effective leader of change should make the reasons for change known, in a language that is accessible to all involved (no jargon, please). After people understand the reason for change, they need to understand what the change will look like, in operational not abstract terms, and how the change might impact their jobs. This communication needs to be ongoing throughout the process and should not be a 'one-off' at the launch of the change initiative. A commitment to the change and consistent messages about the change will reinforce the change behaviours and prevent the organizational inertia mentioned by Connor and Lake.
- Provide training to support the change – Very often when change is occurring, people fear that they will not be able to 'keep up'. Think about what it meant for a typist when organizations were switching to computers! Many simply feared that they wouldn't be able to use the new technology and would lose their jobs. Training on the new equipment would go a long way towards alleviating those fears. Soft skill training may also be necessary. For example, many organizations moved to

team-based structures in the 1990s. This meant an entirely new way of doing things for lots of people. Instead of working rather independently, employees had to work with others in interdependent relationships much of the time. This requires a whole new set of skills – interpersonal skills, teamwork skills and group decision-making skills to name a few.

- Reward changes in the right direction – It is important to set manageable goals and to reward them. This breaks mammoth change into manageable chunks, establishes accountability and creates a positive energy around the change. Too often, a change is 'rolled out' and all of the pieces are expected to fall into place. People are not held accountable, the change seems to be forgotten by the higher-ups and people slip back into their old routines – it is simply easier.

- Commit organizational resources to the change – Very often, especially after the major downsizing in the 1980s, employees are sceptical of change. They feel that somehow they must be being asked to do more with less. A commitment of organizational resources does two things. First, it demonstrates the organization's commitment to the change (putting their 'money where their mouth is'). Second, it helps to alleviate fears that employees are being asked to do more with less. Very often, organizations facing major change simply do not have additional resources to commit to the change. This is where Bratton's strategy of redirecting resources would be useful.

Must the leadership of change happen from the top?

In this section, we will address the second assumption made by most leadership theorists, as introduced in the beginning of the chapter. Indeed, all of the theories discussed so far in this chapter have made the assumption that those leading change are doing so from the top of the organizational hierarchy.

More recently in the organization change literature, theorists have been advocating the concept of change that is 'led from the middle'. Oren Harari is one such advocate. In a 1999 article in *Management Review*, he contends that middle-level management positions are really where the action is – or should be.[27] He suggests that middle-level managers are better placed to understand employees, customers and markets and are the ones doing the exciting things. He offers ten rules for leading change from the middle:

1 Let the customer drive the change process.
2 Develop standards, measurements, processes and rewards based on your customer feedback and follow-up discussions.
3 With rare exceptions, don't ask for permission.
4 Stand by your convictions and stay the course.
5 Make your moves quick, continuous and public.
6 Don't shirk from challenging sacred cows.

7　Act the part of a coach.
8　Demand some quick payoffs.
9　Embrace perpetual change by looking ahead to tomorrow's customer.
10　Stay ahead of change.[28]

Harari offers an interesting view of change and challenges the older notion that change has to start at the top – the very top. However, his suggestions still rely on the notion of positional power, as he is still suggesting that managers (just lower on the ladder) lead the change. Our next theory goes even further, acknowledging the ability of those not in management positions to lead organizational change.

Deborah Meyerson uses the term '*tempered radicals*' to describe *people in organizations who serve as quiet change advocates and start the change ball rolling from the middle – not the top*. In her book, *Tempered Radicals: How People Use Difference to Inspire Change at Work*, she further describes these individuals as 'people who want to fit in without selling out'.[29] She contends that people exist in organizations who remain outside of the mainstream organizational culture and these people, by staying true to their ideals, can bring about significant change. She uses as examples, visible minorities who make it their agenda to encourage workplace diversity by hiring other members of underrepresented groups, environmentalists who encourage green thinking by leading by example and creating awareness, and mothers and fathers who bring attention to and champion family-friendly policies, among others.

Although the nuances of leading change in this way are beyond the scope of this chapter, Meyerson's contribution to the leadership of change should not be overlooked. Indeed, many have taken up the 'tempered radical' banner and are using her suggestions to lead change in their organizations.

Leaders as sensemakers of change

Regardless of positional power and from whence the leaders lead, it can be argued that leaders of change are sensemakers of change.[30] According to Parry and Bryman, 'Leadership is seen as a process whereby the leader identifies for subordinates a sense of what is important – defining organizational reality for others. The leader gives a sense of direction and of purpose through the articulation of a compelling worldview'.[31] Although it appears that Parry and Bryman are speaking of leadership from on high, the same could be said for leaders throughout the organization. The single mother who challenges assumptions about commitment levels of single parents and their abilities to perform; the homosexual who encourages debate and brings to light latent biases and prejudice, thus creating a more open and accepting workplace; and the environmentalist who puts a green bin under everyone's desk are all leading change through sensemaking – identifying what is important and providing a way forward.

End of chapter questions and exercises

1   Do an Internet search of *HealthSouth Corporation*. What has happened since Mr. Scrushy's conviction? How has the organization evolved and who has led the changes?

2   Find three news articles about newly appointed CEOs, CFOs or presidents. Scan all three for the newly appointed individuals' 'selling features'. Which traits or behaviours are used to convince readers and shareholders that the new appointment is a good one? How does this fit with the theories of leadership discussed in this chapter?

3   Do an Internet search of Deborah Meyerson's tempered radicals. How might you become a tempered radical? Which values and principles would you like to promote in an organization?

4   Think about a change in your history that you may have resisted. Why did you resist? Which of the categories of resistance would your resistance fit? How might the person requesting the change have overcome your resistance?

5   Identify someone who you feel is or was a transformational leader. What makes them a transformational leader? Describe their traits and behaviours.

6   Who were/are the leaders in your life? Which types of leaders were they?

7   Do an Internet search on Branch Ricky and the Brooklyn Dodgers. How did Branch Ricky lead change? What was his strategy? Discuss other types of social change that you feel are required. How might change be accomplished?

9 Power and resistance

Objectives of this chapter

By the end of this chapter, you should:

1 Understand the importance of power in the process of organizational change
2 Be familiar with the different perspectives of organizational power and resistance
3 Be critically aware of the relationship between power and resistance in organizations
4 Identify different uses of power across selected change approaches
5 Be able to critically assess the relevant models and theories of power and resistance in adopting different change strategies

Power and resistance at *Nova Scotia Power*[1]

In the mid-1980s, *Nova Scotia Power* was a company that was run according to a combination of hierarchical and expert power. Professional engineers dominated the ranks of management at all levels and ran the company along strict reporting rules. The focus was on building and maintaining a technically advanced organization that served the needs of the population of Nova Scotia. That was the situation when Louis Comeau took over the company as its Chief Executive Officer (CEO).

However, what Comeau found was that little attention had been paid to the various human elements that constitute an effective organization, including employee morale, customer satisfaction and the needs of key stakeholders (the Nova Scotia government, voters, special interest groups). Instead, formal, structural rules had been enacted to deal with these various issues. It was assumed that a focus on technical expertise would take care of customer satisfaction and the voters' sense of value for money. If the voters were happy the government would be happy. A number of recent mergers of smaller power companies throughout the province had also been dealt with through a series of new rules and structures that linked the various units through expanded roles and reporting chains.

Nonetheless, Comeau gained the strong impression that things just weren't working. The newly merged company seemed like a collection of different organizations under one umbrella, each with its own way of doing things, its own organizational culture. The outcome was an organization that lacked a unified sense of direction. Morale also seemed bad and customer/voter satisfaction were low. Subsequent surveys, initiated by Comeau, confirmed that customers saw *Nova Scotia Power* as one big construction company (they were always building new plants) that was somewhat removed from electrical supply; employees saw management as remote and uncaring; voters saw a company that had continually pushed up rates without adequate explanation or obvious improvements. Whatever the truth or otherwise of these perceptions, surveys confirmed that they were strong perceptions that were influencing how people at all levels felt about the company.

Seeking an answer to these problems, Comeau turned to consultants to help him to introduce culture change into the company. It had worked at industry leader *Florida Power & Light* and at many local companies, including *Maritime Telephone & Telegraph* (*MT&T*). The new culture change programme introduced a mission statement built around four core values of valuing the employees, the Province, the customer and the environment. These values were introduced through the existing hierarchical system, with employees being informed that they would be trained in the new culture change. The system broke down when managers were given four-day training programmes, while employees were only offered one-day training. The disparity in time allotments was not purely symbolic. Time away for training was time away from the normal work routines and served as a break. The employees of the heavily unionized Cape Breton area responded to the structural and hierarchical introduction of the new values by walking out of the sessions.

Eventually, by working to build trust and by breaking down many of the symbols of hierarchy (separate canteens for workers and managers were ended; the colours of hard hats changed from white and yellow, for managers and employees respectively, to yellow only), the culture began to take hold with a fair degree of employee buy-in.

In the early 1990s, *Nova Scotia Power* was privatized and gained a new powerful stakeholder – the shareholders. New imperatives were introduced – efficiency and profitability – and shaped the organization once again. This time Comeau drew on the newly popular Business Process Re-engineering (BPR) to help his company meet the new demands. Once again the company was structurally driven, with a whole series of tasks being reorganized around key processes. For example, the jobs of meter reading, meter installation and bill collecting were all seen as aspects of customer contact and made into one new position, that of Customer Service Field Representative (CSFR): the new CSFR people were trained to undertake all three tasks. Unlike the early 1980s, the new structural changes were supported with training programmes designed to build commitment to BPR. Employees and managers who did buy in found themselves leading important aspects of the BPR process and, as a result, some form of promotion. Other employees fared less well as the company began its first ever series of large-scale lay-offs.

At the start of the twenty-first century the company introduced the Balanced Scorecard, complete with a new round of training protocols. The language and the zeal matched that of the introduction of culture change in the 1980s and BPR in the 1990s. Nothing had changed except the people and the cheerleaders as *Nova Scotia Power* gained a reputation not only as a highly competitive power company but also as a successful serial change organization.

Power is rarely, if ever, discussed in the management of change literature.[2] Resistance, on the other hand, has a longer history within studies of change, where it was seen as an illegitimate reaction to management decisions.[3]

It is assumed that power is some*thing* that resides with senior management, major shareholders and/or other stakeholders (e.g. government officials, boards of directors etc.). This notion of power, as a thing, has a long-established history that has provided management scholars with a legitimate framework to assume that power was structural, i.e. resided in the position of the power holder, but also involved psychological elements. As we shall discuss below, an understanding of power is vitally important for understanding the processes of organizational change because such processes are rarely successful if they rely solely, or largely, on appeal to authority; they usually require more detailed attempts to deal with the underlying and contextual psychological factors involved. As we have seen in the preceding chapters, different change approaches have balanced the structural and psychological elements of power in different ways. The various continuous-quality approaches of Total Quality Management (TQM), Business Process Re-engineering (BPR), Six Sigma and the Balanced Scorecard (Chapters 6 and 7), for example, rely very heavily on centralized decision-making and structural solutions to introduce and shape the process. Once the decision has been made and structures are under way, training methods are used to encourage buy-in from managers, front-line supervisors and then employees. OD, Culture Change and the Learning Organization (Chapters 3–5), on the other hand, vary in the extent to which they attempt to bring out change through psychological buy-in, through improved jobs, participation in decision-making, or changing values, beliefs and symbols. In each case an appreciation of power is needed to manage or resist the processes that are being implemented. In the *Nova Scotia Power* case culture change was built around four values designed by a paid consultant in consultation with senior management. Employees were then trained in the values and were expected to espouse and enact them. The problem came when union employees interpreted the culture change through how it was *done* (structurally and with little consultation) rather than what it was trying to *say* (i.e. 'we value employees'). The company was using a method of exercising power that was inconsistent with the new culture that they were trying to build and which was to be based on valuing employees by taking their issues and concerns into account.

Antecedent theories of power

Power can be defined as '*the control that a person has over other people [through] the ability to exact compliance or obedience to his or her will*'.[4] But how do people get power and what does that tell us about change?

Machiavelli, the medieval Italian political philosopher, saw power as some-*thing* to possess, a form of centralized power that gave those with it the ability to control and manipulate others.[5] Indeed, Machiavelli can be read as suggesting that power is not only something that is possessed by the powerful but that some elements of power are generated through the art of manipulation and control. While there has been some discussion of Machiavellian use of power throughout the management literature it is usually negative. Nonetheless, there are numerous examples of organizational leaders who have used this type of approach to effect change, and whether they are successful or not may well depend on the extent to which they are able to manipulate and control people.[6] The problem with this approach is that the chance of buy-in is very limited if employees feel that they are simply being told what to do or, worse, feel that they are being manipulated. If there is a moral here it is a negative one – be very good at impression management!

Thomas Hobbes, the English philosopher of the seventeenth century, also viewed power as central but broadened the notion to see it as control through consensus or contractual agreement.[7] From this perspective, power can be limited and limiting where people feel that it is simply imposed. According to Hobbes, the use of power is more effective where people come to see it as ultimately based on agreement of all to obey a single or selected power holder. By the same token the exercise of power needs to be seen as in the broad interests of everyone involved. From this perspective, change would need to be seen as something that needed to be 'sold' to those directly involved, and sold in a way that appears to be in their interests, as in 'the company's interest'. But Hobbes was thinking of non-elected political leaders and the need to convince people that such rule should be viewed as ultimately based on an unwritten contractual obligation rather than some divine right. In other words, political leaders would appeal to some underlining rationale of leadership rather than divine right. It was left to the German sociologist, Max Weber, some centuries later, not only to translate this into organizational power but also to explain the bases of obedience.

Weber argued that power was at the heart of the modern organization and ultimately managers can enforce compliance based on their ability to hire and fire those in their employ. Such 'power is about getting someone to do something irrespective of their desire to do it'.[8] However, Weber was interested in those forms of power that encouraged people to comply, or 'obey', because they wanted to – he referred to this as 'authority'. Ironically, its very effect is to mask and mediate the underlying power of the organization through layers of authority – that way making it very effective. Indeed, he argued that the bedrock of modern (bureaucratic) organization is acceptance of 'legitimate' authority through a psychological contract where people agree to accept the rules of the game so long as those rules are perceived as fair (i.e. free of patronage and other subjective decisions) and providing of opportunity for others to gain some level of power through authority.[9] Legitimate power assumes some element of psychological acceptance of the power holder, and arguably this is essential for the functioning of modern-day businesses. Weber was interested in why people obey and what gives authority its legitimacy. To answer this question he traced the history of power through three main forms of legitimacy – traditional, charismatic and rational-legal.

Traditional obedience rests on established belief in the sanctity of traditions and the unquestionable right and status of those who exercise authority under those traditions. A modern-day example can be seen in the power given to some religious leaders by their followers. In such cases, change may be less problematic where the leader's appeal rests in an unquestioned divine right to speak for the organization. Its limits, however, may hinge on whether the change flies in the face of tradition and encourages people to question the leader's traditional power. When Pope John XXIII, for example, introduced wide-ranging changes in the Catholic Church in 1962 there were some who saw those changes as being so radical as to question the very basis of his divine right to speak for the Church.[10] Despite the fact that John XXIII did not live to see many of his changes come to fruition some groups questioned his leadership, in particular Sedevacantist and Conclavist groups. These groups went so far as to accuse John XXIII of being an antipope and a secret Freemason.[11] Beyond these small but important constituencies there were many conservative voices that saw these changes as moving the Catholic Church away from the position that it is the one and only true Christian Church, that the Bible is historically inerrant and the Church's emphasis on Death, Judgement, Heaven and Hell.[12] If we return to our opening *Nova Scotia Power* case we can see that, even in bureaucratic organizations, an element of tradition can creep in. In the early to mid-1980s, senior management at *Nova Scotia Power* exercised their authority but with little attempt to deal with the psychological aspects of control. In many ways they expected obedience not because of the fairness of the system but because it is the manager's right (i.e. traditional right) to manage.

Charismatic obedience rests on some form of attraction to the sanctity, heroism or exemplary character of an individual. Hitler provides a powerful but negative image of a charismatic leader that people followed by dint of his personality.[13] Within the change literature there are numerous stories of leaders whose position as CEO enabled them to initiate change but whose charismatic personality allowed them to carry people with them in their enthusiasm for change. Jack Welch is one such example. The lesson for change management would be that top managers should not only be seen to be implementing the changes but also to have a passion and enthusiasm for those changes. As it is often said of Jack Welch, he was 'nuts' for Six Sigma and is credited with being a powerful influence on *GE* and the implementation of Six Sigma. At *Nova Scotia Power* many credit the charisma of Louis Comeau for introducing culture change in a highly resistant organizational culture. In the beginning there were many managers as well as employees who were resistant to change. For unionized employees, for example, the managers might be remote and even authoritarian at times, but at least they knew who they were and what interests they represented (i.e. the company's, not the employees'). Drawing on his charismatic personality Comeau was able to gain sufficient momentum to make the changes and get others to push them through.

Rational-legal obedience rests on a belief in the 'legality', fairness, and rationality (i.e. it makes sense) of a set of rules, and in the right of those implementing the rules to issue commands. According to Weber, as society developed from a traditional to a modern world, we moved from beliefs based in myth, magic and mysticism to one where we valued scientific explanations. We moved from a worldview based on fate and tradition to one where we make rational calculations about our life chances. We moved from acceptance of what we were told to acceptance of something because it was fair. These values all come into play in the modern bureaucratic organization. Through competitive ranks and offices we engage in a system that more or less appears fair because we can get a job and rise on merit rather than on favouritism or patronage. We also know that, through competitive exams, interviews, credentials and other 'objective' factors, we have an opportunity to rise up the ranks and become a senior manager. Thus, we are willing to accept the authority of a whole number of office holders because we know that they obtained the position in a 'fair' way and are operating within a system of rules that are also fair and objective. The process is both rational and part of the broader sets of legal rules that govern commerce. Much of this thinking has been incorporated into standard management approaches but is more geared to stable and routine functions than to techniques of change.[14] However, in terms of change, this at least alerts us to the fact that people are more likely to respond to calls for buy-in and commitment where they feel that the process is fair and legitimate. But it also alerts us to the fact that people's sense of fairness and legitimacy may also be context-specific. For example, towards the end of the 1990s, *Air Canada*, although a stock-holding company, came under government pressure to take over its ailing rival *Canadian Airways*. Both airways operated a system of seniority (i.e. number of years, months and days employed by the airline), which governed many important aspects of employees' working lives. For example, if and when there were lay-offs – and there have been many in the twenty-first century – people with the least seniority would be laid off first. Given that airlines have to operate all year round, both *Air Canada* and *Canadian* had a system of bidding for holidays, where the most senior employees in each category got to bid first. For airline captains the planes they get to fly were also determined by seniority. However, when *Air Canada* finally took over *Canadian Airlines* they merged the seniority of both sets of employees, with serious consequences that have led to problems ever since. This meant that a number of *Air Canada* employees with considerable seniority and expectations of job security, holiday privileges or promotion found themselves much lower down the seniority rankings as former *Canadian Airlines'* employees moved ahead of them in the newly merged company. Thus, while the system of seniority was seen as fair by all employees, the changes in who counted as senior following the merger were seen as unfair by a number of *Air Canada* employees. This has resulted in some bad feelings and demoralization ever since.[15] At *Nova Scotia Power* we can also see that structural routines and changes need to take account of the psychological perception of fairness and rationality. In the mid-1980s, the exercise of authority was not enough to gain more than a perfunctory acceptance of the system. It took a lot of work and a reiteration of core values by Louis Comeau to convince people that there was potentially something fair about rational-legal bureaucracy.

Unlike Weber, two other nineteenth-century sociologists of work and power – Emile Durkheim and Karl Marx – have been neglected by management theory, but for very different reasons. Durkheim was likely ignored because of his focus on small-scale organization as a solution to social integration. Marx was clearly ignored because of his widespread critique of capitalism and the association of his work with communism.[16]

Emile Durkheim suggested that power rested, in part, on acceptance of the rules of social life. Social control – a form of decentralized power – helps us to make sense of the world and feel part of it. Too little social control results in 'anomie' – an inability to understand or associate with the rules of life. But too much social control – as in a strict military regime – can have a similar effect by robbing us of our individuality and thus our ability to react to change.[17]

Durkheim believed that at work, as well as in other communities, we should pay attention to the power of rules and their influence on our sense of self and wellbeing. Durkheim felt that modern organization had the ability to contribute to a sense of wellbeing where the broad rules of the organization provide a sense of guidance, purpose and control to people. Here the concern is with social life, the individual and stability, which perhaps explain why Durkheim's approach was not taken very far in the management and change literatures. Nonetheless, there was an attempt to apply some of the lessons of this approach in the Hawthorne Works of *Western Electric* in the 1920s and 1930s. These studies became known as the Hawthorne Studies.

Basically, the Hawthorne Studies involved a series of experiments, observations and other approaches to the study of behaviour at work. The management theorists involved[18] suggested that the modern organization could serve to integrate people into society. They argued that social solidarity (i.e. feelings of connectedness) could be built inside an organization in ways that would help that organization. Providing people with the opportunity to develop social relations at work could be channelled through (company-appointed and trained) 'informal' leaders in the achievement of the organization's goals.[19] The focus of this research, however, was to affect change that would improve the company's bottom line, and social integration was a means to that end. This may explain why critics have described the Hawthorne Studies as manipulative and intrusive in people's lives.[20] In recent years, some of these insights have appeared in studies of organizational culture and the need to develop strong value systems within an organization. Indeed much of the organizational culture debate has been about encouraging senior managers to develop an organization culture that provides employees with implicit direction and commitment that will provide measures of control through values and beliefs. This much was clear in the *Nova Scotia Power* case and the introduction of culture change.

The work of Marx has been neglected for a number of reasons[21] but primarily because of his revolutionary critique of capitalism and, what he called the 'exploitative' nature of the capitalist relations of production.[22] Nonetheless, much of what he had to say about power often mirrors what is implicit in management theory, that power is controlled by elites whose power rests on economic and ideological bases, i.e. that power – control of human and material resources – depends on economic ownership and the ability to influence ideas through such things as the media, education, religion, etc. This suggests that the management of change ultimately rests on the economic power of the company and its top managers but its effectiveness will depend on how well those managers are able to bring their influence to bear to make the changes seem palatable. Unlike culture change, which is often directed at values and beliefs, BPR and TQM programmes are more likely to reveal power in the senior managers' ability to make sweeping changes not just to the overall structures but in the various ways that tasks are constructed and carried out. However, even proponents of BPR and TQM recognize that these programmes have to be justified and explained to those who will implement them. This usually comes in the form of training that is imbued with a strong ideological content about the value and importance of TQM and/or BPR. When *Nova Scotia Power* introduced BPR in the 1990s, senior management realized that the underlying philosophy (of efficiency and streamlining) would clash with the previous culture change and its focus on values. To that end, the company went to great lengths to call the introduction of BPR the next – 'efficiency' – stage of the culture change. In other words, the company suggested that it would retain and add a value to the existing four values – the new value spoke of valuing the shareholders. The gains of the new culture were now to provide the much-needed strength to gain greater efficiencies for a competitive market. Unfortunately the laying off of over five hundred of sixteen hundred employees did more to strengthen the impression of the exercise of power than any genuine concerns with the psychological concerns of the employees.[23]

Resistance and power in theories of organization and change

Prior to the Second World War, with mass unemployment throughout Western society, senior managers tended to operate with a simple carrot and stick approach. Employees were expected to do what they were told or be fired. Rewards were often based on scientific management or Taylorist principles, where extra payments or 'incentives' were linked to improved performance.[24] This form of management, based largely on the explicit exercise of power and authority, was in part linked to the rise of industrial unionism in the United States and the outbreak of violent unrest across a number of major companies, as employers used force to quash the newly established Congress of Industrial Organizations (CIO).[25] Nonetheless, some of the problems of this form of managing were being identified by the emerging human relations theorists in the late 1920s and early 1930s who argued for socio-psychological and psychological methods for dealing with employee motivation and acceptance of change. One of the central findings from the Hawthorne Studies, for example, was the fact that employees could be encouraged to accept management decisions if they were made to feel part of the organization and were given appropriate leadership.[26]

Following the Second World War, attention shifted within management theory to finding ways to overcome employee resistance to change through psychological and social psychological strategies. An early approach was to involve employees in the decision-making of the change process.[27] This 'employee participation' approach, however, was cautious and only involved the employees in one small routine stage of the overall decision-making process and attempts to reproduce the study with unionized employees produced different results.[28] In the earlier study, there was evidence that the employees were more willing to engage in change if they were consulted on some of the process but in the latter study the employees continued to resist change despite the offer of involvement in the change-making decision. In these and similar studies, the magnitude of the change was quite small, involving small product and/or production changes. These studies were usually of unskilled or, at best, semi-skilled, industrial workers involved in fairly routine tasks.

In the 1960s, there was a considerable move to build on the employee participation approach throughout Western Europe but at the same time there was a dramatic shift towards structural away from psychological solutions as employers adopted a 'worker participation' approach. In this approach, major companies across Western Europe attempted to involve employees in decision-making, usually through the election of union representatives to serve on company boards.[29]

The five bases of power

Towards the onset of the 1960s, John French and his colleagues switched their attention not from resistance but to include power in our understanding of change processes. They came up with the now classic 'bases of power' which argued that there are five areas where people gain some form of power in organizations – legitimate, reward, punishment, expertise and referent. *Legitimate power refers to the power that someone gains as a result of the office they hold.* Thus, a senior manager or CEO has power by dint of their appointment to the office of CEO or senior manager. The power is referential, which means that people respond to the role and generally accept the right of the person to exercise their authority because of their rank or designation. However, behind acceptance of legitimate power is the knowledge that the person has the ability to *reward* or *punish* people. Not all those with legitimate power have the ability to reward or punish. Some managers have neither. They are just administrators who rely on people to obey them by dint of their title. Some managers may be able to discipline employees but have little discretion to reward others. Some managers, however, may have discretionary power to reward people (and hence punish them by not rewarding them). Thus, some managers may have extra bases of power that increases their power.

Expert power refers to the fact that some people – managers and employees alike – may be able to control information because of their specific knowledge and training. Some groups of employees, for example, may be easier to get rid of because they can be replaced with new people who have little or no training. Other groups are harder to replace and thus gain power as a result. In an airline company, it would be far easier to replace a catering employee than a pilot for example. Pilots are well paid in most airlines not only because they do an important and responsible job but also because they are difficult to recruit and hard to replace. Their expert knowledge gives them power over an important aspect of a company's operation.

Finally, *referent power refers to what Weber called charismatic authority*. Here it is through the power of personality that people come to do things for the charismatic person. They gain some kind of trust and guidance through the personality of the person with referent power. That power may be associated with legitimate power as in the case of Jack Welch and Louis Comeau, but it may be with an employee representative, union leader or even informal or unofficial spokesperson who is able to convince people to resist some aspect of the company's policy. A good example of this can be seen in the movie *Norma Rae* where an informal leader is removed from the factory where she works. As security police are escorting her from the factory she stands on a table and holds up a sign that says 'UNION'. Slowly but surely, the rest of the workers respond by turning off their machines in an act of solidarity. They are responding not to the fact that she is an unofficial union organizer but to her sheer force of personality.

Kanter's notion of organizational power

French and Raven's approach was important in pointing out different aspects of organizational power but failed to contextualize those bases or explain how they could be utilized. Rosabeth Moss Kanter, on the other hand, explains how managerial power develops and is maintained. For Kanter, organizational power is 'the ability to mobilize resources (human and material) to get things down'.[30] She begins with the question, 'where does power come from?' And answers that power evolves from two kinds of capacity:

1 Access to the resources, information and support necessary to carry out a task.
2 The ability to get cooperation in doing what is necessary.

These capacities derive from a leader's location in the formal and informal systems of the organization – in both job definition and in connection to other important people in the organization. Looking at this in practice, Kanter argues that there are three main sources of organizational power:

1 *Lines of supply* Influence outward, over the environment, means that managers have the capacity to bring in the things that their own organizational domain needs – materials, money, resources to distribute as rewards and perhaps even prestige. (This is a form of reward power.)
2 *Lines of information* To be effective, managers need to be 'in the know' in both the formal and informal sense.
3 *Lines of support* In a formal framework, a manager's job parameters need to allow for non-ordinary action, for a show of discretion or exercise of judgement. Thus, managers need to know that they can assume innovative, risk-taking activities without having to go through the stifling multilayered approval process. And, informally, managers need the

backing of other important figures in the organization whose tacit approval becomes another resource they bring to their own work, as well as a sign of the manager's being 'in'.

Breaking this down further we can see that power relies upon job activities and political alliances. In Kanter's words, 'Power is most easily accumulated when one has a job that is designed and located to allow *discretion* (non-routinized action permitting flexible, adaptive, and creative contributions), *recognition* (visibility and notice), and *relevance* (being central to pressing organizational problems)'.[31] For Kanter,

> Power also comes when one has relatively close contact with spon-sors (higher-level people who confer approval, prestige or backing), peer networks (circles of acquaintanceship that provide reputation and information, the grapevine often being faster than formal communica-tion channels) and subordinates (who can be developed to relieve man-agers of some of the burdens and to represent the manager's point of view).[32]

Empowerment

Kanter is not only concerned with power and its bases but also with arguing that power should be distributed more equitably around an organization. It is her argument that the concentration of power in a few hands is not likely to be healthy for the organization; that *powerlessness* breeds discontent and contempt: 'Powerlessness . . . tends to breed bossiness rather than true leader-ship. In large organizations, at least, it is powerlessness that often creates ineffective, desultory management and petty, dictatorial, rules-minded man-agerial styles'.[33] Kanter goes on to argue for empowerment. It is her conten-tion that organizational power can actually grow, in part, by being shared: 'Delegation does not mean abdication'.[34] She continues that, 'More powerful leaders are also more likely to delegate (they are too busy to do it all them-selves) to get things done'. Thus, 'people with the tools, information and support to make more informed decisions and act more quickly can often accomplish more. By empowering others, a leader does not decrease his/her power; instead s/he may increase it – especially if the whole organization performs better'.[35] She concludes that, 'the true sign of power . . . is accomplishment – not fear, terror, or tyranny'.[36]

Kanter's approach has various implications for change management. For one thing, to effect change it is important for senior management to provide their change agents with access to human and material resources, support, information and the creation of formal and informal networks that simul-taneously generate support and information. This seems to be recognized by those implementing BPR and TQM. When *Nova Scotia Power* introduced BPR they selected 'champions' from managers and staff to form teams around the various processes. Those teams were empowered to lead the change and keep everyone appraised of the situation. On the other hand, the overall change process also led to the disempowering of existing managers and departments that now became less central to the new processes and structures. At *Nova Scotia Power* two rounds of large-scale lay-offs may have served to deal with the problem through resorting to more obvious sources of power but clearly this approach can cause more problems than it overcomes by encouraging fear and morale problems among remaining employees.

Since the start of the 1990s, empowerment has been a popular way of dealing with change. According to a *Fortune* magazine poll of CEOs at the time virtually all of them said that they shared power more than they did five years previously, and more than their predecessors.[37] The common view was that today's workforce couldn't be managed in the old 'military command-and-control model'. Senior managers need 'to set a strategic direction, get [employees] to agree, give them money and authority, and leave them alone'.[38]

A shift to personal power also started around this time, with *Fortune* magazine arguing that the 'better the leader . . . the more likely he is to reply on the personal sources of power'.[39] The power to punish is the one least likely to be used and only as a last resort. However, the power to reward can be more difficult in corporations that have flattened (i.e. removed layers of hierarchy) their organization, and where there are formalized compensation systems and fewer promotions to hand out.[40] Similarly, empowerment needs some skilful introduction. For one thing, it can be difficult to find people who are willing to take on the extra responsibilities implied in empowerment. For another thing, there can be a shift to renewed emphasis on formal planning alongside decentralization of power, contextualizing empowerment in an increasingly bureaucratized environment. In a flatter organization, empowerment can be experienced as remote as the span of control increases, and empowerment does not necessarily lead to increased communication. More tellingly, strategies of empowerment often ultimately rest on bottom-line results. As one business analyst succinctly puts it: 'Share power, and if profits go up everyone will praise the brilliant way you unleashed the latent energy of your people . . . But if profit goes down, everyone will condemn the sloppy way you lost control of the company. In this world, all that you can do by way of empowerment, teamwork, and participation can't change one central fact: When it comes to power, the bottom line in the bottom line'.[41]

New approaches to power

In recent years the works of Foucault and Weick have garnered attention in the change literature. Michel Foucault, a French philosopher, has argued that power is diffuse and not centralized.[42] It owes its source to 'knowledge' that is generated through discourses. Karl Weick, an American social psychologist, suggests that power depends on a series of socio-psychological properties involved in every organizational decision-making process.

The power of discourse

A discourse can be seen as a set of ideas and viewpoints that arise out of but also inform a set of related practices and are experienced as 'knowledge'. For example, prior to the 1980s, *Nova Scotia Power* had few women employees and none on the Board of Directors. What women the company did employ were in relatively unskilled or routine jobs.[43] The fact that men were considered more suitable for leadership and most skilled jobs was a powerful discourse that was reinforced by the actual practices of the company. It likely did not hit those involved as a prejudicial viewpoint but a 'natural' thing – common knowledge, something that 'we all know'. By the mid-1990s, the company was reflecting a new discourse of employment equity throughout its practices and corporate materials. If the practices still lagged far behind the words, it nonetheless had the feel of a set of ideas embedded in knowledge.[44]

According to Foucault, power is related to 'knowledge' and where we stand in relationship to it. It also has several layers to it. Thus, for example, when Louis Comeau was seeking solutions to his problems of low morale and poor perceptions of *Nova Scotia Power* he turned to culture change. It can be argued that the idea of culture change constituted a powerful discourse that was reinforced through myriad practices as companies across North America and Europe adopted culture change programmes (or at least called what they were doing 'culture change'). In one sense Comeau was exercising his power as CEO to adopt culture change but at another level it was already a powerful pre-existing option that led him to adopt it. In other words, he was a less powerful actor in his choices of adopting culture change or something else. True, he did have choices but he was strongly influenced by the knowledge that culture change was an important ingredient in company success. Once Comeau adopted culture change he needed to employ consultants to introduce and explain the process. In that case the consultants were knowledge experts and stood in a strong situation of power in regard to their understanding of the discourse of culture and change. There is evidence that within *Nova Scotia Power* most people bought into the idea that culture was some-*thing* that needed changing. Most, if not all, employees had heard of culture change – from books, newspapers and from other company practices. It was common knowledge. However, not everyone agreed with the changes. Those that embraced culture change tended to be more empowered while those who resisted were marginalized in the process, being seen as people resisting change. Similarly, when *Nova Scotia Power* introduced BPR many of those who embraced the change gained more power not simply because they gained leadership positions in the process but also because they were seen as having a great understanding and feel for the new discourse of change.[45]

One important lesson for change and resistance here is to recognize knowledge for what it is, the outcome of a series of practices and ideas that are constantly changing with time and challenges to its validity and viability. That could mean, for instance, resisting the introduction of a programme of change simply because it is popular and widespread. Or introducing it with the understanding that it represents a changing discourse that does not need to be reproduced in every detail. Hammer and Champy, best-selling authors of re-engineering, argue that seventy-five per cent of all attempts to introduce BPR is due to incorrect implementation.[46] Indeed, this is often how TQM and Six Sigma programmes are sold to companies: that if they don't implement it correctly it could likely fail. However, that assumes that something has only one way to be implemented and that success is possible in each case but only through complete implementation. It may be that the successful adoption of culture change, TQM, BPR, Six Sigma, or any other programme may be more about perceptions of the process and adaptation to local circumstances. The consultant hired by *Nova Scotia Power* to introduce the culture change had sold an identical programme to the *Nova Scotia Liquor Commission*, complete with a similar mission statement of values, which was prominently displayed in liquor stores throughout the province. However, there is a huge difference between a large power company and a series of liquor stores. If there is any link between culture change and organizational outcomes at *Nova Scotia Power* it is the enacted sense that Louis Comeau was able to impose on the company's impression management.

In terms of resistance, understanding the character of a discourse can provide opportunities for challenging some of the ideas and enacting a different sense of them. For example, in the early days of *Air Canada* (then operating as *Trans-Canada Airways*) the first flight attendants were women and were imaged by the company as flying hostesses. This was very much in line with a powerful discourse of gender at the time, which cast women as glamorous, short-term employees until they married. Women's role was to look good and get married. Lucille Garner, the woman employed to oversee the hiring of the flight attendants, was able to change some of the image towards one of the hard-working stewardess. She was able to trade on the notion of glamour by advertising the job as one that was looking for glamorous but hard-working young women. Eventually that idea became part of company thinking as it was embedded in their recruitment practices.[47] Similarly, senior managers may get around resistance by gearing some of the ideas and practices of change to local conditions. When *Nova Scotia Power* introduced BPR, instead of selling the programme as a revolutionary change to what the company had adopted before, they instead sold it as an extension of the previous culture change.

Power and sensemaking

The idea of power and resistance is implied rather than developed in Karl Weick's notion of organizational sensemaking.[48] Weick talks about *ongoing, social* and *enacted* senses of a situation that influence the way that people make sense of things. Social sensemaking refers to the influence of relevant groups (e.g. a professional association in the narrow sense or a prevalent social attitude in the broader sense). For example, when Louis Comeau was considering sweeping change at *Nova Scotia Power*, he was influenced by the fact that other large companies across various industries were arguing that culture change was the most important way to deal with organizational problems. When Comeau took over *Nova Scotia Power* he faced an ongoing sense of the company as a construction company, run by engineers and run on fairly hierarchical lines. To introduce change he first had to 'shock'[49] the system by hiring consultants to conduct a company-wide attitude survey. The survey didn't simply discover that employee morale and customer satisfaction were low, it also enacted it, i.e. it created a powerful sense of the company's environment, drawing on seemingly scientific and objective measures to establish the situation. This prepared the ground for the introduction of culture change, which, through a large-scale process of training and symbolism, helped to enact culture change. Enactment refers to the fact that a sense of a situation may initially involve various interpretations that are being discussed but eventually a particular view (or competing views) comes to dominate and influence how people understand the situation. In each case people are influenced by the power of social influence (something akin to a discourse), the dominance of an ongoing sense of a situation (people like to feel a sense of ontological security, i.e. they are reassured by sharing a similar view of things with other people),[50] and the fact that something is enacted (i.e. carries more weight because it is circulated through various written and oral pronouncements).

Weick also suggests that dominant ideas of things are powerful because they help people to make *retrospective sense* of what has happened. At *Nova Scotia Power* the introduction of culture change may have helped employees and managers alike to make sense retrospectively of the low morale and other events, which themselves were the products of retrospective sensemaking induced by surveys. Two other aspects of the social psychological process – *cues* and *plausibility* – also help to draw people to a particular enacted sense of reality. Social, ongoing and enacted senses draw attention to certain cues at the expense of others. Culture change, for example, encourages people to pay attention to such things as values and symbols, for example, and ignore other cues that may suggest that there are other ways of dealing with organizational problems. Ultimately, the power to convince someone of a sense of a situation depends on how plausible it is. To be plausible something has to be convincing because it fits in with existing knowledge (e.g. that culture change is an effective method of dealing with company-wide problems), or make a good case for challenging existing knowledge (e.g. that emphasis on cultural problems makes more sense than continuing to focus on technical expertise); that the argument is well structured (e.g. a good case is made for focusing on the 'human element' over other elements); and that the argument is legitimate (i.e. put forward by credible people, such as Louis Comeau and his senior management team).

Finally, Weick argues that a sense of situation is powerful where it meshes with the identity construction of those involved. This can ensure greater buy-in where those involved identify themselves with the projected sense. For example, the culture change at *Nova Scotia Power* allowed Louis Comeau and other managers to position themselves as cutting-edge leaders who were adopting state-of-the-art ideas. At a later stage, when the company adopted BPR, Comeau was able to link BPR to globalization to position himself as the leader of a forward-thinking company. Thus, change programmes stand to face problems where their presentation not only lacks plausibility but also undermines the identity construction of a critical mass or some of the key actors involved. This was the case at *Air Canada* where merger was accompanied by a seniority system that favoured a number of the merging *Canadian Airlines* over *Air Canada* employees. For those *Air Canada* employees not only did the argument lack plausibility (*Canadian Airlines* employees saved their jobs but retained their seniority despite the fact that they were from a defunct airline), it also undermined the identity construc-tions of those who gained a sense of self from their relative position in the seniority roles.

Weick's notion of sensemaking signals but doesn't deal with the influence of power on the sensemaking process. Yet it is clear that some people play more powerful roles in the enactment of ongoing, social and retrospective senses of a situation. It was Louis Comeau, for example, who commissioned surveys to discover low morale, and it was Comeau who introduced culture change and BPR. In the process it was senior managers and a number of supportive employees who helped to enact culture change and BPR on the situation. Beyond this it was the broader social sense of the significance of culture change that was a powerful influence but also helped to make it plausible for Comeau to adopt and enact.

End of chapter questions and exercises

1   Use an Internet and library search to find examples of organizations that have adopted widespread organizational change. Try to find at least one example each of culture change, TQM, BPR, Six Sigma, the Balanced Scorecard and any other approach not listed. Now undertake the follow-ing analysis:

   a   Identify the different strategies of power involved in each approach. Make notes on differences between the approaches in terms of the types of power utilized. What can we learn from this?

   b   What is the role of leadership in the various examples? Makes notes on the differences between different leadership styles and power. What can we learn from this?

2   Use an Internet and library search to find examples of Machiavellian styles of leadership. Make notes on how this style is discussed through-out news reports and scholarly accounts. What does this tell us about the

value and potential of the Machiavellian approach? Where is it more and where less effective?

3 Use an Internet and library search to find examples of organizational resistance. Try to find a range of examples drawing from scholarly discussions of resistance as well as news reports and cases. What are the most obvious examples of resistance and what are the least obvious? What can we learn from this? How are the different examples of resistance related to different exercises of power?

4 Review the chapters on OD, culture change, TQM and BPR, Six Sigma and the Balanced Scorecard. What forms of power are dominant in each and what can we learn from the differences?

5 Using French and Raven's five bases of power, explain how each major change programme could or should make use of each base of power to implement effective change.

6 Using Kanter's model of the bases of organizational power, explain how each major change programme could or should make use of each base of power to implement effective change.

7 Using Foucault's notion of discourse, explain how each major change programme could or should make use of discourse analysis to implement effective change.

8 Using Weick's sensemaking approach, explain how each major change programme could or should make use of the sensemaking properties to implement effective change.

9 Drawing on empirical examples, discuss situations where appeals to charismatic, traditional and/or rational legal authority are more likely to be effective in processes of change.

10 Diversity management

Objectives of this chapter:

By the end of this chapter, you should:

1 Understand what is meant by diversity management
2 Be familiar with the factors most often associated with diversity management success
3 Understand the difference between diversity management initiatives and equal opportunity or affirmative action programmes
4 Understand the criticality of management support for diversity initiatives
5 Understand the importance of measuring the success of diversity management initiatives
6 Be familiar with arguments for and against the implementation of diversity management initiatives

General electric aviation materials **sued for discrimination** [1]

On June 7, 2005 two issues that directly related to gender and diversity issues were being reported by *The New York Times*. The less controversial of the two stories was about *Lowe's* new strategy to appeal to female shoppers. The other story wasn't quite as rosy.

The New York Times reported that the Chief Executive of *GE Aviation Materials*, Marcel Thomas, was suing for racial discrimination. He contends that racial discrimination was not only the source of his own poor treatment (a low-performance evaluation and negligible performance-based compensation increase despite a large increase in his unit's sales), but that it was so pervasive within *GE* that a class action suit was warranted. Officials at *GE* insist that they have a comprehensive diversity programme and that African Americans are faring well within its ranks. They use statistics to support their defence: *GE* has seven black officers, up from four in 2001; two of its 11 business units are run by African Americans; and Marcel Thomas had been promoted three times since joining *GE* and currently earned a salary that ranked him 18th among 314 employees in his grade level.

Marcel Thomas also used statistics. They sang a different song: Only 3.6 per cent of the company's 4,500 junior executives, 4.9 per cent of its senior executives and 3.3 per cent of the officers are African American. Perhaps even more disturbing are the allegations that Mr. Thomas was retaliated against for bringing to light instances of race- and age-related discrimination.

How can companies who pride themselves on diversity initiatives become targets of racial discrimination suits? How can numbers serve as defences for organizations and fodder for lawsuits? Cases such as these are not unusual. As quoted from *The New York Times*, 'Experts in diversity say that, as corporate America becomes more welcoming of African Americans, such mutually exclusive reactions are becoming more common. They note that *GE* joins *Coca Cola, Kodak* and *Xerox* on a growing list of corporations that have been lauded by black organizations for their treatments of minorities, yet have been sued'.[2]

The opening vignette suggests that gender and diversity issues are about more than numbers. Indeed, numbers were used in the case of *GE* to both condemn and defend the organization. This leads us to conclude that the problem is a deeper and less obvious one. So should the fact that of the 71 business leaders discussed in the three major newspapers, only four were women.

The *Society for Human Resource Management* has declared diversity as one of the most important issues facing the human resources field.[3] Additionally, statistics show that more organizations than ever before are attempting to implement diversity initiatives for a variety of reasons.[4] Indeed, more than 75 per cent of *Fortune 1000* companies have instituted some sort of diversity initiative.[5] Some organizations wish to avoid legal remedies while others are cognizant of a moral imperative – doing it because it is right.[6] Several organizations are lured by the promise of financial benefits and others are simply aware that the demographic makeup of the workforce is becoming more and more diverse – the demographic imperative.[7] Regardless of the rationale, it appears that diversity management appears to be (and has been since the 1990s) 'en vogue' in organizations.

Unfortunately, when we take a look at what is happening, the results are not all promising. An extensive review of the literature[8] reveals that not only are organizations making fundamental errors in their efforts to effectively 'manage diversity' but these efforts may in fact be serving to disguise deep-level systemic problems within organizations.[9] Diversity management attempts range from one-day seminars to dynamic, strategic initiatives that upend traditional rewards for conformity. However, many argue that they are essentially too simplistic and fail to recognize the deeply-rooted nature of racial problems and ignore the extent to which such efforts are influenced by both the organizational and societal context.[10] This may be the case in the scenario that opened this chapter and leads to an important question: How can leaders effect successful change in the area of diversity? The following chapter addresses this issue.

It isn't common to find a chapter on diversity in an organization change text. You see, it doesn't fall neatly into any of the more traditional theories of organization change and few 'prescriptions' for success exist. Despite this, the changing face of the workforce, coupled with the desire to provide more inclusive work spaces, makes this an important issue for organization change. The first part of the chapter will look at more traditional attempts to manage diversity, popularized in the 1990s. The second part will provide a more critical look at traditional diversity management initiatives and propose some new lenses through which to examine diversity at work.

What is diversity management?

We shall start with a better understanding of the more traditional notion of diversity management and what it might mean. David Jamieson and Julie O'Mara, authors of *Managing Workforce 2000: Gaining the Diversity Advantage*, explain it in the following way:

> *People are different from one another in many ways – in age, gender, education, values, physical ability, mental capacity, personality, experiences, culture, and the way each approaches work. Gaining the diversity advantage means acknowledging, understanding, and appreciating these differences and developing a workplace that enhances their value – by being flexible enough to meet needs and preferences – to create a motivating and rewarding environment.*[11]

Sounds great, doesn't it? However, explanations like this one don't provide us with much in terms of what the change required to achieve such a rosy state might look like. A quick Internet search of 'diversity management', using Google, results in more than 351,000 hits. Many of these hits describe specific company initiatives, others advertise the services of the thousands of diversity management specialists and consultants that exist and others attempt to explain the 'one best way' to manage diversity. Figure 10.1 presents some of the most common diversity initiatives. Rather than try to summarize all (or even most) of the different approaches, we'll focus on the elements that have variously been described as essential for diversity management programmes.

- Targeted recruitment – These are special recruitment initiatives, aimed at generating applications from certain groups. *McDonald's* did this with a special television campaign that targeted seniors. The *Royal Canadian Mounted Police* did something similar, through school visits, to attract more female applicants.

- Language classes – Classes are often offered to employees who do not have English as their first language in organizations where business is conducted in English. Classes can also be offered to managers to teach them the basics of the language used by a minority group in their business unit. Acadia University offers Chinese name pronunciation classes to its professors. Although the university functions using English as its fist language, many students come from the People's Republic of China. A better understanding of how to pronounce students' names helps build relationships between faculty and students – something Acadia University prides itself on.

- Education and training programmes aimed at underrepresented groups – A good example of this would be a training programme recommended yb a manufacturing facility in rural Nova Scotia. The training programme is offered by a local community college in partnership with the manufacturing company. The course teaches students how to prepare for the employment exam. The organization wanted to employ local workers but found that many were unable to pass the basic mathematics and writing tests that were required for employment. The training programme has been highly successful in employing blue-collar workers.

- Career development – Programmes that focus on career development provide employees with strategies for growth within the company. Employees who might not otherwise move into higher positions are given skills that are needed for promotion. Very often, management skills courses are offered to those hoping to move into low-level management positions but have no formal management training.

- Mentoring – Mentoring is a strategy often aimed at women in organizations. The philosophy is that women paired with other women who are more senior in the organization will learn skills necessary for advancement.

- Flexible work arrangements – These programmes were often aimed at women returning to the workforce after the birth of a child. Arrangements included part-time and flex-time work and telecommuting. More recently, these programmes have been enlarged to include fathers, those taking care of elderly parents, employees who spend a considerable amount of time commuting to and from work.

- Workshops – Organizations often offer mandatory and voluntary workshops in areas where they perceive there to be gaps or problems. Topics include the following:
  Sensitivity training
  Intercultural communication
  Team-building
  Conflict resolution
  Inclusiveness awareness training
  Cultural diversity awareness

Figure 10.1 Popular diversity initiatives.

Significant success factors

Thorough examination of the literature reveals that there are five significant factors that contribute to the success of diversity management initiatives, yet are often lacking in the attempts of organizations to embrace diversity:

1　Differentiation between 'managing diversity' and 'affirmative action' or 'employment equity' initiatives
2　Management support
3　Employee commitment
4　Performance measures and accountability initiatives
5　Evaluation of initiatives

Differentiation between 'managing diversity' and 'affirmative action' or 'employment equity' initiatives

Believe it or not, not everyone feels that diversity initiatives are good for organizations or individuals. Some feel that these initiatives take away from more pressing issues, result in failure to hire 'the right person for the job' or negatively impact their own chances of getting the job or promotion. The negative attention afforded the affirmative action movement in the US and the equal employment opportunities movement in Canada and the UK may be, in large part, responsible for many of the hostile feelings towards diversity management initiatives in organizations. Simply put, the controversies surrounding affirmative action and equal employment opportunity programmes (and there were many), led by legislative attempts to eliminate discrimination in the workplace (i.e. the Civil Rights Act of 1991 and Executive Order 11246), may have spilled over to taint legitimate attempts to manage diversity. Some diversity initiatives are resisted as a result of their inaccurate association with their distant cousins – affirmative action and equal employment opportunity programmes. Figure 10.2 provides the history of employment equity in Canada for comparison purposes.[12]

This confusion is caused by organizations' failure to clearly differentiate between diversity management initiatives and affirmative action or employment equity programmes. The two are not equivalent. Whereas affirmative action or employment equity programmes seek to increase minority representation in various capacities, diversity management seeks to develop an environment that works for all employees.[13] By 'all employees' we mean men and women, mothers and fathers, baby boomers and generation Xers, homosexuals and heterosexuals, visible minority members and visible majority members, and many, many more. Unfortunately, the term 'diversity management' is often used as a more politically correct term for 'affirmative action'.[14] By failing to distinguish between the two, organizations are potentially creating programmes with narrow scopes (i.e. gender and race) and are effectively alienating many employees. In essence, these programmes

- **1960:** The first Canadian Bill of Rights was introduced.

- **1977:** Parliament enacted the Canadian Human Rights Act.

- **1978:** The federal government launched a voluntary Affirmative Action Programme aimed at private industry.

- **1979:** Federal contractors and Crown corporations were included and the programme was administered through the Canada Employment and Immigration Commission. The targeted groups were: Aboriginal peoples; Blacks in Nova Scotia; persons with disabilities; and women.

- **1980:** A pilot Affirmative Action Programme was established in three federal government departments (Canada Employment and Immigration Commission, Secretary of State and Treasury Board Secretariat). In 1983, this initiative was extended to all departments within the federal public service. The groups targeted were: Aboriginal peoples; persons with disabilities; and women.

- **1981:** The government of Canada created a Parliamentary Special Committee on the Disabled and the Handicapped. The report stemming from this committee, entitled Obstacles, was the first federal government examination of the issues faced by persons with disabilities.

- **1983:** The Royal Commission on Equality in Employment was established to address the lack of progress experienced through voluntary affirmative action programmes.

- **1984:** Judge Rosalie Abella released the Commission's report and coined the term Employment Equity to describe the Canadian approach to dealing with employment disadvantage.

- **1985:** In June, the federal government responded to the Commission's report by introducing Bill 62: a bill with respect to Employment Equity.

- **1986:** The Employment Equity Act was passed.

- **1995:** The second Employment Equity Act received royal assent in 1995 and came into force on October 24, 1996. Built on the framework provided by the earlier legislation, it focuses on clarifying and enforcing the employer obligations in the Act. The Act covers private sector employers under federal jurisdiction as well as almost all employees of the federal government.

- **2001–2002:** The Standing Committee on Human Resources Development and the Status of Persons with Disabilities heard testimony from witnesses in response to the Subsection 44(1) review clause.

Figure 10.2 The history of employment equity in Canada.

Source: Adapted from www.labour.gc.ca

merely serve as band-aids on wounds that would heal much faster in the open air. Organizations adopting such programmes appear to have 'dealt with the problem' when in fact they are merely camouflaging deeper diversity issues.

The first thing that has to happen is a clear differentiation between a diversity management initiative and affirmative action or equal opportunity initiatives. This means that organizational members have to understand what is mean by diversity management – the valuing of all diversity, including race, gender, class, native language, national origin, physical ability, age, sexual orientation, religion, professional experience, personal preferences and work styles.[15]

According to diversity specialist Soni, more than just ensuring women and minorities have equal access to positions and promotions within organizations, as affirmative action programmes seem to typify, diversity management programmes need to focus on:

1   increasing sensitivity to cultural differences
2   developing the ability to recognize, accept and value diversity
3   minimizing patterns of inequality experienced by women and minorities
4   improving cross-cultural interactions and interpersonal relationships among different gender and ethnic groups
5   modifying organizational culture and leadership practices.[16]

The goal of affirmative action – assimilation – is vastly different from the goal of diversity management – integration.[17] This difference must be understood and emphasized.

Management support

As with any organizational project, management support is crucial to success. Not only does management generally possess the power to allocate resources to such initiatives, management often determines the level of importance or seriousness granted to the efforts.

Cited as the number one predictor of diversity training success,[18] gaining management support remains one of the biggest challenges facing organizations wishing to capitalize on the benefits of diversity. Diversity Specialist Kay Iwata contends that the problem lies in the failure to differentiate between buy-in and leadership commitment. She argues, '[b]uy-in is expressed by managers who are carrying out directives to implement diversity, without committing to making it actually happen'.[19] She concludes that this passive support is not enough and must be turned into the personal commitment and active involvement of corporate leaders in the initiatives.

As you can imagine, management support must start with the belief that diversity is important. A 1998 study by the Society for Human Resource Management revealed that 80 per cent of executives at *Fortune 500* companies believed that diversity is important but only 26 per cent considered diversity to be 'very important'.[20] In addition, 8 per cent of these executives did not consider diversity important to the bottom line at all.

The question then remains – how can managers be convinced of the importance of diversity management? One important step in the process may be issue-selling. Tired of, or unimpressed by, moral appeals or pretty pictures of harmonious workplaces painted by diversity flag bearers, a new appeal may be required. According to Gilbert, Stead and Ivancevich, that appeal needs to be consistent with business discourse. As noted by Kevin Sullivan, vice president of *Apple Computer*, 'initiatives must be sold as business, not social work'.[21] In essence, leaders need to see the advantages of diversity management on paper through the use of columns and numbers. Fortunately, diversity management initiatives, if implemented correctly, can have a powerful effect on a company's bottom line.[22] Whether the increase in profitability is as a result of more creative decision-making, better relationships with diverse customers, or happier and more productive employees, remains to be determined. Regardless of the precursor to increased profitability, managers need to be made aware that managing diversity is not only the right thing to do, it has positive consequences.

The gaining of initial management support should not lead to a false sense of victory, as verbal support is sometimes not translated into action. Proceeding without true management support that does indeed translate into action can actually have more of a negative effect than not implementing a diversity initiative at all. This is supported by Susan Kirby and Orlando Richard who contend that serious negative consequences have been felt as a result of management's lack of follow-through.[23]

In order to move forward, a deeper level commitment must be made. Management's commitment to the initiative should be more than mere lip service and must be visible as demonstrated through policies, procedures, time spent on the initiative, rewards, personal commitments and behaviour. This level of commitment requires deep, introspective self-reflection by managers to uncover personal biases and prejudices that may serve as barriers to complete commitment to the diversity initiative.[24] Only by identifying these latent biases and prejudices can managers begin to overcome them. For example, a CEO may agree to let the HR department develop a diversity programme for the organization. A budget may be allocated and the department may get the 'green light' to proceed. However, if this particular CEO has latent biases about what type of work is appropriate for women, his/her hiring decisions may not reflect support for the initiative. This type of contradiction does not go unnoticed by employees. If the CEO is able to identify these biases (blindly acquired as the result of societal conditioning), she/he may be able to overcome them.

Employee commitment

Researchers have found that employees' attitudes and behaviours may be one of the barriers for implementing 'inclusive policies' in the workplace. In today's 'politically correct' environment, employees may be embarrassed to show their ignorance about other cultures or may feel threatened by other people who may take their jobs.[25]

Clearly, if the benefits of diversity are to be maximized in organizations, organizational members should value diversity. If organizational members do not value the differences that exist within their work groups, they probably will not be committed to the diversity programmes. There are three key factors leading to willing participation in diversity initiatives by employees. The first of these is fairness.

Much of the success or failure of diversity management programmes can be attributed to whether employees believe the programmes to be fair and equitable.[26] Employees do not want to feel that individuals, regardless of which group they belong to, are being unjustly rewarded. When employees feel that programmes are not fair and that people are getting jobs, promotions or rewards that are undeserved, especially if it negatively affects them, resentment can occur. It is apparent, once again, that the line between affirmative action and managing diversity is not clear and it is this confusion that causes employees to question the fairness of diversity initiatives.

The second key factor is inclusion. It is important, when developing diversity management initiatives within organizations, to include members who are representative of the organization's demographics. Many organizations recognize this and make an effort to ensure that the needs of all minority groups are met. However, the needs of the majority (often white males) are frequently overlooked.[27] Studies indicate that a great deal of resistance to diversity initiatives is the direct result of this oversight.[28]

The third, and most difficult, factor to overcome is prejudice. Cox contends, 'While it is not clear whether prejudice is declining, what is clear is that a considerable amount of prejudice and discrimination continues to occur'.[388] This is supported by research conducted by Ann Morrison. After surveying managers from 16 corporations, she defines prejudice as 'equating a difference with a deficiency'.[29] She also states, 'Prejudice, in its many subtle forms, continues to pervade decisions made in organizations, even in the 1990s.'[30] Morrison believes that learning, communication and dialogues are the keys to reducing prejudices in the workplace.

Although one of the most difficult areas in which to effect change, organizations appear to be recognizing the need for education and training in this area. In a survey conducted by Sara Rynes and Benson Rosen, it was revealed that the most common topic areas addressed through diversity training are subconscious stereotypes, assumptions and biases.[31] Unfortunately, many current diversity initiatives are isolated or episodic events that fail to effect deep change.[32] Simply asking participants to engage in a one-day workshop designed to educate about prejudices is usually not enough. In fact, studies show that these often awkward, public discussions in the presence of organizational 'higher-ups' can often do more harm than good.[33] Training in this area should be ongoing and should provide participants with 'safe environments' for self-discovery and growth.

Although the three factors noted above are the most predominant in current literature written in this area, there are many other, more subtle, factors that affect employees' perceptions and acceptance of diversity management initiatives. Unfortunately, no one solution will address all employees' concerns about diversity initiatives. However, Vindu Soni[34] offers a fairly comprehensive solution. Soni suggests that organizations can improve employee receptivity to diversity initiatives by doing the following:

1   Improving perceptions of discrimination, exclusion and inhospitable organizational climate on the part of women and minorities
2   Making systematic and concerted efforts to communicate diversity goals to employees
3   Training managers and supervisors to build their diversity management competence[35]

Performance measures and accountability initiatives

Researchers seem to agree that one of the key factors often overlooked by organizations when implementing diversity management initiatives is accountability.[36] Often, comprehensive diversity management initiatives are developed and implemented but there is a failure to identify who is responsible for the outcome of the initiative. For example, an SHRM/CCH survey found that only 20 per cent of its respondents who conduct diversity training reward managers for increasing the diversity of their work groups.[37] There is a failure to link performance measures and accountability with the initiative.[38]

Not only do performance measures and accountability initiatives provide managers with concrete incentives to implement programmes, they help to maintain momentum. It is often too easy for managers to put the project, once implemented, on the back burner in favour of other, more visible, projects. In order for diversity initiatives to maintain momentum, accountability measures must be in place. This could take the form of monthly diversity meetings where managers discuss progress and/or challenges in rolling out the initiative, or a spot on annual performance evaluation reports where goals can be set and results measured. In terms of accountability and 'who's in charge' of the project, establishing a Diversity Advisory Committee is a good idea.[39]

Evaluation

The SHRM/CCH survey found that only 30 per cent of its respondents who conduct diversity training go on to measure resulting behaviour at work.[40]

This is consistent with other findings discussed in the literature. It appears that, although many organizations are committing considerable resources to managing diversity, the effectiveness of these projects is often not being measured. That doesn't seem to make sense – a project that is not evaluated and changed according to desired outcomes is merely a static directive that could as effectively be disseminated through a company policy manual. To deliver a static diversity initiative is to pay mere lip service to such a dynamic issue.

Evaluation of diversity management initiatives is important for many reasons, three of which are:

1   *Cost–benefit analysis*
    The average diversity expert cost $2,000 per day in 1993 (and much more now) and the much-touted cultural audits can cost up to $100,000.[41] It seems absurd that a company would dedicate such financial resources to projects without measuring their effectiveness. However, this is indeed quite common. For example, a study of American universities found that US colleges and universities have invested substantial resources in diversity workshops without seeing or seeking any empirical assessment of return on their investment.[42]

2   *Possible negative impacts of diversity initiatives*
    Poorly implemented diversity management initiatives can have adverse effects. These include 'the possibility of post-training participant discomfort, reinforcement of group stereotypes, perceived disenfranchisement or backlash by white males, and even lawsuits based on managers' exposure of stereotypical beliefs exposed during "awareness-raising" sessions'.[43] Without constant evaluation and feedback, negative consequences may not be recognized and resulting backlash cannot be minimized.

3   *Control*
    One could assume that most diversity management initiatives are proposed in good faith and that employers have genuine reasons for embracing diversity. From this, we might conclude that employers want the initiatives to have positive effects on their organizations. Following this, it seems strange to expect an initiative to have a positive outcome if it is not monitored, evaluated and adjusted in accordance with organizational needs.

One of the difficulties of measuring the success of diversity management initiatives is the lack of a measurement tool or standard. Although it is fairly easy to measure minority representation in the workplace, representation of women and minorities in management, and promotions of women and minorities, these measures simply evaluate affirmative action initiatives and serve to further blur the line between affirmative action and equal employment opportunity initiatives and initiatives that truly focus on managing diversity. For example, a 1998 study by *Korn/Ferry International* revealed that women and minorities are making strong advances in the boardrooms of corporate America and cites statistics showing growth in the number of women and/or minorities who sit on corporate boards.[44] Unfortunately, these numbers reflect attempts to 'equal out the numbers' but do not measure the success of true diversity management initiatives. Once again, managers may be patting themselves on the back for 'valuing diversity' when what they have really done is fuelled anger and mistrust among employees.

A scorecard evaluation system, using the indicators described above, may be the first step in developing much needed measurements. Guidelines for such a scorecard are provided by Ivancevich and Gilbert, 'A sound evaluation should allow for the identification of important criteria targeted by the programme, which criteria have changed, whether these changes are the result of the diversity management training, whether the same changes will occur in future replications of the programme in the same firm with different training participants, and whether the changes will occur in the same training programme in a different organization'.[45]

Diversity management initiatives became popular in the 1990s, and can be found in one form or another in most organizations. Their successes vary. As we saw in the opening vignette, the existence of a diversity management programme does not ensure success. In fact, if implemented less than adequately, such programmes may provide 'fuel for the fire'.

A more critical look at diversity

Some argue that the trend in the 1990s towards surface level, isolated or episodic diversity initiatives (like the ones just discussed) serve only to commodify diversity,[46] and fails to deal with deeper cultural and societal issues. They feel that, in order to be effective, diversity management initiatives need to actively challenge latent biases and prejudices[47] – something that cannot be done through a one-day workshop on sensitivity training. Even if we wanted to challenge latent biases and prejudices, is this the role of the organization? Is it appropriate for organizations to require this level of analysis and scrutiny of its members? We may say with certainty that this is a very difficult area and offers no easy answers.

Additionally, by commodifying diversity, we may be silencing voices or hiding deeper issues. Let's think of it this way: When an organization says that they 'value diversity' and put resources behind this notion through programmes, policies and equity officers, organizational members are probably less likely to complain about perceived injustices. For example, at a university in Nova Scotia, Canada, there exists the position of 'equity officer'. Additionally, employees are sent the standard policies on discrimination and harassment annually. However, these efforts target the more 'traditional' injustices in organizations, and do little to address deeper issues – such as masculinist cultural norms; unspoken, informal rules that hinder employees' abilities to care for their families or contribute to their communities by establishing work practices that are not conducive to these efforts, or a lack of awareness and acceptance of diverse sexual orientations or lifestyles. The individuals concerned might not even recognize these issues because they understand their organization to be a fair one due to the espoused commitment to diversity.

These arguments are important and should encourage you to question the validity of some diversity management initiatives. The main problem may lie in the fact that many consider diversity to be an HR issue that can be taken care of with a well-intentioned diversity management programme. As demonstrated by the opening vignette, this isn't always the case. Perhaps this 'handing off' of the diversity issue is not the best way forward. Shouldn't the embracing of differences be something for which all organizational members should be responsible?

The final criticism of diversity management initiatives that will be addressed comes from a sensemaking perspective. Traditional diversity initiatives are often seen as necessary, not for legislative reasons but for business reasons. In essence, organizations are keen to 'embrace diversity' in order to recruit the best talent, to have more creative work teams and to better represent their customer base (the belief is that an African American salesperson is better to handle African American customers, and so on). This is known as the business case for managing diversity and it is used to help managers 'make sense' of the need for diversity initiatives. However, some argue that a focus on the advantages of hiring people from diverse groups causes us to ignore issues of inclusion.[48] You see, by focusing on 'using' people from diverse groups, we are assuming that they are being 'included' – very different things. Inclusion suggests that networks of information, opportunity, access to resources and decision-making influence are shared by all.[49] However, these issues are rarely addressed in more traditional diversity management initiatives and research. In response to this issue, a new discourse has emerged which uses the language of *inclusion* instead of diversity. It is beyond the scope of this chapter to delve into the conceptual and practical distinctions between the two. However, it certainly provides food for thought.

Some concluding thoughts

The purpose of this chapter has been to bring to your attention one of the areas of change management that is often overlooked in organization change textbooks – the issue of diversity management. Although not a prescriptive chapter in terms of providing you with a toolbox or list of steps for implementation of a successful diversity initiative, this chapter should have introduced you to some of the elements fundamental to success and some, perhaps disturbing, shattering of the diversity management myth.

End of chapter questions and exercises

1   Using the Internet, find an organization in your area that has a diversity management programme. Use the criteria outlined in the chapter to evaluate the programme. What might you do differently?

2   Conduct an Internet search of 'diversity management'. Identify three companies that provide consulting services in this area. How much do they charge? Summarize their offerings.

3   Research your school or organization's policies and programmes in terms of diversity management. Do they appear adequate? What changes might you make?

4   Find the outcome of the *GE Aviation Materials* discrimination case. What do *GE*'s policies look like now. Is their commitment to diversity apparent on their website?

5   *Wal-Mart* has been the target of several discrimination suits. Research the issues and write a one-page opinion paper on the results of your research.

6   Design a hypothetical scorecard that could be used to measure performance in terms of a manager's success with a diversity management initiative.

7   Assume that you work in the Human Resource department of an organization and wish to bring in a diversity management programme. How would you convince top management to spend money on the initiative? What kinds of arguments would you use?

8   Do an Internet search of the equity legislation in your area. Prepare a one-page memo as if you are reminding managers in an organization about their legal requirements.

9   Use the Internet to find companies that have programmes or policies that address ageism, discrimination based on sexuality or discrimination based on disability. Were these easy or difficult to find? Prepare a short report of your findings.

10   Assume that you are a business owner. How would you gain employee support for a diversity initiative? What might your initiative look like?

11 Institutionalization and change

Objectives of this chapter:

By the end of this chapter, you should:

1 Understand what is meant by management fads and fashions
2 Be familiar with the organizational change imperative
3 Be familiar with the notion of institutionalization
4 Understand what is meant by the various forms of isomorphism
5 Be familiar with the concepts of discourse and organizational knowledge
6 Understand the relationships between sensemaking, institutionalization and change management

---

Obituary: *Ben's Restaurant*, Montreal, 1908–2006 [1]

It may seem strange to announce the closure of a restaurant in the form of an obituary. As if someone or something had died. Yet, that is how many people felt about the little delicatessen on the corner of Metcalfe and de Maisonneuve that had become a Montreal institution. Founded in 1908 by Latvian immigrants Ben and Fanny Kravitz, the restaurant steadily gained a reputation for its smoked meat sandwiches – and its cultural life. Over the years *Ben's* hosted politicians (it was said to have been a favourite of Prime Minister Pierre Trudeau, nationalist leaders René Lévesque and Jacques Parizeau), hockey players (particularly the Montreal *Canadiens*), singers and musicians (from Leonard Cohen to Bette Midler). It was even a meeting place for spies, including, in the mid-1940s, at least one well-known member of the Israeli paramilitary *Haganah* who was said to have conducted arms deals from the tables of the restaurant.

Originally established on St. Laurent Boulevard, *Ben's* moved down-town in 1929 and then in 1950 to its current location where it 'remained stubbornly unchanged while the city grew modern around it'.[2] Indeed, its failure to change became part of its charm and, as local interest waned, its growing attraction to tourists. What started as a 1950s diner ended, more than half a century later, as a 1950s-*style* diner. For the longest time the unchanging and 'authentic' atmosphere of *Ben's* was what kept the customers coming. As one writer describes his first visit to the restaurant in 1986, the 'place was *authentic*. It wasn't just recreating 1950s kitsch – it had never gotten over 1950s kitsch!'[3] The tables were Formica, the plates were Melmac, and the 'dad-aged man-waiters' were dressed in black pants and white shirts. Yet, despite the aging Formica and drab appearance *Ben's* retained a fading charm for those who entered.

In the end, it was a combination of factors that killed off *Ben's*, including the waning interest in the business by the descendants of the founders, a failure to update the restaurant's appearance and a protracted labour dispute. Various commentators date the root of *Ben's* demise in the early 1990s when Ben Kravitz died and his son Irving inherited the restaurant. When Irving died a few years later his wife Jane and her son took over but did little or nothing to update the restaurant. In the words of one reviewer, 'by not changing anything in the restaurant [these] disinterested heirs changed the one thing that made *Ben's* great: its vitality'.[4] From the mid-1990s the seventy-five staff began to unionize as conditions deteriorated. By July 2006, the staff – now numbering less than thirty – went on strike for a 40-cent increase on their $8-an-hour wages. After a few months the owners announced that they were closing the business, arguing that they 'could not operate a profitable business in the current economic climate with unionized staff'.[5]

In today's business environment, where 'change' is almost an imperative, it is rare that we stop to reflect on the value and importance of stability. Failure to change is seen as a recipe for disaster. Successful change averts potential threats to organizational survival and bestows prestige on those associated with the change. Senior managers who adopt wide-reaching change projects appear in the press – and the business textbooks – as exemplars of the modern leader.[6] Globalization, as a force for change, is often cited as the overriding reason for developing change strategies.[7] Leadership in a global environment is a privileged status that is accorded to the few.

Yet, in the midst of this powerful discourse there are organizations whose very success relies on the fact that they have not changed over the years, and, in some cases, may have single-mindedly resisted change. Indeed, stability and a relative lack of change is the very definition of enduring *institutions*, such as the Catholic Church. That is in large part why people referred to *Ben's* as a Montreal 'institution'. Not a real institution in the classic sense of the word, *Ben's* nonetheless appears to have earned that reputation because of its longevity and its unchanging character over the past half-century. Interestingly enough, of the numerous commentaries on the demise of *Ben's* none mentioned its failure to change so much as its need to have paid attention to the appearance of the décor and to the needs of its dwindling staff.

While *Ben's* was closing in Canada another 'institution' was under threat of closure in Britain – this time the *Little Chef* restaurant chain. Established in 1958, *Little Chef* was much younger than *Ben's* but shared an important similarity – a menu and décor that remained pretty much unchanged over the past fifty years. As one food critic expressed it, the *Little Chef* restaurants 'still looked like they belonged in the 50s',[8] while another described the chain as being 'stuck in a 1970s timewarp . . . with only a nod to the 21st century'.[9] But the timewarp, which had been the essence of its charm for forty years, became a liability in the new century. This was partly due to a failure to update the appearance of many of the restaurants. What had the potential to 'seem quirky' was lost in the fact that many of the restaurants 'just looked run-down and out of date'.[10] The failure of *Little Chef* was also due to the fact that, as a chain, it faced stiff competition from a growing fast-food market and a changing national diet focused increasingly on 'healthy eating'.[11] By the beginning of 2007, the restaurant chain had been taken over in a 'rescue deal' by *RCapital*, a UK private equity group, for less than £10m. Thirty-eight of the 235 branches were closed immediately, but the remaining restaurants continue to operate normally. Whether the chain will survive may ultimately depend on the types of survival strategies the new company adopts.

The experiences of *Ben's* and *Little Chef* raise interesting questions for change management. To begin with, they both survived for a considerable period of time by not changing. They did not resist change so much as they sold a sense of stability. Customers entering a *Little Chef* in 1997 would have found it relatively unchanged from when they entered the same restaurant in 1967. Indeed, that may well have been the reason they continued to seek out the restaurant, 'you know what you are getting'. On the other hand, factors did eventually intervene to threaten the survival of these companies. What can we learn from their survival and their demise?

Making sense of change and stability

Throughout this book we have examined organizational change, change strategies and change techniques. However, as we emphasized in Chapter 1, an important ingredient in any focus on change is sensemaking. In other words, when a senior manager focuses on change he or she, whether consciously or otherwise, is making a sensemaking decision to highlight one important aspect of the operating environment to the exclusion of others. That is not to suggest that this 'decision' is always a free choice. Far from it. The senior manager facing spiralling losses is forced to seek some form of change strategy, at which point pre-existing change strategies can have a powerful influence. On the other hand, the senior manager can choose at any given time to focus on stability. Of course, it is highly likely that the average manager will focus on stability and change at any given point but it is also likely that one of these two sensemaking devices will be dominant and will have powerful consequences for further action. Louis Comeau of *Nova Scotia Power* chose to focus on change as a defining characteristic of his company's management practices. Ben Kravitz of *Ben's Restaurant* chose to focus on stability and an unchanging environment.

Management fads and fashions

One of the major problems for senior managers in recent years has been the proliferation of change programmes and their adoption by an increasing number of companies. So powerful and yet so fleeting have many of these programmes been that some management theorists have referred to them as management fads and fashions.[12] For example, when Louis Comeau was seeking for a way to better integrate employees into *Nova Scotia Power* in the mid-1980s he turned to culture change as the solution. He was in good company. The local telephone company, *Maritime Telephone and Telecommunications (MTT)* had recently introduced a culture change and heralded its many successes in the media. Comeau was also well aware that industry leader *Florida Power & Light* had also successfully introduced a culture change. Thus, it wasn't a stretch for Comeau to adopt this relatively new and popular change programme. Indeed, organizational culture change was the single most popular change programme at the time.[13] When *Nova Scotia Power* was privatized in the early 1990s Comeau turned to Business Process Re-engineering to address his new concerns of efficiency and global competitiveness. Once again he was in good company when he adopted the most popular change programme of that period. When Comeau's successor, David Mann, introduced strategic business units in the late 1990s he looked around for new formulas to help him manage. It was not totally unsurprising that he adopted the then current Balanced Scorecard approach.[14]

We can observe three things from events at *Nova Scotia Power*: (1) Senior managers, busy people at the best of times, often search for ready-made (popular) solutions;[15] (2) Packaged change programmes, which have become very popular since the onset of the 1980s, are a powerful option for managers seeking widespread change; (3) The content and focus of packaged change programmes have changed significantly over the same period.

The organizational change imperative

What is less obvious is the fact that organizational change has become an 'imperative' rather than a strategic choice.[16] Managers feel compelled to adopt, rather than consider the option of, organizational change. This was the case at two major Eastern Canadian organizations (a hospital and a college) where a recent study found that senior managers and employees alike felt that the change process they were undergoing was an *inevitable* response to environmental factors.[17]

A look inside today's companies

If we return to our list of companies from Chapter 1 (see Figure 1.1) we will see that many of those listed introduced programmatic change of one kind or another. *Abbott Laboratories*, for example, introduced TQM, BPR and Balanced Scorecard. *Bank of America* employed TQM and Six Sigma, and *Bombardier* went through Culture Change, Balanced Scorecard and Six Sigma. If we take a closer look at these companies we find that each felt compelled to introduce programmatic change. Each sought the popular change programme of the day. Yet, in their day-to-day operations, each of these companies also highlights stability as an important part of their identity.

At the September 14, 2007 board meeting of *Abbott Laboratories*, the company 'declared a quarterly common dividend of 32.5 cents per share', adding this marked the company's '335th consecutive quarterly dividend' since 1924.[18] In other words, the company is a successful, stable and reliable company to invest in. For those looking for a long-term career it is, according to *Abbott*'s website, also a good company to work for: with a '100+ year history' the company is a 'global, broad-based health care company', which 'employs 65,000 people and markets its products in more than 130 countries'.[19] It is a 'global citizen' that cares about people and the environment, inviting people to become a part of the *Abbott* 'team' and enjoy 'a wide range of career opportunities' and 'extensive learning and development programs'.[20]

In a similar vein, *Bombardier* makes much of its history. Its website, for instance, has pages on 'product milestones' and the company's 'historical background'.[21] Six pages are devoted to *Bombardier*'s founding as *L'Auto-Neige Bombardier Limitée* in 1942, through its name change to *Bombardier Limited* in 1967 and several other milestones on the road to the company's financial standing in 2005. Like *Abbott*, *Bombardier* sees itself as a 'global leader',[22] which grew 'from a small entrepreneurial company [. . .] into a global organization that straddles continents'.[23] Even references to global change are linked to company history and stability. For example, in a tribute to *Bombardier* employees the company's annual report refers to the fact that the global markets in which it operates are much more competitive than a decade earlier, making it 'incumbent on every employee and manager to focus on the qualities that got us here'.[24]

Boots, the UK pharmaceutical company, talks about its 'heritage', and the fact that 'not many companies today can claim that their core business activity benefits from the cumulative experience of trading in the 19th, 20th and now 21st centuries'.[25] Like *Bombardier*, *Boots* links its approach to change to its 'long and successful business history, which has developed in the face of an ever-changing economic, social and political climate in the United Kingdom and worldwide'.[26] That history is explored at length on the company website, with four pages devoted to 'timelines' (from 1849–2007) and eight pages of 'history' (dealing with the birth of founder John Boot in 1815, through to the company's acquisition by *AB Acquisitions Limited* in 2007).

Institutionalization

As the examples from *Abbotts, Bombardier* and *Boots* indicate, change is a regular and important aspect of a company's operations. But change, defined as 'perceived and felt differences',[27] should not be confused with organizational change (as so often occurs in the literature on organizational change[28]), which we defined in Chapter 1 as 'an alteration of a core aspect of an organization's operation'. This is different again from programmatic change, which refers to 'pre-packaged change programmes, such as Total Quality Management and Business Process Re-engineering, which focus on changing core organizational processes through the application of a series of elaborate rules and guidelines'.

Change happens but organizational change is linked to institutionalization. What does this mean? First, we should start with an understanding of an *institution as an organization (or social practice) that is characterized by the predominance of recurring and continuous behaviours that are deeply rooted in a relatively stable and unchanging value system*. The term is usually reserved for long-established government organizations, such as the *British Broadcasting Corporation* (*BBC*), the *United States Army*, or the *Canadian Broadcasting Company* (*CBC*), but also influential religious bodies, such as the Catholic and Anglican Churches. It is also used to describe less formal but enduring social entities, such as 'the family'. The term has also been extended to include other organizations, including businesses that have become an established part of a nation's economic identity. The *Hudson Bay Company* (the *Bay*) is a clear example of a Canadian institution and *Boots* is an equally clear example of a UK institution. In the United States you couldn't find a better example than *The New York Times*. Nonetheless, for our purposes, the term can be extended to any organization that meets the criteria of a relatively stable value system that strongly influences recurring behaviours and activities that characterize the organization's core operations. *McDonald's* is a good example. The company claims a history that goes back to 1955, when Ray Kroc opened his Des Plains restaurant. However, the company wasn't so much built from its hamburgers, its restaurant layout or its carefully structured system of delivering a fast service (i.e. 'fast food'), so much as its philosophy of franchising the business and ensuring that the central qualities of food, structure and layout are carefully reproduced in each new franchise. That underlying philosophy, or value, has contributed to the corporate identity of *McDonald's*, with its standardization of service across sixty-seven thousand restaurants worldwide.

Institutionalization and change

Institutionalization refers to the processes by which an organization becomes an institution. *Institutionalization is a process where organizational activities come to form a pattern of behaviour through frequent and habitual reproduction by members of the organization, and where a number of patterns of behaviour build up over time to shape the character of the organization.*[29] Thus, an institution is characterized by the existence of 'predefined patterns of conduct' that control the members' actions, by channelling them in certain directions.[30]

Organizational change is thus constrained by established practices but is also targeted at changing some of those practices. That is arguably why some programmatic change initiatives fail where they are unable to account for and overcome certain established practices. For example, when *Nova Scotia Power* was going through a culture change process that included the 'valuing of employees' it encountered fierce opposition from unionized employees. A long-established class system of separate car parks and canteens for employees and managers had encouraged the prevalent employee view that managers were out to manipulate them. This notion was reinforced when the company attempted to provide one-day (time from work) training sessions to employees but four-day sessions to managers. A union walkout ensued because the workers came to feel that this unequal use of time for training was evidence of a continuance of the old class-divided system rather than the new employee-valuing culture.[31]

Macro or 'field' institutionalization

Over the past thirty years there has been increasing research into the macro or 'field' influences on institutionalization. This research looks at how organizations, particularly those within the same field (e.g. a collection of organizations that are somehow linked to each other as competitors, suppliers, customers, or, in some cases, geographically – as in aspects of the tourist industry) increasingly come to look like each other in terms of structure, process, rules and/or personnel.[32] A good example of a 'field' is higher education where, despite some apparent differences, universities tend to look very similar to each other in the way they recruit, educate and reward faculty and students.

It is argued that the process of *homogenization* (i.e. *the similarity of organizations across a particular field*) is caused by three central factors, known as 'isomorphic' pressures – mimetic, normative and coercive isomorphic pressures. One of the ways that organizations come to look like each other is through legal and socio-economic pressures.

Coercive isomorphic pressures are where companies feel compelled to con-form to the standards, processes, structures and/or regulations of other more powerful organizations due to legal, economic or other perceived social threat. Organizations that are in the process of being established need to attract and maintain source funding; customers, clients, staff and/or members; and legal approvals. Legal approvals are usually not granted to those organizations that seems unable to conform to existing legal requirements. For example, an airline has to assure government agencies that it has the capabilities, funding and personnel to develop and maintain minimum safety practices; similarly a restaurant has to comply with legal regulations about the provi-sion of adequate rules of cleanliness. Beyond formal, legal requirement, socio-economic pressures can be used as powerful coercive pressures on a company. The pricing policies of *Wal-Mart*, for example, have a powerful influence on those suppliers who do business with the company. Failure to conform to *Wal-Mart*'s pricing decisions can lead to the economic demise of a supplier company and thus coerce it to adjust its operations. There are numerous examples of suppliers who attempted to avoid or resist *Wal-Mart* requirements only to be denied shelf space for any of their products.[33] Less obvious but equally powerful can be social pressures that threaten the legiti-macy of an organization, and thus its ability to operate. A good example is the current trend among university business schools in North America, Australia, New Zealand and Northern Europe to seek accreditation from the *Association to Advance Collegiate Schools of Business* (*AACSB*). In recent years, despite the fact that business schools owe their legitimacy to the fact that they are part of the university system, an increasing number of business schools have sought *AACSB* accreditation in order to attract students and faculty. In the mid-1990s, the *Canadian Federation of Deans of Business Schools* voted against *AACSB* accreditation for member schools – viewing it as a US system of accreditation that was not needed in Canada. A decade later, under competitive pressure to attract increasing numbers of foreign students, the majority of Canadian business schools were involved in *AACSB* accredit-ation and were willing to change their curriculum, structure and staffing policies to achieve it.[34]

Normative isomorphic pressures are where a company comes to adopt the existing practices, structures or regulations of other organizations because they share similar values, beliefs, goals and legitimacy needs. The best example of this kind of pressure is professionalization. As you read this sentence, many of tomorrow's dentists, doctors, lawyers, social workers, bankers and man-agers are being trained and educated in the professional schools of a variety of universities. In the process they are acquiring a relatively standardized set of beliefs and practices that they will carry with them into their chosen pro-fession by way of a specific organization. This will mean that dental practices, hospitals, law firms, social work agencies, banks and a variety of management teams will be staffed with people with similar training, education and out-looks. While professionals may differ on a number of things (e.g. the type of change programme that should be adopted), the fact that they share a num-ber of fundamental views on the nature of the profession itself will serve to shape the organization's structures and practices. For example, when business schools develop masters' degrees more often than not they include a Masters in Business Administration (MBA), which conforms for the most part to other MBA programmes across universities. This can be explained by the fact that the professors developing the degree have an MBA degree and want to reproduce the courses and subject matter that they had to study. In addi-tion, there is some pressure to offer a degree that is seen as legitimate by other business educators and so normative pressures combine with coercive pressures to create a relatively standard MBA degree across universities.

Mimetic isomorphic pressures occur where an organization attempts to deal with uncertainty or adopt what it sees as a winning formula by copying many of the attributes of successful organizations in the field. When, in 1930, *United Airlines* became the first airline in the world to employ female flight attend-ants it dealt with uncertainty through the recruitment of young women with certified nursing qualifications.[35] In this way the airline was able to claim that the women were hired for their medical skills rather than simply their looks or appearance.[36] The 'experiment' proved to be a success and other airlines quickly followed suit, copying *United*'s hiring practice, right down to the requirement of nursing qualifications. Despite the fact that nursing qualifica-tions played little part in the routine activities of the female flight attendant it remained a hiring practice of most US, Canadian and British airlines until the end of the 1950s.[37] Developing MBA programmes and seeking *AACSB* accreditation can also be the result of mimetic, as well as normative and coercive, pressures as a business school seeks to be successful by copying the successful efforts of other business schools. The influence of ISO accreditation on business organizations can be seen in Figure 11.1 overleaf.

Discourse and organizational knowledge

Beyond isomorphic pressures, there is evidence that powerful sets of ideas, beliefs and practices strongly influence the way that organizations are estab-lished and maintained. These sets of interrelated ideas and practices are called *discourses* where they *confront us as knowledge about how the world works and who and what should be valued.*[38] Take, for example, the idea that women are not capable of being engineers. This idea was dominant in the UK, Canada and the United States for much of the twentieth century and didn't really weaken in the periods of the world wars (1914–18, 1939–45) when women were hired to do engineering work to replace the men called into the armed forces.[39] This powerful idea was based on a broader notion of woman as domestic, caring yet technically inept.[40] This powerful idea about women's capabilities was kept alive through a whole series of practices that

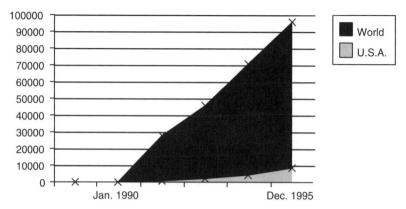

Figure 11.1 Growth in ISO 9000 Registrations, 1990–95.

Source: Adapted from Uzumeri, 1997: 27 (see Hatfield & Mills, 1997)

included men-only hiring and recruitment policies. *Globalization* is another powerful set of ideas. At one level *globalization* is simply a term that is meant to describe a whole series of new and unique practices (e.g. the influences of worldwide events on business practices and/or the way that new technologies have made worldwide business relationships both possible and rapid). However, definitions of *globalization* differ and range from excitement[41] to fear[42] of global business relationships. In the process there has developed a discourse around *globalization* that has a powerful influence on business operations and leadership.

We can see the influence of *globalization* discourse in the statements of many of our featured companies. *ABN/Amro*, for example, refers to itself as 'a leading global asset management group'; arguing that, 'With the globalization of investment consulting, it was clear that ABN/Amro Asset Management needed to mirror this development in the provision of information. By creating a dedicated RFP team, which has the latest company and product information, we ensure that a globally consistent message is delivered'.[43] *Corus Entertainment* sees itself building a 'sustainable and vibrant entertainment industry that is truly Canadian and globally competitive'.[44] *Nortel* offers 'global communication solutions' and claims that its 'ongoing spirit of innovation' is linked to its 'agility to respond to an ever-changing world'.[45] *Abbott*, as we saw earlier, views itself as a 'global citizen', and includes no fewer than twenty-one references to its global activities in its annual report.[46] The company's approach to *globalization* is to establish itself as cutting edge by 'globalizing' its strategies and products but also by meeting the challenge of the 'global community' through the 'expansion of affordable health care services and needed medicines' for the poor and underserved.[47] In the process, the company uses the term 'global' in the designation of several executive ranks (e.g. 'Executive Vice President Global

Nutrition'). *Bombardier* also believes in a strategy of corporate responsibility designed to manage 'the challenges and opportunities of a rapidly changing global environment',[48] and devotes its 2006 Annual Report to the 'Global View'.[49] It is a company that sees itself as having a 'global presence' in which it has attained 'global leadership by exercising foresight, perseverance and innovation'.[50]

Call centres and the management of change

The last twenty-five years of the twentieth century witnessed the rapid growth of a new form of organization called the call centre (or call center). The call centre is an organization that is set up in the form of a centralized office to handle large volumes of information over the telephone and the Internet.[51] Employees normally sit in open-plan rooms at desks equipped with telephones, headsets and computer monitors. There are two major types of call centre – in-house and outsourcer centres. The in-house call centre is usually part of an existing company that has centralized much of its operations (such as sales, technical help and/or customer service) to online services. An outsourcer call centre is one that operates services on behalf of a particular company but is not part of that company. *Air Canada*, for example, has an in-house call centre to take care of its customer relations. *Singapore Airlines*, on the other hand, outsourced its information technology work in 2001: this included its 'data centre, help desk and end-user computing support'.[52]

According to a number of organizational scholars, the call centre is dramatically changing the nature of organizational structure and employment in the twenty-first century.[53] Extensive research indicates that call centres are structured along highly formalized lines, operated along scientific management principles, with high levels of control and surveillance. While earlier forms of the call centre had limited control mechanisms (some form of telephone monitoring was available), today the level of technology makes it possible to exercise tight control over call centre employees, with various technologically mediated indicators that measure employee performance through voice and keystroke recording.[54]

By the end of the 1990s, it was reported that millions of workers throughout the world were working in call centres, including up to seven million in the United States (in 70,000 call centres), 160,000–200,000 in the United Kingdom, 65,000 in Germany and around 60,000 in Australia.[55] At that point the growth rate was 20–30 per cent annually and saw the addition of hundreds of thousands of new employees each year.[56] Since the turn of the new century Canada has been one of the top growth areas for call centre development,[57] particularly in the Eastern region, where approximately one in twenty of the working population of New Brunswick, and one in ten of the workforce of Halifax, Nova Scotia work in such a centre.[58] Companies operating call centres in the Eastern region include several from our list of newsworthy organizations (listed in Figure 1.1) – the *Canadian Imperial Bank of Commerce*, the *Royal Bank of Canada*, *Rogers AT&T*, *Nortel* and *IBM*, as well as a number of other important companies such as *UPS, Xerox, Marriott Hotels, Cendant, Federal Express* and *AOL*.

Rapid growth is also occurring in Europe, Asia, Africa and the Caribbean. In Europe, the Middle East and Africa the number of call centres was estimated at 45,000, employing over two million people by the start of 2008.[59] This includes around half a million employees in the UK alone, 50,000 in Eastern Europe and 130,000 in Sweden.[60] In the Caribbean and Central America, the Dominican Republic – the leading call centre nation in the region – has 18,000 people employed in forty centres, Jamaica has 10,000 (in forty centres), Panama 9,500 agents, Costa Rica 4,500 and El Salvador 4,000 agents.

Paradoxically, this truly worldwide phenomenon is both an outgrowth of technological change and a change strategy that encourages the development of more conservative, stable and relatively inflexible new forms of organization.[61] While call centre organization has been associated with sustaining and driving substantial economic growth,[62] it has also been associated with a number of problems that include burnout, stress, problematic emotional labour, low compensation, restrictive working practices, repetitive job tasks, poor working conditions, excessive control systems, overly scripted service and many other employee- and customer-focused problems.[63]

Sensemaking, institutionalization and change management

Institutionalization and the development of powerful discourses tell us a lot about the process of change management. Centrally, they inform us that there are powerful pressures on managers to conform to existing organizational structures and procedures (institutionalization), while attempting to deal with global change (discourse). These pressures are sometimes complementary (e.g. where a company feels it has to adopt similar change strategies to others in the field), and sometimes contradictory (e.g. where a company tries to stabilize its operations while trying to adopt change strategies that radically alter those operations). The good news here is that these pressures can be understood for what they are – social and ongoing *sensemaking*, as opposed to concrete facts or knowledge that has to be adhered to.

In broad terms, managers can make strategic choices[64] that include prediction, alignment or avoidance.[65] *A strategy of prediction refers to the development of a plan of action that attempts to assess the next wave of management practices and implement them ahead of competitors.* For example, in the late 1970s *Scandinavian Airlines System* (*SAS*) was one of the very first companies in the world to introduce an organization-wide culture change.[66] Over the next decade or so, thousands of major companies followed *SAS*'s example.[67] *A strategy of alignment is a choice that a company makes to develop management strategies that are in line with cutting-edge companies. British Airways* (*BA*) is a prime example. Shortly following *SAS*'s success in turning the company's economic fortunes around through a culture change *BA* introduced its own culture change and employed the same change agents as *SAS*. *A strategy of avoidance is less used and refers to a conscious decision to resist going with the flow and follow other companies just because they are popular and widespread.* A classic example is a religious organization, such as the Catholic Church, that makes a concerted effort to retain its value system by resisting a number of social changes. To a lesser extent this strategy can refer to companies that set out to market themselves as unchanging or traditional. *Ben's* is a good example of this approach.

Thus, senior managers who are aware that organizational change is largely a sensemaking process are better placed to develop strategies for dealing with the pressures. The successful adoption of a strategy, whether it involves going with the flow, alignment or avoidance, will depend on the utilization of important sensemaking properties.

Strategy of prediction

In many ways this is a very difficult (sensemaking) strategy. The key problem with a strategy of prediction is that it is not that easy to make plausible yet single accurate predictions in today's business world. It involves huge risks.

Senior management has to be prepared to adopt and sell the idea of themselves as innovators. This will be more or less difficult depending on the existing projected identities of the senior managers involved. Usually this approach works best with leaders who are new to the organization. Jan Carlzon had already established a track record for turning around failing companies when he took control of *SAS* in 1981. Prior to joining *SAS* he was portrayed as having reversed the economic decline of Swedish airline *Vingresor*, despite the fact that the industry was 'in a tailspin because of the first economic crisis'.[68] Much was also made of Carlzon's age, given that he had taken over *Vingresor* at the age of 32.[69] Carlzon went on to establish a strategy of culture change that became a benchmark not only for commercial aviation but also for business as a whole.

These strategies can work with insiders who manage to project themselves as agents of change. When Doug Robinson was appointed as President of *Lowe's Canada* he announced that the company would be focusing on female shoppers. This unique strategy was seen as a way of positioning the company in a crowded Canadian home improvement market. Although an insider – he was formerly a company vice president – Robinson was ideally placed to project himself as the ideal leader of *Lowe's* new Canadian operations. Announcing the company's new strategy of targeting the 'Canadian handywoman', the business press pointed out that Robinson was 'no stranger to Canada', citing the fact that he had previously headed up *Beaver Lumber* and *ARXX Building Products* in the 1990s before joining *Lowe's* in 2003.[70]

We may note that the projected innovative leadership of Carlzon, Robinson and others depends on how plausible they are as innovators and how plausible their change ideas are. *SAS* had posted an $8 million loss in the year prior to Carlzon's appointment and so were prepared to accept even fairly radical changes that would turn their fortunes around. Carlzon's leadership was made plausible through emphasis on those cues that made him appear to have experience (he had run other airlines), new ideas (he was young) and a success record (he had successfully turned companies in similar situations). Robinson's plausibility rested in large part on the fact that *Lowe's* were planning to expand into Canada and so needed someone with knowledge and experience of that market. Thus, much was made of Robinson's experience in the home improvement business (twenty years), his leadership position within *Lowe's* (as a vice president) but also his track record within Canadian companies (he was an American who had successfully run Canadian businesses). His decision to focus on the female shoppers was made plausible through reference to successful strategies of marketing to women and the need to do something radically different in the face of 'fierce competition in a "crowded sector" '.[71]

In terms of the risks involved, the more plausible the strategies are the more likely that people will buy in and share the risk. Thus, if things go wrong the senior manager may be able to successfully develop a retrospective sense of the situation that is enacted through reference to selected aspects of the previously plausible account. For example, when Louis Comeau took over *Nova Scotia Power* (*NSP*) in the early 1980s he introduced a culture change programme that highlighted the important role of the employee. The strategy was largely successful when measured against employee satisfaction in the crown-owned corporation. However, when, in the midst of this programme, the government privatized the company in the early 1990s five hundred workers were laid off in a new drive for efficiencies. At this stage *NSP* introduced Business Process Re-engineering to effect dramatic changes. Instead of arguing that the company had changed its focus on the employee to a primary concern with shareholder needs, senior managers at NSP presented the changes as the next – 'efficiency' – stage of the culture change. In other words, they drew on the established plausibility of culture change to explain contradictory changes.

Strategy of alignment

In many ways a strategy of alignment is the easiest (sensemaking) strategy, especially where senior managers are proposing to follow well-established and widespread strategies. All they really need to do is to emphasize the plausibility of a proposed strategy through the fact that it is popular across industry and/or with highly successful companies. The real sensemaking strategy may be in convincing the organization to change its ways in order to buy into a strategy that radically alters the way people do their jobs. In the late 1980s, the business schools of two Canadian universities – the University of Alberta and the University of Calgary – gained accreditation from the *Assembly of*

American Colleges of Schools of Business (AACSB).[72] In 1994, the *Canadian Federation of Business School Deans (CFBSD)* reviewed the issue of *AACSB* accreditation and reported that the majority of its 51 business schools did not support *AACSB* accreditation. The process was too time-consuming and costly to warrant the required changes.[73] Not only were the respective deans not convinced but they would have had a difficult time making sense of accreditation to their institutional managers (i.e. university vice presidents and presidents). However, the *AACSB* made a concerted effort to sell its service in Canada and across the world, including dropping 'American' from its title to make it seem an international rather than purely US organization. The strategy worked. Between 2000 and 2005, the number of *AACSB*-accredited business schools in Canada grew from seven to fifteen, with a further seventeen seeking accreditation. It had now become an imperative to gain *AACSB* accreditation as an increasing number of business schools sought to remain credible, leading-edge and not left behind.[74] Nonetheless, there were many in the business schools that argued against accreditation for a variety of reasons, including protecting academic freedom, avoiding the standardization of business education, and for the very fact that business school accreditation is ultimately rooted in the character of the respective universities.[75]

It is at the point where something is widespread and popular that senior managers have to ask themselves, 'Is the current pressure to change a fad or fashion or is it something worth the time and effort to pursue?' To make a viable assessment, senior managers should conduct a sensemaking audit. This would involve an assessment of the extent to which a particular change initiative is rooted in a tangible need for change (e.g. a drive by educational institutions to send their students *only* to *AACSB*-accredited universities) or is largely the outcome of reactions to pressures to conform. This could be uncovered through analysis of sensemaking cues (e.g. claims that *AACSB* accreditation bestows some kind of honour on the university) and plausibility (e.g. claims that *AACSB* accreditation improves student education) to reveal the substantive nature of the supposed pressures to change.

Strategy of avoidance

This brings us to the third, and the most difficult (sensemaking) strategy. The risk here is that by avoiding a popular trend an organization and its managers can be seen as backward-thinking, out of touch and 'behind the times'. It may be that the organizational managers or leaders want to maintain a look, an operation or a service that gives them a unique appeal; it may be that they want to resist what they see is a fad or fashion; or they may want to emphasize the unchanging values and beliefs that give them their unique identity and appeal.

Ben's and *Little Chef* typify the first approach. They both did well by selling the idea of an unchanging food environment. The fact that both organizations went through a crisis in the end may be less to do with a lack of change – many organizations that introduced widespread change have also gone through crises – than with the fact that they lost sight of the need to constantly sell the idea of an unchanging product, operation and/or service.

The *CFBSD* typifies the second approach. For a long time the *CFBSD* successfully resisted *AACSB* accreditation but largely because they acted collectively. An in-depth discussion of the 1994 decision will likely reveal how certain leading deans made reference to ongoing sensemaking about universities, and not outside agencies, as the legitimate source of accreditation. Study of the Canadian business school in the early twenty-first century will likely show that a new ongoing sense of *AACSB* as a critical agent of legitimacy, made plausible by the growing number of *AACSB*-accredited schools, was used to encourage individual business schools to join rather than resist a growing trend. Research indicates that many of the cues that are used to build a plausible case for becoming *AACSB*-accredited have more to do with the fact that other business schools are buying into it (ongoing sensemaking) and that there are a number of subsidiary and indirect benefits, such as encouraging faculty to rethink the curriculum (social sensemaking), rather than any proven concrete benefits linked to measurable outcomes.[76]

Religious and political parties typify the third approach. These organizations develop from particular values and beliefs that not only give them a unique identity but also ground them in a powerful sense of the world and their role in it. Thus, not unexpectedly, they usually attempt to maintain those values and beliefs and the practices that reinforce them. In the process they come across a number of pressures to change as other social groups and values change around them. Clearly, many church organizations and political parties have changed over time. The British Labour Party under Tony Blair is a good example. Blair and his associates were able to capitalize on the fact that the old 'Socialist' Labour Party did not seem capable of winning elections and so had to be reformed into a 'New Labour' party of social justice (rather than socialism). However, some political parties and religious organizations have worked hard to avoid change. Take for example, the ordination of women by church groups. Women have been ordained by religious organizations since the mid-nineteenth century but in the past three decades there have been struggles within several churches to increase and to decrease the ordination of women. The Roman Catholic Church, the Church of Jesus Christ of the Latter-day Saints, a minority of provinces within the Anglican Community, many Fundamentalists and Evangelical Protestant denominations, and all Eastern Orthodox churches continue to refuse to ordain women.[77] Two churches that have reversed the ordination of women are the Presbyterian Church of Australia (in 1991) and the Southern Baptist Convention (in 2000). In the latter case, fundamentalists were able to successfully argue, 'While both men and women are gifted for service in the church, the office of pastor is limited to men as qualified by Scripture'. In this case, a strategy of avoidance was successful through a plausible argument that appealed not only to Scripture (the source of ultimate appeal) but also to modernist values (of female ability and 'gifts').[78] Thus, while conceding that women have the ability to become pastors, fundamentalists cited both Timothy 2:9–14 as contending that it is not permitted for 'a woman to teach or to have authority over a man', and the Church's own 1998 ruling that a wife should 'submit herself graciously to the servant leadership of her husband.[79] Despite the contested nature of both these statements – moderate Southern Baptists believe that an anonymous author reversed some of Paul's and Jesus' teachings on women – opponents were unable to successfully enact an alternative (retrospective) sensemaking account.

End of chapter questions and exercises

1   Use an Internet and library search to find examples of two organizations that have adopted a strategy of avoidance; two that have adopted a strategy of prediction; and two that have adopted a strategy of alignment. That is six companies in total. Where possible, try to find companies that appear on the list in Figure 1.1 in Chapter 1. Gather as much information as you can on each of the organizations. Write short notes on how difficult it was to find examples of each. What can managers learn from the simple exercise of attempting to find these examples? What are the strengths and limitations of the information sources? Was there evidence of alternative strategies?

2   Using the sensemaking framework (Table 1.1) in Chapter 1, write short notes, with examples, on how each company uses the eight sensemaking properties to develop, explain and/or present their strategy.

3   What similarities can you find in the way each strategy is made plausible? What can we learn from this?

4   What are some of the differences in the way each strategy is made plausible? What can we learn from this?

5   Make notes on how key managers are presented in corporate accounts. What is the role of identity construction in these accounts both for the managers and for others? What can we learn from this?

6   What 'pressures' to change can you identify in each company case? What pressures, if any, are similar across all companies? What, if any, are different? What can we learn from this?

7   Choose ten companies at random from the list in Figure 1.1 (Chapter 1) and gather as much information as possible. Undertake a discourse analysis to discover what appear to be common themes and 'knowledge' across the companies. What are main assumptions about stability and change? What does the ideal company, the ideal manager and the ideal employee look like?

8   Drawing on all sixteen companies (the six from question 1, and the ten from question 7), find examples of coercive, normative and mimetic

isomorphism. Do companies differ in terms of isomorphic pressures? What can we learn from this?

9   From all the companies that you have studied throughout this course, what have been the main drivers of organizational change? What can we learn from this?

10   What are the pros and cons of a sensemaking approach to the management of organizational change?

Endnotes

Chapter 1

1 In fact, his work on leadership style began in the pre-Second World War era. The research focused on the impact of 'democratic' (i.e. involvement of group members in decision-making), 'authoritarian' (i.e. telling group members what to do) and 'laissez-faire' (i.e. a complete lack of leadership intervention in group decision-making) styles of leadership on group morale and productivity. The research indicated that a democratic style of leadership is associated with higher levels of productivity and morale – see Lewin, Lippitt, & White (1939).

2 See Cooke (1999; 2001; 2006) for a discussion of how the social community intent of Lewin's theory of change management was 'written out' of management theory over time.

3 See for example Blanchard & Johnson's *One Minute Manager* (1981) or Peters & Waterman's *In Search of Excellence* (1982).

4 For the role of sensemaking in business decision-making see Gioia & Chittipeddi (1991), Gioia & Mehra (1996), Helms Mills (2003), Helms Mills & Weatherbee (2006), Weick (1996; 1993; 1995a) and Yue & Mills (1994).

5 Hammer and Champy (1993) estimate that 75 per cent of all attempts to implement BPR end in failure due to the ineptitude of the managers involved.

6 One of the classic cases of this was the 1985 decision of *Coca-Cola Company* to cease production of their popular Coca-Cola and replace it with 'New Coke'. Widespread customer complaints led to the reintroduction of (the now renamed) 'Classic Coke' – see Oliver (1986).

7 See Helms Mills (2003) for a listing of some of the major companies to adopt programmatic change models over the past decade.

8 A term originally coined by Helms Mills (2006) for *Nova Scotia Power*'s adoption of several change programmes.

9 For example, *TransAlta*, the primary electrical company in Alberta, Canada, paid *Symmetrix*, a US-based consulting firm, $24 million to help reengineer the company in the mid-1990s (Kay, 1996).

10 http://cibc.com/ca/pdf/investor/2006-review-en.pdf.

11 At that point, *ING Bank* had 3,000 employees using the scorecard applications and 'planned to roll them out to all 10,000 employees over the next few years'. See http://www.itworld.com/App/220/IW010108hnetrend/.

12 Meadus (2006, p.28).

13 Byrne (1998).

14 Crawley, Mekechuk, & Oickle (1995).

15 Calabro (2001).

16 http://main.isixsigma.com/forum/showmessage/.asp?messageID=16321.

17 Jackson (2001).

18 Keleman (1999).
19 Helms Mills (2003).
20 For discussion on the adoption of different change methods and the fads and fashions they have gone through see Abrahamson (1996), Jackson (2001), Kieser (1997).
21 Jick (1993).
22 Grint (1994).
23 Galt (1996).
24 Analysis of 138 business school texts published between 1960 and 2000 shows that re-engineering was discussed in sixty per cent of the relevant texts, Total Quality Management forty-seven per cent, organizational culture in sixty-nine per cent and organizational development in sixty-seven per cent – see Mills (2001). Relevant textbooks are those that were published since the advent of the new change programmes (i.e. OC, TQM, BRP, etc).
25 Huczynski (1993).
26 Helms Mills (2003).
27 Weick (1995a); Helms Mills (2003).
28 Weick (1995a, xi) describes sensemaking as 'developing a set of ideas with explanatory possibilities'.
29 See in particular Weick's (1995a; 2001) work on organizational sensemaking. Gephart (2003; 1984), for example, takes a different approach to sensemaking from that of Weick – see Helms Mills, Weatherbee, & Colwell (2006).
30 Weick (1995a; 2001). For a short and readable account of the sensemaking perspective see Helms Mills (2004).
31 The eighth property comes from Helms Mills (2003).
32 All examples are taken from Helms Mills (2003).
33 This excellent question was adapted from Palmer, Dunford, & Akin (1996, p.191).

Chapter 2

1 Milton (2005).
2 Taylor referred to this workplace attitude, whereby employees would try to control their work environment by limiting their productivity and work output, as 'systematic soldiering'.
3 A.J.J. Mills, Helms Mills, Bratton, & Foreshaw (2005).
4 These were men whose job it was to lift and shovel 100 pound slabs of iron onto railway cars.
5 Ibid.
6 See Gilbreth (1911).
7 Gilbreth (1911).
8 http://gilbrethnetwork.tripod.com/front.html.
9 Taylor (1911).
10 Nadworny (1957).
11 See Mayo (1933).
12 Trist & Bamforth (1951).
13 Woodward (1958).
14 Thompson (1967).
15 Perrow (1986).
16 See F. Herzberg (1959); F.L. Herzberg (1966, 1968)
17 Also known as 'the hygiene-motivator theory'.
18 J.R. Hackman & Oldham (1980); J.R. Hackman & Oldham (1974); J. Richard Hackman & Suttle (1977).
19 Walton (1973).

20 Although the project was deemed successful, economic conditions forced Volvo to close the plant and revert to more traditional structures. For more details see Blackler & Brown (1978).
21 J.C. Helms Mills (2003).
22 See K Lewin (1951).
23 J.C. Helms Mills (2003).
24 K.E. Weick (1995b).
25 J.C. Helms Mills (2003).
26 See Abrahamson (1996); Jackson (2001); Kieser (1997).
27 Rüling (1998).
28 J.C. Helms Mills (2003).
29 Foucault (1979).
30 Galt (1996).
31 Legge (1996).
32 Jackson (2001).
33 Ibid.
34 Abrahamson (1996).
35 Howes (1994).
36 Helms Mills, J. (2003).

Chapter 3

1 Much of this information comes from www.asda-corporate.com; www.iht.com; www.4ni.co.uk.
2 Hayes (2002, p.169).
3 Marrow (1969, p.15).
4 Ibid.
5 Burnes (2004); Cooke (1999).
6 Marrow (1969).
7 Schellenberg (1978).
8 Ibid.
9 D.K. Smith (1996)
10 French & Bell (1978, p.17).
11 Ibid.
12 Kemmis & McTaggart (1988).
13 Marrow (1969).
14 Marrow (1969, p.30).
15 Marrow (1969); Schellenberg (1978).
16 Marrow (1969, p.34).
17 K. Lewin (1939).
18 Marrow (1969, p.168).
19 Schellenberg (1978, p.78).
20 Ibid.
21 K. Lewin (1945).
22 K. Lewin (1945, p.130).
23 K. Lewin (1945, p.135).
24 K. Lewin (1947).
25 E. Schein (1988, p.239).
26 Burnes (2004).
27 Ibid (2004, p.82).
28 Beckhard (1969, p.9).
29 Burnes (2004).
30 Argyris (1962, p.ix. in Burnes, 2004).
31 French & Bell (1978, p.18).

32 French & Bell (1978 p.18).
33 French & Bell (1978, pp.30–37)
34 Kotter (1996).
35 Connor (1977, p.635).
36 White and Wooten (1983).
37 Schein (1988).

Chapter 4

1 Eldridge (1997); Pettigrew (1979).
2 This was an NBC news story produced in 1980.
3 B. Turner (1988).
4 http://www.walmartstores.com/GlobalWMStoresWeb/navigate.do?catg=259.
5 Ouchi (1981).
6 The cover of *Business Week*, October 27, 1980 featured a story on organizational culture.
7 Ouchi (1981); Pascale & Athos (1981).
8 Martin, J. (1992).
9 Ott, S.J. 1989.
10 Louis (1980).
11 Deal & Kennedy (1982); Albert J. Mills & Stephen J. Murgatroyd (1991).
12 Geertz (1973); Edgar Schein (1991).
13 Deal & Kennedy (1982); Peters & Waterman (1982).
14 Smircich (1983).
15 Wikipedia (2006).
16 Schein (1984); (1985); (1990).
17 Albert J. Mills & Stephen J. Murgatroyd (1991).
18 Imahal (2002).
19 Joanne Martin (1992); (2002).
20 Simons & Roberson (2003).
21 Deal & Kennedy (1982).
22 Peters & Waterman (1982).
23 http://www.forbes.com/2002/09/30/0930booksintro.html.
24 Peters & Waterman (1982).
25 Carlzon (1987).
26 Albert J. Mills & Stephen J. Murgatroyd (1991).
27 Jick (1993).
28 J.C. Helms Mills (2003).
29 http://www.themanufacturer.com/uk/detail.html?contents_id=1946.

Chapter 5

1 Prokesch (1997).
2 This vignette was written by Amy Thurlow.
3 Agashae & Bratton (1999).
4 H.A. Simon (1969).
5 Fiol & Lyles (1985).
6 Argyris & Schon (1974).
7 Argyris & Schon (1978).
8 McShane (2001).
9 Ibid.
10 Senge (2007).
11 Senge (1994).
12 Garavan, Thomas (1997).

13 Pedlar, Mike, John Burgoyne and Tom Boydell.
14 Agashae & Bratton (1999).
15 Cyert, R. and J.G. March.
16 Matthews (1999).
17 Garavan, Thomas (1997).
18 K.E. Weick (1995a).
19 Ibid.
20 Smircich (1983).
21 Matthews (1999).
22 Agashae & Bratton (1999); Fenwick (1998).
23 Garvin (1993).
24 Townley (1994).
25 Agashae & Bratton (1999).
26 Agashae & Bratton (1999).
27 T. Fenwick (1998).
28 Ibid.
29 D. Garvin (1993).
30 Cooperrider (2007).
31 Cooperrider (1987).
32 Cooperrider & Dutton (1999).
33 Cooperrider (1987).
34 Cooperrider (2007).
35 http://appreciativeinquiry.case.edu/.
36 Gergen & Whitney (1996).
37 www.vancouver.anglican.ca/Portals/0/GetFit/PDF%20files/
   AI%20Doing%20an%20Appreciative%20Inquiry.pd.
38 Paddock (2004).

Chapter 6

1 General (2001) http://media.gm.com/us/saturn/en/company/awards_non_
   product.html.
2 Referred to as the 'Masters' of quality management by Bruce Brocka and M.
   Suzanne Brocka in their 1992 book, *Quality Management: Implementing the Best
   Ideas of the Masters.*
3 W.E. Deming (1953).
4 Anschutz (1995).
5 Ibid.
6 Ibid.
7 W.E. Deming (1982).
8 Anschutz (1995).
9 'Total Quality Management' – http://www.asq.org/learn-about-quality/total-
   quality-management/overview/overview.html.
10 Anschutz (1995).
11 J.C. Helms Mills (2003).
12 'International Organization for Standardization' – http://www.iso.org/iso/en/
   ISOOnline.frontpage.
13 Spector & Beer (1994).
14 Connor (1997).
15 J.C. Helms Mills (2003).
16 J.C. Helms Mills (2003).
17 Kettinger, Teng, & Guha (1997).
18 Cummings & Worley (2001).
19 J.C. Helms Mills (2003).

20 McKinley & Scherer (2000).
21 '83% of Companies Practising Business Process Redesign', 2002 – http://www.cut-ter.com/research/2002/edge020827.html.
22 Ibid.

Chapter 7

1 Birkenshaw & Mol (2006, pp.86–87) credit Art Scheiderman, the manager at *Analog Devices*, with developing the prototype of BSC in 1987. Robert Kaplan first wrote a teaching case on *Analog Devices* and featured Schneiderman's 'corporate scorecard'. He then highlighted the idea in an article in *Harvard Business Review*, before eventually working with David Norton to codify the process and make it more generally applicable across companies and industries.
2 See http://en.wikipedia.org/wiki/Balanced_scorecard.
3 Davey (1971).
4 Davis (1996).
5 http://www.1000ventures.com/ebooks/bec_mc_25lessons_welch.html   (Retrieved December 22, 2007).
6 See Morris (2006).
7 Ibid.
8 See Paton (2002); Birkenshaw & Mol (2006).
9 http://www.corporate-ir.net/ireye/ir_site.zhtml?ticker=hot&script=410&layout=6&item_id=149848 (Retrieved 13 December, 2007).
10 http://www.starwoodhotels.com/corporate/careers/paths/description.html?category=200000304 (Retrieved 13 December, 2007).
11 Ibid.
12 See for example *3M* – http://solutions.3m.com/wps/portal/3M/en_US/electronics/home/productsandservices/products/MicrointerconnectSolutions/SixSigma/;
Amazon – http://www.sixsigmacompanies.com/archive/six_sigma_at_amazon-com.html; *Boeing* – http://www.boeing.com/news/frontiers/archive/2003/july/i_ca1.html; *Ford* – http://www.qualitydigest.com/sept01/html/ford.html.
13 Paton (2002).
14 Morris (2006).
15 Morris (2006).
16 Birkenshaw & Mol (2006, p.85).
17 Birkenshaw & Mol (2006, p.87).
18 See Kaplan & Norton (1992; 2000).
19 Books include Banker, Janakiraman, & Konstans (2001), Best Practices LLC. (2001), Brown (2007), Ceynowa & Coners (2002), De Marco, Salvo, & Lanzani (1999), Fleetwood & Anstey (2003), Gilles (1976), Hannabarger (2007), Nair (2004), Niven (2005), Smith (2007) and many others.
20 The Missouri Small Business Development Centers – http://www.missouri business.net/consulting/docs/introduction_balanced_scorecard.pdf
21 Ibid.
22 Missouri Small Business Development Centers, 'The Balanced Scorecard', http://www.missouribusiness.net/consulting/docs/introduction_balanced_scorecard.pdf.
23 Kocakulah & Austill (2007).
24 Ibid.
25 Ibid.
26 Armstrong, Armstrong, Choiniere, Mykhalovskiy, & White (1997).
27 Kocakulah & Austill (2007, p.78).
28 Davey (1971).
29 Missouri Small Business Development Centers, 'The Balanced Scorecard', http://www.missouribusiness.net/consulting/docs/introduction_balanced_scorecard.pdf.

30 Kocakulah & Austill (2007, pp.80–81); The Balanced Scorecard Institute provides numerous examples of not-for-profit organizations that have successfully adopted BSC. See http://www.balancedscorecard.org/BSCResources/ExamplesSuccess Stories/tabid/57/Default.aspx.

31 Missouri Small Business Development Centers, 'The Balanced Scorecard', http://www.missouribusiness.net/consulting/docs/introduction_balanced_scorecard.pdf.

32 Missouri Small Business Development Centers, 'The Balanced Scorecard', http://www.missouribusiness.net/consulting/docs/introduction_balanced_scorecard.pdf.

33 See, for example, Gygi, DeCarlo, & Williams (2005); Chadwick (2003) – who calls Smith the 'Father of Six Sigma'; http://www.motorola.com/content.jsp?global ObjectId=3079 (Retrieved December 6, 2007); http://en.wikipedia.org/wiki/Six_Sigma (Retrieved December 6, 2007).

34 Paton (2002).

35 http://www.sei.cmu.edu/str/descriptions/sigma6_body.html.

36 Chadwick (2003).

37 Quoted Chadwick (2003).

38 Eckes (2003); Jones (2002) – who calls Harry 'the father of Six Sigma'.

39 Pande, Neuman, & Cavanagh (2000).

40 Pande, Neuman, & Cavanagh (2000).

41 Eckes (2003).

42 Pande, Neuman, & Cavanagh (2000).

43 Quoted in Paton (2002).

44 Paton (2002).

45 Ramias (2005).

46 Ramias (2005).

47 Ramias (2005).

48 Quoted in Chadwick (2003).

49 Ramias (2005).

50 Chadwick (2003).

51 Quoted in Chadwick (2003).

52 Quoted in Chadwick (2003).

53 Books include Breyfogle (1999), Breyfogle, Cupello, & Meadows (2001), Eckes (2001a; 2001b; 2003), Gygi et al., (2005), Pande et al., (2000), Pyzdek (2001).

54 ASQ, quoted in Jones (2002).

55 Jones (2002).

56 Jones (2002).

57 Jones (2002).

58 Quoted in Jones (2002).

59 Quoted in Jones (2002).

60 Jones (2002).

61 Quoted in Jones (2002).

62 http://en.wikipedia.org/wiki/Six_Sigma

63 http://www.sei.cmu.edu/str/descriptions/sigma6_body.html.

64 http://www.sei.cmu.edu/str/descriptions/sigma6_body.html.

65 http://www.sei.cmu.edu/str/descriptions/sigma6_body.html.

66 http://www.skymark.com/resources/methods/sixsigmaquality.asp.

67 For an excellent example of how this might look with attempting to fill 10 lb bags of potatoes see http://www.sei.cmu.edu/str/descriptions/sigma6_body.html.

68 http://www.sei.cmu.edu/str/descriptions/sigma6_body.html.

69 http://www.sei.cmu.edu/str/descriptions/sigma6_body.html.

70 Six Sigma consultants usually refer to measurable factors as 'metrics'.

71 http://www.sei.cmu.edu/str/descriptions/sigma6_body.html;   http://en.wikipedia.org/wiki/Six_Sigma (Retrieved December 6, 2007).

72 http://en.wikipedia.org/wiki/Six_Sigma (Retrieved December 6, 2007).

73 http://en.wikipedia.org/wiki/Six_Sigma (Retrieved December 6, 2007).
74 See for example http://www.6sigma.us/six-sigma-black-belt.php.
75 See for example http://www.6sigma.us/six-sigma-green-belt.php.
76 Jones (2002).
77 Professor Vijay Govindarajan of Dartmouth's Tuck School of Business, quoted in http://www.businessweek.com/magazine/content/07_24/b4038406.htm?chan= top+news_top+news+index_best+of+bw.
78 Armstrong et al. (1997), Ashkanasy, Wilderom, & Peterson (2000), Helms Mills (2003), Helms Mills & Mills (2000), Martin (2002), Peters & Waterman (1982), Schein (1992).
79 Voelpel, Leibold, Eckhoff, & Davenport (2005).
80 This example is drawn from: http://www.businessweek.com/magazine/content/07_24/b4038409.htm.
81 Weick (2001) refers to interruptions in the way people are thinking about a situation as shocks to the 'ongoing sensemaking'.
82 Weick (2001).

Chapter 8

1 The information contained in this vignette comes from several sources: *The New York Times*, June 7, 2005; *The Wall Street Journal*, June 29, 2007; USATODAY. com.
2 *The Wall Street Journal*, June 29, 2005.
3 *Globe & Mail*, June 7, 2005.
4 Pfeffer, J. (1977).
5 Phills, J. (2005).
6 Burke, W (2002), Weiner & Mahoney (1981), Barrik, Day, Lord, & Alexander (1991), Burke & Trahant (2000).
7 Burns, J.M. (1978).
8 Bass, B.M., (1985).
9 Kuhnert, K & Lewis, P. (1987).
10 Avolio, B.J., Bass, B.M., & Jung, D.I. (1999).
11 Quoted directly from Parry, W. & Bryman, A. (2006).
12 Parry, W. & Bryman, A. (2006).
13 Alimo-Metcalfe, B. & Alban-Metcalf, R.J. (2001).
14 Ibid.
15 Ibid.
16 Ibid.
17 Leavy, S. & Wilson, D. (1994).
18 C., Lawrence, T.B., & Nord, W. (2006).
19 Kanter, R.M. (1983).
20 Paton, R. & McCalman, J. (2000).
21 Kanter, R.M. (1989).
22 Kim, C.W and Mauborgne, R. (2003).
23 Ibid.
24 Ibid.
25 Ibid.
26 Ibid.
27 Connor, P. and Lake, L. (1988).
28 Harari, O. (1999).
29 Quoted directly from Harari, O. (1999).
30 Meyerson, D. (2001).
31 Parry, W. & Bryman, A. (2006).
32 Ibid.

Chapter 9

1 See Helms Mills (2003; 2005; 2006).
2 Clegg (1989), Hardy & Clegg (1996).
3 See, for example, Coch and French (1948).
4 Taken from Mills, Simmons, & Helms Mills (2005, p.317).
5 Machiavelli lived from 1469 to 1527. See *The Prince* (1996).
6 Robert Jackall's (1988) account of organizational morality is interesting in this regard. See also Kets de Vries (1989; 1991) and Kets de Vries & Miller (1984; 1986).
7 Hobbes lived from 1588 to 1679. See *Leviathan* (Hobbes, Schuhmann, & Rogers, 2003).
8 Jackson & Carter (2007, p.97).
9 Weber lived from 1864 to 1920. See *The Theory of Social and Economic Organization* (1947).
10 The changes were made through a series of pronouncements of the Second Vatican Council (1962 to 1965).
11 See http://en.wikipedia.org/wiki/Pope_John_XXIII#Criticism.
12 http://en.wikipedia.org/wiki/Second_Vatican_Council.
13 Here we are only talking about the millions of devoted and fanatical followers. Clearly there were millions of others who were not swayed by his personality and/or who only obeyed the broader pronouncements of Hitler out of fear. See Hunt (2005), Lucacs (1997).
14 See for example Dubin (1968), Behling & Schriesheim (1976), Daft (1986), Jones (1995), Johns & Saks (2008).
15 Interviews with former and existing *Air Canada* employees.
16 References to Marx tended to appear, albeit rarely, during the height of the Cold War and usually as part of a discussion of the value of capitalism as compared with communism – see Mills & Helms Hatfield (1998). An example of this kind of approach can be found in Wheeler (1962).
17 Durkheim lived from 1858 to 1917. See *The Division of Labour in Society* (Durkheim, 1964).
18 Including Elton Mayo (1933), Fritz Roethlisberger and W.J. Dickson (1939).
19 Bendix (1974), Rose (1978).
20 See Brown (1967), Rose (1978).
21 In some earlier, post WWII, management texts Marx was sometimes dealt with as someone whose ideas were either dangerous or outmoded or both (Griffin, Ebert, & Starke, 2002; Gutenberg, 1968; Kelly, 1974; Rogers, 1975; Steiner & Steiner, 1977, 1997; Zimet & Greenwood, 1978).
22 Marx lived from 1818 to 1883. See in particular *Capital* (Marx, 1999).
23 Helms Mills (2003; 2005; 2006).
24 Bendix (1974), Rose (1978).
25 Filippelli & McColloch (1956), Goldstein (1978), Stolberg (1938).
26 In the 1920s, *Western Electric* commissioned a series of studies at its Hawthorne Works in Chicago to deal with issues of morale and motivation. The studies involved a number of phases and lasted into the 1930s. The various findings of the studies indicated that employees should be seen as 'social beings' who needed social solidarity, attention and leadership at work. These various studies became known as the Hawthorne Studies, and are seen as the beginning of the human relations school of management because of the focus on change through 'manipulation' of workplace relations (Acker & van Houten, 1974; Brown, 1967; Mills et al., 2005; Rose, 1978).
27 See Coch & French (1948).
28 French, Israel, & Aas (1960).

29 Despite some apparent success with improved working conditions in times of economic growth (European Foundation for the Improvements of Living and Working Conditions, 1983) the worker director or worker participation approach is more problematic when issues of widespread changes to jobs, pay cuts and lay-offs are involved (Brannen, 1976; Guest & Fatchett, 1974; Heckscher, 1981; Pylee, 1975)

30 Kanter (1979).

31 Ibid.

32 Ibid.

33 Ibid.

34 Ibid.

35 Ibid.

36 Ibid.

37 Stewart (1989).

38 Ibid.

39 Ibid.

40 Ibid.

41 Ibid.

42 Michel Foucault was born in 1926 but died an untimely death in 1984. On discourse and knowledge see in particular Foucault (1979; 1980).

43 Helms Mills (2005).

44 Ibid.

45 Helms Mills (2003).

46 Hammer & Champy (1993).

47 Mills & Helms Mills (2004).

48 On organizational sensemaking see Weick (1995; 2001). Helms Mills (2003) has pointed out that Weick does not adequately deal with power, a fact that has since been recognized by Weick and his colleagues (Weick, Sutcliff, & Obstfeld, 2005). A focus on power and the structural contexts of sensemaking has led to the generation of a critical sensemaking approach that has been explored through a number of studies of organizations and change – see, for example, Helms Mills & Weatherbee (2006), Helms Mills, Weatherbee & Colwell (2006), Mullen, Vladi, & Mills (2006), O'Connell & Mills (2003).

49 This is one of Weick's (1995) terms for talking about changes to ongoing sensemaking.

50 The term 'ontological security' is from Giddens (1976).

Chapter 10

1 Deutsch, C. (2005).

2 Deutsch, C. (2005).

3 Kersten (2000).

4 Caudron (1998a); Kirby & Richard (2000); Recascino & Tschirhart (2000); Rynes & Rosen (1995); Wise & Tschirhart (2000).

5 Daniels (2001).

6 Cox (1994).

7 Barak (2000); Von Bergen, Soper, & Foster (2002); Berger (2001)

8 This study was presented at the Atlantic Schools of Business Conference by Kelly Dye in 2003.

9 Barak (2000); Dolan & Giles-Brown (1999).

10 Kersten (2000).

11 Jamieson & O'Mara (1991, pp.14–15).

12 www.hrsdc.gc.ca.

13 Carnevale & Stone (1994, p.2).

14 Wise & Tschirhart (2000, p.2).
15 Carnevale & Stone (1994, p.1).
16 Soni (2000) p.2.
17 Gilbert, Stead, & Ivancevich (1999); Lorbiecki (2001).
18 Rynes & Rosen (1994).
19 Carnevale & Stone (1994, p.5).
20 Caudron (1998b).
21 Ivancevich & Gilbert (2000, p.79).
22 Carnevale & Stone (1994); Hall & Parker (1993); Dolan & Giles-Brown (1999); Prasad & Mills (1997); Lorbiecki (2001).
23 Kirby & Richard (2000).
24 Fletcher & Kaplan (2000).
25 Barak (2000).
26 Kirby & Richarch (2000, p.2).
27 Carnevale & Stone (1994).
28 Soni (2000).
29 Cox (1994, p.73).
30 (Carnevale & Stone (1994, p.3).
31 Ibid.
32 Rynes & Rosen (1994, p.2).
33 Dass & Parker (1999); Lorbiecki (2001).
34 Gingrich (2000).
35 Soni (2000).
36 Quoted directly from Soni (2000, p.22).
37 Cox, Hall, & Parker (1994); Caudron, Carnevale, & Stone (1998a); and Rynes & Rosen (1994).
38 Carnevale & Stone (1994).
39 Dass & Parker (1999); Kelly & Dobbin (1998).
40 Kossek, Lobel, & Brown (2006).
41 Carnevale & Stone (1994).
42 Rynes & Rosen (1994).
43 McCauley, Wright, & Harris (2000, p.11).
44 Rynes & Rosen (1994, p.2).
45 Caudron (1998b).
46 Invancevich and Gilbert (2000, p.84).
47 Kersten (2000).
48 Noon (2007).
49 Roberson (2006); Prasad (2001).
50 Roberson (2006).

Chapter 11

1 The title and much of the story is based on material on the website http://benson-strike.zoomshare.com/.
2 Ingrid Peritz (2006) 'A legendary sandwich shop is toast', *Globe and Mail*, cited on http://bensonstrike.zoomshare.com/.
3 From 'Obituary: Ben's Restaurant, Montreal, 1908–2006', http://bensonstrike.zoomshare.com/.
4 http://bensonstrike.zoomshare.com/.
5 http://bensonstrike.zoomshare.com/.
6 See Helms Mills (2003).
7 See Egelhoff (1998) and Senior (2002).
8 http://www.answers.com/topic/little-chef.
9 Helen Carter, 'End of the road for the Little Chef? Restaurant chain "stuck in a

1970s timewarp" may close after 50 years', *The Guardian*, Saturday, December 30, 2006, http://business.guardian.co.uk/story/0,,1980148,00.html.

10 http://www.answers.com/topic/little-chef.

11 http://www.answers.com/topic/little-chef.

12 See Abrahamson (1996), Jackson (2001) and Kieser (1997).

13 Helms Mills (2003), Kieser (1997).

14 Kaplan & Norton (2000).

15 Simon (1976) argues that senior managers often act under conditions of 'bounded rationality', where due to time constraints decisions have to be made without full or new information.

16 Helms Mills (2003: 73) argues that, over the years, the focus on organizational change 'has shifted from the strategic choice (Child, 1972) of the actor to one of incontrovertible external forces that managers need to anticipate, react to and manage. It is contended that organizational change as an imperative has become an important management discourse (Foucault, 1979) that can be witnessed in the discursive practices of companies throughout North America and Europe (Cooke, 1999)'.

17 See Thurlow (1996) and Thurlow & Helms Mills (1996).

18 *Abbott Laboratories* website; home page http://www.abbott.com (accessed September 20, 2007).

19 Ibid.

20 Ibid.

21 http://www.bombardier.com/.

22 *Bombardier* Annual Report, January 31, 2007, p.2.

23 Annual Report, p.11.

24 Annual Report, p.11.

25 http://www.boots-the-chemists.co.uk/.

26 http://www.boots-the-chemists.co.uk/.

27 Mills & Murgatroyd (1991, p.97).

28 Mills & Murgatroyd (1991, p.100).

29 For a deeper and more detailed understanding of institutionalization see Berger & Luckmann (1967).

30 Berger & Luckmann (1967, pp.70–72).

31 See Helms Mills (2003).

32 See DiMaggio & Powell (1983); Pyper (2009).

33 See http://www.larouchepub.com/other/ 2003/3046wal-mart_pricing.html; http://www.laborrights.org/projects/ corporate/walmart/Supplier-Standards-2005.pdf; http://www.fastcompany.com/magazine/77/walmart.html.

34 McKee, Mills, & Weatherbee (2005).

35 Nielsen (1982).

36 Barry (2007), Mills (2006).

37 The main exception to this hiring rule was during WWII when nurses were in high demand and airlines were forced to alter their hiring requirements (A.J. Mills, 2006).

38 Here we are using a much simplified definition that is drawn from the work of Foucault (1972; 1979; 1980).

39 See Beauman (1971), Escott (1989), Higonnet et al. (1987), Pugh (1992), Roberts (1988), Rowbotham (1999).

40 Cockburn (1985; 1991), Franklin (1990), Rothschild (1988), Rowbotham (1999).

41 Hill (2008), Wolf (2004).

42 Buckman (2004), Laxer (1993).

43 http://www.pragmatech.com/CustomerSuccess/CaseStudies/Profile-ABN-AMRO.aspx.

44 http://www.corusent.com/corporate/about/index.asp.

45 http://www.nortel.com/corporate/corptime/index.html.
46 http://www.abbott.com/static/content/microsite/annual_report/2006/support_files/abbott_ar06_editorial.pdf.
47 Ibid.
48 http://www.bombardier.com/.
49 http://www.bombardier.com/en/0_0/0_0_1_7/0_0_1_7_4/pdf/annual_report_2007.pdf.
50 Ibid.
51 See http://en.wikipedia.org/wiki/Call_center.
52 http://www.jobcyclone.com/news/Singapore_jobs_news_26.php.
53 See Batt & Moynihan (2002), Carroll & Helms Mills, (2005), Carroll, Mills, & Helms Mills (2006), Dewett & Jones (2001), Loebbecke & Wareham (2003).
54 Carroll, Mills & Helms Mills (2006).
55 http://www.wsws.org/news/1998/dec1998/call-d09.shtml.
56 Ibid.
57 Datamonitor (2003a; 2003b).
58 Province of New Brunswick (2003), Mills, Helms Mills, Forshaw & Bratton (2007, p.168). By the end of the 1990s, with only 1 in 50 of the workforce involved, New Brunswick was being called the 'Call Centre Capital of North America' (http://www.emergence.nu/news/cccap.html).
59 http://networks.silicon.com/telecoms/0,39024659,39120264,00.htm.
60 http://networks.silicon.com/telecoms/0,39024659,39120264,00.htm;   http://www.nada.kth.se/~tessy/NormanK.pdf.
61 Ellis & Taylor (2006).
62 Dewett & Jones (2001), Gans, Koole, & Mandelbaum (2003), Miciak & Desmarais (2001).
63 http://www.nada.kth.se/~tessy/NormanK.pdf;   http://www.wsws.org/news/1998/dec1998/call-d09.shtml; http://en.wikipedia.org/wiki/Call_center; Bain & Taylor (2000), Deery, Iverson, & Walsh (2002), Ellis & Taylor (2006), Holman (1999), Mirchandani (1998).
64 See Child (1972).
65 These terms are taken from Mills, Helms Mills, Bratton, & Foreshaw (2006, pp. 49–88).
66 See Carlzon (1987).
67 See Helms Mills (2003).
68 http://www.harpercollins.com/authors/1516/Jan_Carlzon/index.aspx?authorID=1516.
69 Ibid.
70 Information from *The Globe and Mail*, Business Section, pp. B1, B7, June 7, 2005.
71 Ibid.
72 It has since been renamed the *Association to Advance Collegiate Schools of Business*, but retains the initials *AACSB*.
73 Coleman, Wright, & Tolliver (1994).
74 See McKee, Mills, & Weatherbee (2005).
75 McKee, Mills, & Weatherbee (2005).
76 McKee, Mills, & Weatherbee (2005).
77 See http://www.religioustolerance.org/femclrg13.htm.
78 Cited in http://www.religioustolerance.org/femclrg13.htm.
79 Cited in http://www.religioustolerance.org/femclrg13.htm.

Bibliography

'83% of Companies Practicing Business Process Redesign'. (2002). Retrieved May 8, 2007, from http://www.cutter.com/research/2002/edge020827.html.

Abrahamson, E. (1996). 'Management Fashion'. *Academy of Management Review*, *21*(1), 254–285.

Acker, J. & van Houten, D.R. (1974). 'Differential Recruitment and Control: The Sex Structuring of Organizations'. *Administrative Science Quarterly*, *9*(2), 152–163.

Agashae, Z. & Bratton, J. (1999). 'Exploring the Adult Learning-Leadership Interface: A Case Study in a Canadian Energy Company'. *Paper presented at the Research Work and Learning: A First International Conference*, Leeds, UK.

Alimo-Metcalfe, B. & Alban-Metcalf, R.J. (2001) 'The Development of a New Transformational Leadership Questionnaire'. *Journal of Occupational and Organizational Psychology*, 74, 1–28

Anschutz, E.E. (1995). *TQM America: How America's Most Successful Companies Profit From Total Quality Management*. Bradenton, FL: McGuinn & McGuires Publishing Inc.

Argyris, C. & Schon, D. (1974). *Theory in Practice: Increasing Performance Effectiveness*. San Francisco: Jossey-Bass.

Argyris, C. & Schon, D. (1978). *Organizational Learning: A Theory of Action Perspective*. Reading, MA: Addison-Wesley.

Armstrong, P., Armstrong, H., Choiniere, J., Mykhalovskiy, E., & White, J. (1997). *Medical Alert: New Work Organizations in Health Care*. Toronto: Garamond Press.

Ashkanasy, N., Wilderom, C., & Peterson, M. (Eds.). (2000). *Handbook of Organizational Culture and Climate*. Thousand Oaks, CA: Sage.

Avolio, B.J., Bass, B.M., & Jung, D.I. (1999) 'Re-examining the Components of Transformational and Transactional Leadership Using the Multifactor Leadership Questionnaire'. *Journal of Occupational and Organizational Psychology*, 72, 441–462.

Bain, P. & Taylor, P. (2000). Entrapped by the 'Electronic Panopticon'? Worker Resistance in the Call Centre. *New Technology, Work, and Employment*, *15*(1), 2.

Banker, R. D., Janakiraman, S. N., & Konstans, C. (2001). *Balanced Scorecard: Linking Strategy to Performance*. Morristown, NJ: Financial Executives Research Foundation.

Barak, M., 'The Inclusive Workplace: An Ecosystems Approach to Diversity Management', *Social Work*, 45 (July 2000), 339+.

Barrik, Day, Lord & Alexander (1991). 'Assessing the Utility of Executive Leadership'. *Leadership Quarterly*. 2, 9–22.

Barry, K.M. (2007). *Femininity in Flight. A History of Flight Attendants*. Durham, NC: Duke University Press.

Bass, B.M. (1985). *Leadership and Performance Beyond Expectations*. New York: Free Press.

Batt, R. & Moynihan, L. (2002). 'The Viability of Alternative Call Centre Production Models'. *Human Resource Management Journal, 12*(4), 14.

Beauman, K.B. (1971). *Partners in Blue. The Story of Women's Service with the Royal Air Force*. London: Hutchinson.

Beckhard, R. (1969). *Organization Development: Strategies and Models*. Reading, MA: Addison-Wesley.

Behling, O. & Schriesheim, C. (1976). *Organizational Behavior. Theory, Research and Application*. Boston: Allyn and Bacon, Inc.

Bendix, R. (1974). *Work and Authority in Industry*. Berkeley, CA: University of California Press.

Berger, N. (2001). 'Musavi-Lari: An Experimental Exercise in Diversity Awareness', *Journal of Management Education*, 25 (December), 737–745.

Berger, P.L. & Luckmann, T. (1967). *The Social Construction of Reality*. New York: Doubleday Anchor.

Best Practices LLC (2001). *Developing a Balanced Scorecard of Performance Measures*. Chapel Hill, NC: Best Practices.

Birkenshaw, J. & Mol, M. (2006). 'How Management Innovation Happens'. *Sloan Management Review, 47*(4), 80–88.

Blackler, F.H.M., & Brown, C.A. (1978). *Job Redesign and Management Control: Studies in British Leyland and Volvo*. Saxon House.

Blanchard, K. H. & Johnson, S. (1981). *The One Minute Manager*. New York: William Morrow and Co.

Brannen, P. (1976). *The Worker Directors: A Sociology of Participation*. London: Hutchinson.

Bratton, J., Helms Mills, J., Pyrch, T. & Sawchuck, P. (2004) *Workplace Learning. A Critical Introduction*. Toronto: Garamond Press.

Breyfogle, F.W. (1999). *Implementing Six Sigma: Smarter Solutions Using Statistical Methods*. New York: John Wiley.

Breyfogle, F.W., Cupello, J.M., & Meadows, B. (2001). *Managing Six Sigma: A Practical Guide to Understanding, Assessing, and Implementing the Strategy that Yields Bottom Line Success*. New York: John Wiley.

Brocka, B., & Brocka, S. (1992). *Quality Management: Implementing the Best Ideas of the Masters*. Homewood, IL: Business One Irwin.

Brown, J.A.C. (1967). *The Social Psychology of Industry*. Harmondsworth: Penguin.

Brown, M.G. (2007). *Beyond the Balanced Scorecard: Improving Business Intelligence with Analytics*. New York: Productivity Press.

Buckman, G. (2004). *Globalization – Tame It or Scrap It?* London: Zed.

Burke, W. (2002) *Organization Change Theory and Practice*. Thousand Oaks, CA: Sage.

Burke and Trahant (2000). *Business Climate Shifts: Profiles of Change Makers*. Boston: Butterworth Heineman.

Burnes, B. (2004). *Managing Change* (4th ed.). Harlow: Prentice Hall.

Burns, J.M. (1978) *Leadership*. New York: Harper & Row.

Byrne, J.A. (1998). 'How Jack Welch Runs GE'. *Business Week*. Retrieved 31 October, 2006, from http://www.businessweek.com/1998/23/b3581001.htm.

Calabro, L. (2001). 'On Balance. *CFO Asia*'. Retrieved November 1, 2006, from http://www.cfoasia.com/archives/200103-59.htm.

Carlzon, J. (1987). *Moments of Truth*. Cambridge, MA: Ballinger Publishing Co.

Carnevale, A. and Stone, S., 'Diversity: Beyond the Golden Rule', *Training & Development*, 48 (October 1994), 22–39.

Carroll, W. R. & Helms Mills, J. (2005). 'Identity and Resistance in Call Centres: Toward A Critical Sensemaking Approach'. *Paper presented at the Annual Conference of the Administrative Sciences Association of Canada*, Toronto, May 28–31.

Carroll, W. R., Mills, A. J., & Helms Mills, J. (2006). 'Managing Power and Resistance: Making Critical Sense of Call Centre Management'. *Paper presented at the Critical Management Studies Interest Group of the Academy of Management, Annual Meeting*, Atlanta, August 15.

Caudron, S., 'Diversity Watch', *Black Enterprise*, 28 (February 1998a), 141–144.

Caudron, S., 'Diversity Watch', *Black Enterprise*, 29 (September 1998b), 91–94.

Ceynowa, K. & Coners, A. (2002). *Balanced Scorecard für Wissenschaftliche Bibliotheken*. Frankfurt am Main: V. Klostermann.

Child, J. (1972). 'Organisation Structure, Environment and Performance – the Role of Strategic Choice'. *Sociology*, 6(1), 1–22.

Clegg, S.R. (1989). *Frameworks of Power*. Newbury Park, CA: Sage.

Coch, L. & French, J.R.P. (1948). 'Overcoming Resistance to Change'. *Human Relations*, 1, 512–532.

Cockburn, C. (1985). *Machinery of Dominance*. London: Pluto Press.

Cockburn, C. (1991). *Brothers. Male Dominance and Technological Change*. London: Pluto Press.

Coleman, D.F., Wright, P.C., & Tolliver, J.M. (1994). 'American-style Accreditation and its Application in Canada: Perceptions of Utility'. *Revue Canadienne des Sciences de l'Administration*, 11(2), 192.

Connor, P.E. (1977). 'A Critical Inquiry into Some Assumptions and Values Characterizing OD'. *The Academy of Management Review*, 2(4), 635–644.

Connor, P. E. (1997). 'Total Quality Management: A Selective Commentary on its Human Dimensions, with Special Reference to its Downside'. *Public Administration Review*, 57(6), 501–509.

Connor, P. & Lake, L. (1988). *Managing Organizational Change*. New York: Praeger Publishers.

Cooke, B. (1999). 'Writing the Left out of Management Theory: The Historiography of the Management of Change'. *Organization*, 6(1), 81–105.

Cooperrider, D.L. (1987). 'Appreciative Inquiry in Organizational Life'. *Reseach in Organizational Change and Development*, 1, 129–169.

Cooperrider, D.L. (2007). Appreciative Inquiry Commons Case Western Reserve.

Cooperrider, D.L. & Dutton, J.E. (1999). *Organizational Dimensions of Global Change: No Limits to Cooperation*. Thousand Oaks, CA: Sage Publications.

Cooperrider, D.L. and D. Whitney. 'A Positive Revolution in Change Appreciative Inquiry'. Appreciative Inquiry Commons, 1999.

Cox, T. (1994). *Cultural Diversity in Organizations*, San Francisco, CA: Berrett-Koehler Publishers.

Crawley, W., Mekechuk, B., & Oickle, G.K. (1995, June/July 1995). 'Powering Up for Change'. *CA Magazine, June/July*, 33–38.

Cummings, T.G. & Worley, C.G. (2001). *Organization Development and Change* (7th ed.). Ohio: South-Western College Publishing.

Daft, R.L. (1986). *Organization Theory and Design* (Second ed.). St. Paul, MN: West.

Daniels, C. (2001). 'Too Diverse for Our Own Good'. *Fortune*, 144, p. 116.

Dass, P. & Parker, B., 'Strategies for Managing Human Resource Diversity: From Resistance to Learning', *The Academy of Management Executive*, 13 (May 1999), 68–80.

Datamonitor. (2003a). *Opportunities in North American Call Center Markets to 2007*. New York: Datamonitor.

Datamonitor. (2003b). *Profiting from Canadian Call Centre Outsourcing: Lowering Risks and Maximizing Savings*. New York: Datamonitor.

Davey, N.G. (1971). *The External Consultant's Role in Organizational Change*. [East Lansing]: Division of Research Graduate School of Business Administration, Michigan State University.

Davis, T.R.V. (1996). Developing an Employee Balanced Scorecard: Linking Frontline Performance to Corporate Objectives. *Management Decision*, *34*(4), 14–18.

De Marco, M., Salvo, V., & Lanzani, W. (1999). *Balanced Scorecard, Dalla Teoria alla Pratica : Metodi e Strumenti per Orientare le Iniziative Aziendali al Raggiungimento dei Risultati Strategici* (3a ed.). Milan, Italy: FrancoAngeli.

Deal, T.E. & Kennedy, A.A. (1982). *Corporate Cultures*. Reading, MA: Addison-Wesley.

Deery, S., Iverson, R., & Walsh, J. (2002). 'Work Relationships in Telephone Call Centres: Understanding Emotional Exhaustion and Employee Withdrawal'. *Journal of Management Studies*, *39*(4), 471–496.

Deming, W.E. (1953). 'Statistical Techniques and International Trade'. *Journal of Marketing*, *17*(4), 428–433.

Deming, W.E. (1982). *Quality, Productivity, and Competitive Position*. Cambridge, MA: MIT, Center for Advanced Engineering Study.

Deming, W.E. (1986). *Out of the Crisis*. Cambridge, MA.: MIT-CAES.

Deutsch, C. (2005). 'Black, White or Grey'. *The New York Times*, June 7.

Dewett, T. & Jones, G. (2001). 'The Role of Information Technology in the Organization: A Review, Model, and Assessment'. *Journal of Management*, *27*(3), 313.

DiMaggio, P.J. & Powell, W. (1983). The Iron Cage Revisited: Institutional Isomorphism and Collective Rationality in Organizational Fields. *American Sociological Review*, *48*, 147–160.

Dolan, J. & Giles-Brown, L., 'Realizing the Benefits of Diversity: A Wake-Up Call', *The Public Manager: The New Bureaucrat*, 28 (Spring 1999), 51–54.

Dubin, R. (1968). *Human Relations in Administration*. Englewood Cliffs, NJ: Prentice-Hall.

Durkheim, E. (1964). *The Division of Labour in Society*. New York: Free Press.

Eckes, G. (2003). *Six Sigma for Everyone*. Hoboken, N.J.: Wiley.

Egelhoff, W.G. (1998). *Transforming International Organizations*. Cheltenham, UK; Northampton, MA: E. Elgar.

Eldridge, C.C. (1997). *Kith and Kin : Canada, Britain, and the United States from the Revolution to the Cold War*. Cardiff: University of Wales Press.

Ellis, V., & Taylor, P. (2006). ' "You Don't Know What You've Got Till It's Gone": Recontextualizing the Origins, Development and Impact of the Call Centre'. *New Technology, Work, and Employment*, *21*(2), 107–122.

Escott, B.E. (1989). *Women in Air Force Blue*. Northamptonshire: Patrick Stevens.

European Foundation for the Improvements of Living and Working Conditions.

(1983). *The Worker Director and his Impact on the Enterprise*. Shankill, Co. Dublin: E.F.I.L.W.C.

Farrell, G. (2006) *Scrushy Guilty of Bribery in Case Involving Ex-Governor*. USA TODAY, June 30, 2006. USATODAY.com.

Fenwick, T. (1998). 'Questioning the Concept of the Learning Organization'. In S. Scott (Ed.), *Learning for Life*: Thompson Educational Press.

Fiol, C.M. & Lyles, M.A. (1985). Organizational Learning. *Academy of Management Review, 10*(4), 801–813.

Fleetwood, T. & Anstey, M. (2003). *Using the Balanced Scorecard to Assess the Impact of a Staff Scheduling Initiative: A Case Study in the Retail Sector*. Port Elizabeth: Labour Relations Unit, University of Port Elizabeth.

Fletcher, S. & Kaplan, M., 'The Diversity Change Process: Integrating Sexual Orientation', *Diversity Factor*, 9 (Fall 2000), 34–38.

Foucault, M. (1972). *The Archaeology of Knowledge*. London: Routledge.

Foucault, M. (1979). *Discipline and Punish: The Birth of the Prison*. New York: Vintage Books.

Foucault, M. (1980). *Power/Knowledge*. New York: Pantheon.

Franklin, U. (1990). *The Real World of Technology*. Toronto: CBC Enterprises.

French, J.R.P., Israel, J., & Aas, D. (1960). An Experiment on Participation in a Norwegian Factory. *Human Relations, 13*, 3–19.

French, W.L., & Bell, C. (1978). *Organization Development: Behavioral Science Interventions for Organization Improvement* (2nd ed.). Englewood Cliffs, N.J.: Prentice-Hall.

Galt, V. (1996, December 19). 'Universities Look for Corporate Support in Research'. *The Globe and Mail*.

Gans, N., Koole, G., & Mandelbaum, A. (2003). 'Telephone Call Centers: Tutorial, Review, and Research Prospects'. *Manufacturing & Service Operations Management, 5*(2), 79.

Garvin, D. (1993). 'Building a Learning Organization'. *Harvard Business Review, 71*(4), 78–91.

Geertz, C. (1973). *The Interpretation of Cultures*. New York: Basic Books.

General, M. (2001). 'Saturn Recognition & Awards: Non-product'. Retrieved June 11, 2007, from http://media.gm.com/us/saturn/en/company/awards_non_product. html.

Gephart, R.J. (2003). 'Making Sense of the Risks of Organizational Action: An Ethnostatistical Study of the Regulation of Sour Gas Drilling'. *Paper presented at annual meeting of Academy of Management conference* (August 1–6).

Gephart, R.P. (1984). 'Making Sense of Organizationally Based Environmental Disasters'. *Journal of Management, 10*(2), 205–225.

Gergen, K. & Whitney, D. (1996). 'Technologies of Representation in the Global Corporation: Power & Polyphony'. In D.M. Boje, R.P. Gephart & T.J. Thatchenkery (Eds.), *Postmodern Management and Organization Theory* (pp. 331–357). Thousand Oaks, CA: Sage.

Gilbert, J., Stead, B., & Ivancevich, J., 'Diversity Management: A New Organizational Paradigm', *Journal of Business Ethics*, 21 (August 1999), 61–76.

Giddens, A. (1976). *New Rules of Sociological Method: A Positive Critique of Interpretative Sociologies*. London: Hutchinson.

Gilbreth, F.B. (1908a). *Concrete System*. New York: The Engineering News Publishing Company.

Gilbreth, F.B. (1908b). *Field System*. New York and Chicago: The M. C. Clark Publishing Co.

Gilbreth, F.B. (1911). *Motion Study*. Easton, PA: Hive Publications.

Gilbreth, F.B., Jnr & E.G. Carey (1963). *Cheaper by the Dozen*. New York: Thomas Y. Crowell Co.

Gillespie, D.F., Mileti, D. S., & Perry, R. W. (1976). *Organizational Response to Changing Community Systems*. [Kent, Ohio]: Comparative Administration Research Institute Graduate School of Business Administration Kent State University: distributed by Kent State University Press.

Gingrich, B., 'Individual and Organizational Accountabilities Reducing Stereotypes and Prejudice Within the Workplace', *Diversity Factor*, 8 (Winter 2000), 14–19.

Gioia, D. & Chittipeddi, K. (1991). 'Sensemaking and Sensegiving in Strategic Change Initiation'. *Strategic Management Journal*, *12*, 433–448.

Gioia, D.A. & Mehra, A. (1996). 'Sensemaking in Organizations'. *Academy of Management Review*, *21*(4), 1226–1231.

Goldstein, R.J. (1978). *Political Repression in Modern America. 1870 to the Present*. Cambridge, MA: Schenkman Publishing Co. Inc.

Griffin, R.W., Ebert, R.J., & Starke, F.A. (2002). *Business. Fourth Canadian Edition*. Toronto: Prentice Hall.

Grint, K. (1994). 'Re-engineering History: Social Resonances and Business Process Re-engineering'. *Organization*, *1*(1), 179–201.

Guest, D. & Fatchett, D. (1974). *Worker Participation: Individual Control & Performance*. [S.l.]: Instit. Personnel Management.

Gutenberg, A.W. (1968). *Dynamics of Management*. Scranton, PA: International Textbook Company.

Gygi, C., DeCarlo, N., & Williams, B. (2005). *Six Sigma for Dummies*. Hoboken, NJ: Wiley Pub.

Hackman, J.R. & Oldham, G. (1980). *Work Redesign*. Reading, MA: Addison-Wesley.

Hackman, J.R. & Oldham, G.R. (1974). 'The Job Diagnostic Survey: An Instrument for the Diagnosis of Jobs and the Evaluation of Job Redesign Projects'. *Catalog of Selected Documents in Psychology*, *4*(M.S. No.810), 148.

Hackman, J.R., & Suttle, J.L. (1977). *Improving Life at Work: Behavioral Science Approaches to Organizational Change*. Santa Monica, CA.: Goodyear Pub. Co.

Hall, D. & Parker, V., 'The Role of Workplace Flexibility in Managing Diversity', *Organizational Dynamics*, 22 (Summer 1993), 4–18.

Hammer, M. & Champy, J. (1993). *Re-engineering the Corporation*. New York: HarperCollins.

Hannabarger, C. (2007). *Balanced Scorecard Strategy for Dummies* (1st ed.). Indianapolis, IN: Wiley Pub., Inc.

Harari, O. (1999). 'Leading Change from the Middle', Feb. 1999, 88, 2, pp.29–32.

Hardy, C. & Clegg, S.R. (1996). 'Some Dare Call it Power'. In S. Clegg, C. Hardy & W. Nord (Eds.), *Handbook of Organization Studies* (pp.622–641). London: Sage.

Hatfield, J. & Mills, A.J. (1997). Guiding Lights and Power Sources: Consultants Plug into the Management of Meaning in an Electrical Company. *Paper presented at the Colloquium of European Group for Organisational Studies*, Budapest.

Hayes, J. (2002). *The Theory and Practice of Change Management*. New York: Palgrave.

Heckscher, C.C. (1981). *Democracy at Work: In Whose Interests?: The Politics of Worker Participation*. Cambridge, MA: Harvard University Press.

Helms Mills, J.C. (2003). *Making Sense of Organizational Change*. London: Routledge.

Helms Mills, J. (2005). 'Representations of Diversity and Organizational Change in a North American Utility Company'. *Gender, Work & Organization, 12*(3), 242–269.

Helms Mills, J. (2006). 'Lightco: The Case of the Serial Changers'. In G. Jones, A.J. Mills, T.G. Weatherby, & J. Helms Mills (Eds.), *Organizational Theory, Design and Change*. Toronto: Pearson.

Helms Mills, J.C.C. & Mills, A.J. (2000). 'Rules, Sensemaking, Formative Contexts and Discourse in the Gendering of Organizational Culture'. In N.M. Ashkanasy, C.P.M. Wilderom, & M.F. Peterson (Eds.), *Handbook of Organizational Culture and Climate* (pp. 55–70). Thousand Oaks, CA: Sage.

Helms Mills, J. & Weatherbee, T. (2006). 'Hurricanes Hardly Happen: Sensemaking as a Framework for Understanding Organizational Disasters'. *Culture and Organization, 12*(3), 265–279

Helms Mills, J., Weatherbee, T.G., & Colwell, S.C. (2006). 'Ethnostatistics and Sensemaking: Making Sense of Business School Rankings'. *Organizational Research Methods, 9*(4), 1–25.

Herzberg, F. (1959). *The Motivation to Work* (2nd ed.). New York,: Wiley.

Herzberg, F.L. (1966). *Work and the Nature of Man*. Cleveland, OH: World.

Herzberg, F.L. (1968). 'One More Time: How do You Motivate Employees?' *Harvard Business Review, 46*(1), 53–62.

Higonnet, M.R., Jenson, J., Michel, S., & Weitz, M.C. (Eds.). (1987). *Behind the Lines. Gender and the Two World Wars*. London: Yale University Press.

Hill, C.W.L. (2008). *Global Business Today* (5th ed.). Boston: McGraw-Hill Irwin.

History of Employment Equity. Human Resources and Social Development Canada Website. Accessed November 28, 2007. http://www.hrsdc.gc.ca/en/lp/lo/lswe/we/information/history.shtml

Hobbes, T., Schuhmann, K., & Rogers, G.A.J. (2003). *Thomas Hobbes Leviathan*. Bristol: Thoemmes.

Holman, P. & Devane, T. (1999). *The Change Handbook: Group Methods for Shaping the Future*. San Francisco: Berrett-Koehler Publishers.

Howes, C. (1994, January 23). 'Employees "reeling" from new fads'. *The Sunday Daily News*.

Huczynski, A. (1993). *Management Gurus: Who Makes Them and How to Become One*. London: Routledge.

Hunt, I.A. (2005). *On Hitler's Mountain. Overcoming the Legacy of a Nazi Childhood*. New York: Harper.

Imahal. (2002). Academic Success and Stanford: Interview with Joanne Martin.

International Organization for Standardization. Retrieved May 16, 2007, from http://www.iso.org/iso/en/ISOOnline.frontpage.

Ivancevich, J. & Gilbert, J., 'Diversity Management: Time for a New Approach', *Public Personnel Management*, 29 (Spring 2000), 75–92.

Jackall, R. (1988). *Moral Mazes*. Oxford: Oxford University Press.

Jackson, B. (2001). *Management Gurus and Management Fashions*. London: Routledge.

Jackson, N. & Carter, P. (2007). *Rethinking Organisational Behaviour. A Poststructuralist Framework*. London: FT Prentice Hall.

Jamieson, D. & O'Mara, J. (1991). *Managing Workforce 2000: Gaining the Diversity Advantage*, San Francisco: Jossey-Bass Publishers.

Jick, T. (1993). *Managing Change. Cases and Concepts*. Boston: Irwin McGraw-Hill.

Johns, G. & Saks, A.M. (2008). *Organizational Behaviour: Understanding and Managing Life at Work*. Toronto: Pearson Prentice Hall.

Jones, D. (2002). 'Feds May Unleash Six Sigma on terrorism' [Electronic Version]. USATODAY.com. Retrieved 13 December, 2007 from http://www.usatoday.com/money/companies/management/2002-10-30-sixsigma_x.htm.

Jones, G.R. (1995). *Organizational Theory*. Reading, MA: Addison-Wesley.

Kanter, R.M. (1979). 'Power Failure in Management Circuits'. *Harvard Business Review*, *57*(4), 65–75.

Kanter, R.M. (1983). *The Change Masters: Corporate Entrepreneurs at Work*. New York: Thomson.

Kanter, R.M. (1989). *When Giants Learn to Dance; Mastering the Challenges of Strategy, Management and Careers in the 1990s*. London: Unwin Hyman.

Kaplan, R.S. & Norton, D.P. (1992). 'The Balanced Scorecard: Measures That Drive Performance'. *Harvard Business Review* (January–February), 71–79.

Kaplan, R.S. & Norton, D.P. (2000). *The Strategy-Focused Organization*. Cambridge, MA: Harvard Business School Press.

Kay, E. (1996, November). 'Trauma in Real Life'. *The Globe and Mail Report on Business Magazine*, 82–92.

Keleman, M. (1999). 'Total Quality Management in the UK Service Sector: A Social Constructivist Study'. In S.R. Clegg, E. Ibarra-Colado, & L. Bueno-Rodriquez (Eds.), *Global Management*. London: Sage.

Kelly, E. & Dobbin, F., 'How Affirmative Action Became Diversity Management', *The American Behavioral Scientist*, 41 (April 1998), 960–984.

Kelly, J. (1974). *Organizational Behaviour*. Homewood, IL: Richard D. Irwin.

Kersten, A., 'Diversity Management: Dialogue, Dialectics and Diversion', *Journal of Organizational Change Management*, 13 (2000), 235–248.

Kets de Vries, M.F.R. (1989). 'The Leader as Mirror: Clinical Reflections'. *Human Relations*, *42*(7), 607–623.

Kets de Vries, M.F.R. (1991). *Organizations on the Couch: Clinical Perspectives on Organizational Behavior and Change* (1st ed.). San Francisco: Jossey-Bass.

Kets de Vries, M.F.R. & Miller, D. (1984). *The Neurotic Organization*. San Francisco: Jossey-Bass.

Kets de Vries, M.F.R. & Miller, D. (1986). 'Personality, Culture and Organization. *Academy of Management Review.*, *11*(2), 266–279.

Kettinger, W., Teng, J., & Guha, S. (1997). 'Business Process Change: A Study of Methodologies, Techniques, and Tools'. *MIS Quarterly*, *21*(1), 55–80.

Kieser, A. (1997). 'Rhetoric and Myth in Management Fashion'. *Organization*, *4*(1), 49–74.

Kim, C.W & Mauborgne, R. (2003). 'Tipping Point Leadership', *Harvard Business Review*, April 2003, pp. 60–69.

Kirby, S. & Orlando, R., 'Impact of Marketing Work-Place Diversity on Employee Job Involvement and Organizational Commitment', *The Journal of Social Psychology*, 140 (June 2000), 367+.

Kocakulah, M.C. & Austill, A.D. (2007). 'Balanced Scorecard Application in the Health Care Industry: A Case Study'. *Journal of Health Care Finance*, *34*(1), 72–99.

Kodak Canada Inc., *The Globe and Mail*, June 7, 2005.

Kossek, E., Lobel, S., & Brown, J. (2006). 'Human Resource Strategies to Manage

Workforce Diversity', in (Eds) Konrad, A., Prasad, P., & Pringle, J. (2006) *Handbook of Workplace Diversity*, London: Sage Publications Ltd.

Kotter, J.P. (1996). *Leading Change*. Boston, MA.: Harvard Business School Press.

Kuhnert, K. & Lewis, P. (1987). Transactional and Transformational Leadership: A Constructive/Developmental Analysis. *Academy of Management Review*, 12 (4), 648–657.

Laxer, J. (1993). *False God : How the Globalization Myth Has Impoverished Canada*. Toronto, Ont.: Lester Pub.

Learning, 32 (September 2001), 345–361.

Leavy, S. & Wilson, D. (1994) *Strategy and Leadership*. London: Routledge.

Lee, Y.-T. (1994). 'Why Does American Psychology Have Cultural Limitations?' *American Psychologist*, 49(6), 524.

Legge, K. (1996). 'On Knowledge, Business Consultants and the Selling of TQM'. University of Lancaster.

Levinson, E. (1956). *Labor on the March*. New York: University Books.

Lewin, K. (1939). 'Field Theory and Experiment in Social Psychology: Concepts and Methods'. *The American Journal of Sociology*, 44(5), 868–896.

Lewin, K. (1945). 'The Research Center for Group Dynamics at Massachusetts Institute of Technology'. *Sociometry*, 8(2), 126–136.

Lewin, K. (1947). Frontiers in Group Dynamics. *Human Relations*, *1*, 2–38.

Lewin, K. (1951). *Field Theory in Social Science*. New York: Harper and Row.

Lewin, K., Lippitt, R., & White, R.K. (1939). 'Patterns of Aggressive Behavior in Experimentally Created "Social Climates"'. *Journal of Social Psychology*, *10*, 271–299.

Loebbecke, C. & Wareham, J. (2003). 'The Impact of eBusiness and the Information Society on "Strategy" and "Strategic Planning": An Assessment of New Concepts and Challenges'. *Information Technology and Management*, 4(2–3), 165.

Lorbiecki, A., (2001) 'Changing Views on Diversity Management: The Rise of the Learning Perspective and the Need to Recognize Social and Political Contradictions', *Management Learning*, Vol. 32, No. 3, 345–361.

Louis, M.R. (1980). 'Surprise and Sense Making: What Newcomers Experience in Entering Unfamiliar Organizational Settings'. *Administrative Science Quarterly*, 25(2), 226–251.

Lukacs, J. (1997). *The Hitler of History*. New York: Vintage Books.

McCauley, C., Wright, M., & Harris, M., 'Diversity Workshops on Campus: A Survey of Current Practice at U.S. Colleges and Universities', *College Student Journal*, 34 (March 2000), 100+.

McKee, M.C., Mills, A.J., & Weatherbee, T.G. (2005). 'Institutional Field of Dreams: Exploring the AACSB and the New Legitimacy of Canadian Business Schools'. *Canadian Journal of Administrative Sciences*, 22(4), 288–301.

McKinley, W. & Scherer, A.G. (2000). 'Some Unanticipated Consequences of Organizational Restructuring'. *Academy of Management Review*, 25(4), 735–752.

McShane, S. (2001). *Canadian Organizational Behaviour*. Toronto: McGraw-Hill Ryerson.

Machiavelli, N. (1996). *The Prince*. Atlantic Highlands, N.J.: Humanities Press.

Marrow, A.F. (1969). *The Practical Theorist. The Life and Work of Kurt Lewin*. New York: Basic Books, Inc.

Martin, J. (1992). *Cultures in Organizations: Three Perspectives*. Oxford: Oxford University Press.

Martin, J. (2002). *Organizational Culture. Mapping the Terrain.* Thousand Oaks, CA: Sage.

Marx, K. (1999). *Capital: A Critical Analysis of Capitalist Production.* (Abridged ed.). London: Oxford University Press.

Matthews, P. (1999). 'Workplace Learning: Developing an Holistic Model'. *The Learning Organization, 6*(1), 18–29.

Mayo, E. (1933). *The Human Problems of an Industrial Civilization.* New York: MacMillan.

Meadus, K.-A. (2006, Nov/Dec). 'She's the Boss!' *Atlantic Business, 17*, 26–45.

Meyerson, D. (2001). *Tempered Radicals: How People Use Difference to Inspire Change at Work.* Cambridge, MA: Harvard Business School Press.

Miciak, A. & Desmarais, M. (2001). 'Benchmarking Service Quality Performance at Business-to-Business and Business-to-Consumer Call Centers'. *The Journal of Business & Industrial Marketing, 16*(5), 340.

Mills, A.J. (2001). 'Gendering Organizational Analysis – A Retrospective'. In P. Tancred (ed.), *Feminism(s) Challenge the Traditional Disciplines* (pp. 13–25). Montreal: McGill University, MCRTW Monograph Series, No.1.

Mills, A.J. (2006). *Sex, Strategy and the Stratosphere: The Gendering of Airline Cultures.* London: Palgrave Macmillan.

Mills, A.J. & Helms Hatfield, J. (1998). 'From Imperialism to Globalization: Internationalization and the Management Text'. In S.R. Clegg, E. Ibarra, & L. Bueno (Eds.), *Theories of the Management Process: Making Sense Through Difference* (pp. 37–67). Thousand Oaks, CA: Sage.

Mills, A.J. & Helms Mills, J.C. (2004). 'When Plausibility Fails: Towards a Critical Sensemaking Approach to Resistance'. In R. Thomas, A.J. Mills, & J.C. Helms Mills (Eds.), *Identity Politics at Work: Resisting Gender and Gendered Resistance* (pp. 141–159). London: Routledge.

Mills, A.J. & Helms Mills, J. (2006). 'Masculinity and the Making of Trans-Canada Air Lines, 1937–1940: A feminist poststructuralist account'. *Canadian Journal of Administrative Science, 23*(1), 34–44.

Mills, A.J. & Murgatroyd, S.J. (1991a). *Organizational Rules: A Framework for Understanding Organizational Action.* Milton Keynes, UK: Open University Press.

Mills, A.J. & Murgatroyd, S.J. (1991b). *Organizational Rules: A Framework for Understanding Organizations.* Milton Keynes: Open University Press.

Mills, A.J., Simmons, T., & Helms Mills, J. (2005). *Reading Organization Theory: A Critical Approach to the Study of Organizational Behaviour and Structure.* Third Edition. Toronto: Garamond Press.

Mills, A.J., Helms Mills, J., Bratton, J., & Foreshaw, C. (2005). *Organizational Behaviour in Context.* Toronto: Garamond Press.

Mills, A.J., Helms Mills, J., Bratton, J., & Foreshaw, C. (2006). *Organizational Behaviour in a Global Context.* Peterborough, ON: Broadview Press.

Milton, R. (2005). *Speaking Notes for Robert A. Milton, Chairman, President and CEO of ACE Aviation Holding.* Montreal.

Mirchandani, K. (1998). ' "No longer a struggle?": Teleworkers' Reconstruction of the Work Non-Work Boundary'. In P.J. Jackson & J.M. Van Der Wielen (Eds.), *Teleworking: International Perspectives.* (pp. 118–135). London: Routledge.

Morris, B. (2006). 'New Rule: Look Out, Not In' [Electronic Version]. *Fortune.*

Retrieved 22 December 2007 from http://money.cnn.com/2006/07/10/magazines/fortune/rule4.fortune/index.htm.

Morse, D., Terhune, C. & Carrns, A. (2005). Clean Sweep – HealthSouth's Scushy is Acquitted. *The New York Times*, June 29, 2005.

Mullen, J., Vladi, N., & Mills, A.J. (2006). 'Making Sense of the Walkerton Crisis'. *Culture and Organization, 12*(3), 207–220.

Nadworny, M. (1957). 'Frederick Taylor and Frank Gilbreth: Competition in Scientific Management'. *The Business History Review, 31*(1), 23–34.

Nair, M. (2004). *Essentials of Balanced Scorecard*. Hoboken, N.J.: John Wiley & Sons.

Nielsen, G.P. (1982). *From Sky Girl to Flight Attendant. Women and the Making of a Union*. New York: ILR Press.

Niven, P.R. (2005). *Balanced Scorecard Diagnostics: Maintaining Maximum Performance*. Hoboken, N.J.: Wiley.

Noon, M. (2007). 'The Fatal Flaws of Diversity and the Business Case for Ethnic Minorities'. *Work, Employment & Society*, 21, pp.773–784.

O'Connell, C.J. & Mills, A.J. (2003). Making Sense of Bad News: The Media, Sensemaking and Organizational Crisis. *Canadian Journal of Communication, 28*(3), 323–339.

Oliver, T. (1986). *The Real Coke, The Real Thing*. New York: Random House.

Osborne, E., 'The Deceptively Simple Economics of Workplace Diversity', *Journal of Labor Research*, 21 (Summer 2000), 463+.

Ouchi, W. (1981). *Theory Z*. Reading, MA: Addison-Wesley.

Paddock, S.S. (2004). *Appreciative Inquiry and the Catholic Church*. Bend, OR: Thin Book Publishing Company.

Palmer, I. & Dunford, R. (1996). 'Conflicting Uses of Metaphors: Reconceptualizing their Use in the Field of Organizational Change'. *Academy of Management Review, 21*(3), 691–717.

Pande, P.S., Neuman, R.P., & Cavanagh, R.R. (2000). *The Six Sigma Way: How GE, Motorola, and Other Top Companies Are Honing their Performance*. New York: McGraw-Hill.

Parry, W. & Bryman, A. (2006) *Leadership in Organizations*. pp.447–468 in (Eds) Clegg, S.R, Hardy, C., Lawrence, T.B., & Nord, W. (2006) *The Sage Handbook of Organization Studies*, 2nd Edition, London: Sage Publications.

Pascale, R.T. & Athos, A.G. (1981). *The Art of Japanese Management: Applications for American Executives*. New York: Simon & Schuster.

Paton, R. & Dempster, L. (2002). 'Managing Change from a Gender Perspective'. *European Management Journal, 20*, 539–548.

Paton, R. & McCalman, J. (2000). *Change Management: A Guide to Effective Implementation*. London: Sage Publications.

Perrow, C. (1986). *Complex Organizations* (3rd ed.). New York: Random House.

Peters, T. & Waterman, R. (1982a). *In Search of Excellence – Lessons from America's Best-Run Companies*. New York: Warner Communications.

Peters, T. & Waterman, R. (1982b). *In Search of Excellence*. New York: Harper & Row.

Peters, T.J. & Waterman, R.H. (1982c). *In Search of Excellence: Lessons from America's Best-Run Companies* (1st ed.). New York: Harper & Row.

Pettigrew, A. (1979). 'On Studying Organizational Cultures'. *Administrative Science Quarterly, 24*, 570–581.

Pfeffer, J. (1977). 'The Ambiguity of Leadership'. *Academy of Management Review*, January 1977, 104–112.

Phills, J. (2005). 'Leadership Matters – Or Does It?' *Leader to Leader*, Spring 2005, 46–52.

Prasad, A. (2001). 'Understanding Workplace Empowerment as Inclusion'. *Journal of Applied Behavioral Science*, 37, 51–69.

Prasad, P., Mills, A.J., Elmes, M., & Prasad, A., (1997). *Managing the Organizational Melting Pot: Dilemmas of Workplace Diversity*. Newbury Park, CA.: Sage.

Prokesch, S.E. (1997). 'Unleashing the Power of Learning: An Interview with British Petroleum's John Browne'. *Harvard Business Review*, 147–168.

Province of New Brunswick. (2003). *Call Centre Employment in the Province of New Brunswick*. Fredericton, NB: Government of New Brunswick.

Pugh, M. (1992). *Women and the Women's Movement in Britain 1914–1959*. London: MacMillan.

Pylee, M.V. (1975). *Worker Participation in Management: Myth and Reality*. New Delhi: N.V. Publications.

Pyper, R. (2009). 'Isomorphism'. In A.J. Mills, G. Durepos, & E. Wiebe (Eds.), *Sage Encyclopedia of Case Study Research*. Thousand Oaks, CA: Sage.

Pyzdek, T. (2001). *The Six Sigma Handbook: A Complete Guide for Greenbelts, Blackbelts, and Managers at All Levels*. New York: McGraw-Hill.

Ramias, A. (2005). 'The Mists of Six Sigma' [Electronic Version]. *BPTrends*, October. Retrieved 2 January, 2008 from http://www.ispi.org/proComm/resources/TheMistofSixSigma.pdf.

Richard, O., McMillan, A., Chadwick, K., & Dwyer, S. (2003). 'Employing an Innovation Strategy in Radically Diverse Workforces: Effects on Firm Performance'. *Group and Organization Management*, 28(1), 107–126.

Roberts, E. (1988). *Women's Work 1840–1940*. Macmillan: London.

Roberson, Q. (2006). 'Disentangling the Meanings of Diversity and Inclusion in Organizations'. *Group & Organization Management*. Apr. 2006, 32, 2, 212–236.

Roethlisberger, F.J., & Dickson, W.J. (1939). *Management and the Worker*. Cambridge, MA: Harvard University Press.

Rogers, R.E. (1975). *Organizational Theory*. Boston: Allyn and Bacon, Inc.

Rose, M. (1978). *Industrial Behaviour*. Harmondsworth: Penguin.

Rothschild, J. (1988). *Teaching Technology From a Feminist Perspective*. New York: Pergamon Press.

Rowbotham, S. (1999). *A Century of Women. A History of Women in Britain and the United States*. London: Penguin.

Rüling, C.-C. (1998). 'Exploring Management Fashion: Refining A Sociological Approach. *Paper presented at the 14th Colloquium of the European Group for Organisation Studies (EGOS)*, Maastricht, the Netherlands, July 9–11.

Rynes, S. & Rosen, B., 'What Makes Diversity Programs Work?', *HR Magazine*, 39 (October 1994), 67+.

Rynes, S. & Rosen, B., 'A Field Survey of Factors Affecting the Adoption and Perceived Success of Diversity Training', *Personnel Psychology*, 48 (Summer 1995), 247–270.

Schein, E. (1984). 'Coming to a New Awareness of Organizational Culture'. *Sloan Management Review*, 25(2): 3–16.

Schein, E.H. (1985). *Organizational Culture and Leadership*. San Francisco: Jossey-Bass.

Schein, E. (1988). 'What are the Lessons of the OD Fable?' *Group and Organization Studies*, 13(1), 29.

Schein, E.H. (1990). 'Organizational Culture'. *American Psychologist*, 45(2): 109–119.

Schein, E. (1991). 'What is Culture?' In P.J. Frost, L.F. Moore, M.R. Louis, C.C. Lundberg & J. Martin (Eds.), *Reframing Organizational Culture* (pp. 243–253). Newbury Park, CA: Sage.

Schein, E. (1992). *Organizational Culture and Leadership* (2nd ed.). San Francisco: Jossey-Bass.

Schellenberg, J. (1978). *Masters of Social Psychology: Freud, Mead, Lewin, and Skinner*. New York: Oxford University Press.

Schifo, R. (2004). 'OD in Ten Words or Less: Adding Lightness to the Definitions of Organizational Development'. *Organization Development Journal*, *22*(3), 74–85.

Senge, P. (1994). *The Fifth Discipline: The Art and Practice of the Learning Organization*. New York: Doubleday.

Senge, P. (2007). 'Dance of Change: Timelines of Learning Organization Concepts'. Fieldbook.com.

Senior, B. (2002). *Organizational Change*. London: Prentice Hall.

Simon, B. (2003). 'Air Canada is Granted Bankruptcy Court Protection', *The New York Times*. New York.

Simon, H. (1976). *Administrative Behavior*. New York: The Free Press.

Simon, H.A. (1969). *Sciences of the Artificial*. Cambridge, MA: MIT. Press.

Simons, T. & Roberson, Q. (2003). 'Why Managers Should Care About Fairness: The Effects of Aggregate Justice Perceptions on Organizational Outcomes'. *Journal of Applied Psychology*, 88(3), 432+.

Smircich, L. (1983). 'Concepts of Culture and Organizational Analysis'. *Administrative Science Quarterly* (28), 339–358.

Smith, D.K. (1996). *Taking Charge of Change: 10 Principles for Managing People and Performance*. Reading, MA: Addison-Wesley.

Smith, R.F. (2007). *Business Process Management and Balanced Scorecard: Using Processes As Strategic Drivers*. Hoboken, N.J.: J. Wiley & Sons.

Soni, V., 'A Twenty-First-Century Reception for Diversity in the Public Sector: A Case Study', *Public Administration Review*, 60 (September 2000), 395+.

Spector, B. & Beer, F. (1994). 'Beyond TQM Programmes'. *Journal of Organizational Change Management*, 7(2), 63–70.

Steiner, G.A. & Steiner, J.F. (1977). *Issues in Busines and Society* (2nd ed.). New York: Random House.

Steiner, G.A. & Steiner, J.F. (1997). *Business, Government, and Society* (8th ed.). New York: McGraw-Hill.

Stewart, T.A. (1989). 'New Ways to Exercise Power'. *Fortune*, 6 (11).

Stolberg, B. (1938). *The Story of the CIO*. New York: The Viking Press.

Stutz, J. & Massengale, R., 'Measuring Diversity Initiatives', *HR Magazine*, 42 (December 1997), 84–88.

Taylor, F.W. (1911). *Principles of Scientific Management*. New York: Harper & Row.

Thomas, D. & Ely, R., 'Making Differences Matter: A New Paradigm for Managing Diversity', *Harvard Business Review*, 74 (September/October 1996), 79–90.

Thomas, R., Mills, A.J., & Helms Mills, J. (2004). *Gender and the Micropolitics of Organizational Resistance*. London: Routledge.

Thompson, J.D. (1967). *Organizations in Action*. New York: McGraw-Hill.

Total Quality Management. Retrieved June 1, 2007, from http://www.asq.org/learn-about-quality/total-quality-management/overview/overview.html.

Townley, B. (1994). *Reframing Human Resource Management: Power, Ethics and the Subject at Work*. London: Sage.

Trist, E.L. & Bamforth, K. (1951). 'Some Social and Psychological Consequences of the Longwall Method of Coal Getting'. *Human Relations, 4*, 3–38.

Turner, B. (1988). 'Connoisseurship in the Study of Organizational Cultures'. In A. Bryman (Ed.), *Doing Research in Organizations* (pp.108–123). London: Routledge.

Turner, J.R., Grude, K.V., & Thurloway, L. (1996). *The Project Manager As Change Agent: Leadership, Influence and Negotiation*. London; New York: McGraw-Hill.

Uzumeri, M.V. (1997). 'ISO 9000 and Other Metastandards: Principles for Management Practice?' *The Academy of Management Executive*, XI(1): 21–36.

Voelpel, S.C., Leibold, M., Eckhoff, R.A., & Davenport, T.H. (2005). 'The Tyranny of the Balanced Scorecard in the Innovation Economy'. *Proceedings of Fourth Critical Management Studies Conference*, Cambridge University, July 4–6.

Von Bergen, C., Soper, B. and Foster, T., 'Unintended Negative Effects of Diversity Management', *Public Personnel Management*, 31 (Summer 2002), 239–251.

Walton, R.E. (1973). 'Quality of Working Life: What Is It?' *Sloan Management Review, 15*(1), 11–21.

Weber, M. (1947). *The Theory of Social and Economic Organization* (A.R. Henderson & T. Parsons, Trans.). London: Free Press.

Weick, K.E. (1993). 'The Vulnerable System: An Analysis of the Tenerife Air Disaster'. *Journal of Management, 16*(3), 571–593.

Weick, K.E. (1995a). *Sensemaking in Organizations*. London: Sage.

Weick, K.E. (1995b). *Sensemaking in Organizations*. Thousand Oaks: Sage.

Weick, K.E. (1996). 'Drop Your Tools: An Allegory for Organizational Study'. *Administrative Science Quarterly, 41*, 301–313.

Weick, K.E. (2001). *Making Sense of the Organization*. Oxford: Blackwell.

Weick, K.E., Sutcliff, K.M., & Obstfeld, D. (2005). 'Organizing and the Process of Sensemaking'. *Organization Science, 16*(4), 409.

Weiner & Mahoney (1981). 'A Model of Corporate Performances As a Function of Environmental, Organizational, and Leadership Influences'. *Academy of Management Journal*, 24, 453–470.

Wheeler, B.O. (1962). *Business. An Introductory Analysis*. New York: Harper & Row.

White, L.P. & Wooten, K.C. (1983). 'Ethical Dilemmas in Various Stages of Organizational Development'. *The Academy of Management Review, 8*(4), 690–697.

Whitney, D. & Trosten-Bloom, A. (2003). *The Power of Appreciative Inquiry: A Practical Guide to Positive Change*. San Francisco: Berrett-Koehler Publishers.

Wikipedia. (2006). 'Edgar Schein' (Vol. 2006).

Wise, L. & Tschirhart, M., 'Examining Empirical Evidence on Diversity Effects: How Useful is Diversity Research for Public-Sector Managers', *Public Administration Review*, 60 (September 2000), 386+.

Wolf, M. (2004). *Why Globalization Works*. New Haven: Yale University Press.

Woodward, J. (1958). *Management and Technology*. London: HMSO.

Zimet, M. & Greenwood, R.G. (1978). *The Evolving Science of Management. The Collected Papers of Harold Smiddy and Papers by Others in His Honor*. New York: Manhattan College of Business.

Index

Accounting, Business & Financial History

An International and Comparative Review

EDITORS:

John Richard Edwards, *Cardiff Business School, UK*
Trevor Boyns, *Cardiff Business School, UK*

Accounting, Business & Financial History is a major journal which covers the areas of accounting history, business history and financial history. As well as providing a valuable international forum for investigating these areas, it aims to explore:

- the inter-relationship between accounting practices, financial markets and economic development.
- the influence of accounting on business decision-making.
- the environmental and social influences on the business and financial world.

The special features of *Accounting, Business and Financial History* include:

- an on-going record and analysis of past developments in business and finance history.
- explanations for present structures and practices.
- a platform for solving current problems and predicting future developments.

SUBSCRIPTION RATES

2008- *Volume* 18 (*3 issues per year*)
Print ISSN 0958-5206
Online ISSN 1466-4275
Institutional rate (print and online): US$548; £332; €438
Institutional rate (online access only): US$520; £315; €416
Personal rate (print only): US$188; £111; €150

Business History

Celebrating 50 years

**Listed in the ISI Social Science Citation Index
(Business; History of Social Sciences)**

New for 2008: Manuscript Central online submission system

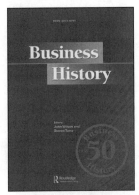

EDITORS:

John Wilson, *University of Central Lancashire, UK*
Steven Toms, *University of York, UK*

Business History is an international journal concerned with the
long-run evolution and contemporary operation of business systems
and enterprises. Its primary purpose is to make available the
findings of advanced research, empirical and conceptual, into
matters of global significance, such as corporate organization and
growth, multinational enterprise, business efficiency, entrepreneurship,
technological change, finance, marketing, human resource
management, professionalization and business culture.

The journal has won a reputation for academic excellence and has a wide readership amongst
management specialists, economists and other social scientists and economic, social, labour and
business historians.

SUBSCRIPTION RATES
2008 - *Volume 50 (6 issues per year)*
Print ISSN 0007-6791
Online ISSN 1743-7938
Institutional rate (print and online): US$826; £486; €661
Institutional rate (online access only): US$784; £461; €627
Personal rate (print only): US$166; £111; €133

informaworld™

eupdates
Taylor & Francis Group

A world of specialist information for the academic, professional and business
communities. To find out more go to: **www.informaworld.com**

Register your email address at **www.informaworld.com/eupdates** to receive information
on books, journals and other news within your areas of interest.

For further information, please contact Routledge Customer Services at either of the following:
T&F Informa UK Ltd, Sheepen Place, Colchester, Essex, CO3 3LP, UK
Tel: +44 (0) 20 7017 5544 Fax: 44 (0) 20 7017 5198
Email: tf.enquiries@informa.com
Taylor & Francis Inc, 325 Chestnut Street, 8th Floor, Philadelphia, PA 19106, USA
Tel: +1 800 354 1420 (toll-free calls from within the US)
or +1 215 625 8900 (calls from overseas) Fax: +1 215 625 2940
Email: customerservice@taylorandfrancis.com

When ordering, please quote: XF25601A

View an online sample issue at:
www.informaworld.com/BusinessHistory